D0910910

Also by Doug Zahn

The Human Side of Statistical Consulting (with J. R. Boen)

Quality Management Plus: The Continuous Improvement of Education (with R. Kaufman)

STUMBLING **BLOCKS** TO STEPPING STONES

A Guide to Successful Meetings and
Working Relationships

DOUG ZAHN

STUMBLING BLOCKS TO STEPPING STONES
A GUIDE TO SUCCESSFUL MEETINGS AND WORKING RELATIONSHIPS

Copyright © 2019 Doug Zahn.

All rights reserved. No part of this book may be used or reproduced by any means, graphic, electronic, or mechanical, including photocopying, recording, taping or by any information storage retrieval system without the written permission of the author except in the case of brief quotations embodied in critical articles and reviews.

iUniverse books may be ordered through booksellers or by contacting:

iUniverse
1663 Liberty Drive
Bloomington, IN 47403
www.iuniverse.com
1-800-Authors (1-800-288-4677)

Because of the dynamic nature of the internet, any web addresses or links contained in this book may have changed since publication and may no longer be valid. The views expressed in this work are solely those of the author and do not necessarily reflect the views of the publisher, and the publisher hereby disclaims any responsibility for them.

Any people depicted in stock imagery provided by Getty Images are models, and such images are being used for illustrative purposes only. Certain stock imagery © Getty Images.

ISBN: 978-1-5320-6088-5 (sc)
ISBN: 978-1-5320-6087-8 (hc)
ISBN: 978-1-5320-6086-1 (e)

Library of Congress Control Number: 2018913397

Print information available on the last page.

iUniverse rev. date: 03/18/2019

To all the Brendas to whom I owe thanks for what
they have taught me in the course of my career

CONTENTS

TABLES

FIGURES

FOREWORD

Most people don't read forewords. I hope this one will be different, for this book is special and worthy of your attention, consideration, and application.

- It is special because it emphasizes that both technical expertise and relational expertise are as necessary for success in consulting as is looking both left and right in crossing a street. Developing your relational expertise will enhance your effectiveness as a consultant. This is the core concept in this book.
- It is worthy of your attention, consideration, and application because it will guide you in working with a partner and video to improve your relational expertise using video data rather than anecdotes.
- Its goal is to give you an opportunity to learn how to produce systematic self-improvement and success.

Doug Zahn has developed *a user's guide that intentionally produces satisfaction for both client and consultant*, based on many of his experiences and much rigorous self-reflection—actually applying to himself what he is suggesting for us.

Unlike most other self-help books, this one takes the time to really develop the concepts and then provides validated tools for successful interactions—all kinds of interactions: meetings, consultations, disciplinary sessions—in short, any purposeful activity involving two or more persons. In a conversational style, Dr. Zahn has provided us both the guidance for planning as well as delivering the fruits that can come from successful interactions: meetings that end in a plan that all parties agree on and implement, yielding results that all stakeholders regard as successful. And, perhaps most importantly, the client will want to work with this consultant again.

I have personally experienced Doug's approach. Some years ago when we were working together, he gave me valuable insights, including the importance of realizing that every mistake is a friend in disguise because it allows you to know what to change and why. Such insights are throughout this book.

Roger Kaufman, PhD, CPT, ABPP;
fellow, American Psychological Association;
fellow, American Educational Research Association

Dr. Kaufman helps clients to describe the world they desire for their grandchildren and then consults with clients to develop a path toward this vision. He has published forty-one books and more than 285 articles on strategic planning, performance improvement, quality management, needs assessment, and evaluation. He consults worldwide with public and private organizations, the most recent of which include the president and minister of tourism of Panama, the University of Puerto Rico, and the Civil Service Commission of Taiwan.

ACKNOWLEDGMENTS

Wholehearted thanks to Andrea Zahn, Donna Crowley, Paul Lavell, William Krebs, Rob Fowler, Derek Zahn, Devin Zahn, Dan Boroto, Duane Meeter, Heather Smith, Larry Barlow, Robin Daniels, Tim White, Eric Vance, and Tom Corneil. I'm grateful for the contributions made by all students and colleagues who assisted in the development of the Florida State University (FSU) consulting courses. I also thank all who participated in the Consultancy Skills Courses in the UK Office of National Statistics. A special thank-you goes out to all Virginia Tech, Cal Poly, University of Georgia, and Penn State students who read and commented on an earlier version of part 1 of this book.

ACKNOWLEDGMENTS

The Client Who Turned My Life Upside Down

A young student, whom I will call Brenda, came to my office to make an appointment for help with her master's degree study. She submitted a New Client Information Form that described the topics she wished to discuss. Over the weekend, I reviewed the form and learned that she intended to construct an experiment and analyze the results without the advantage of the appropriate coursework in statistics. I began to wonder how to help her while avoiding statistical jargon. I continued to ponder her situation and spent a considerable amount of time in preparation.

In keeping with my department's new video-based consulting course, I arranged to video the session with Brenda after she agreed to this. Despite the fact that I had been videoed three times before, I was apprehensive about the presence of the camera and my promise that the video would be reviewed in a consulting class.

As the appointment time approached and passed, I became irritated with Brenda before I had even met her because she appeared to be a no-show. However, eventually I found her waiting outside my office where my new secretary had sent her. This error occurred because I had failed to apprise my new secretary that I met my consulting clients in the video room rather than in my office. My upset initially shifted from Brenda to my secretary until I realized that it was *my* mistake that had initiated this state of confusion.

As Brenda and I walked to the video room, I was still stewing. At the same time, I realized that I had to settle down in order to concentrate on the upcoming consultation.

At the start of the session, Brenda informed me that she was enrolled in the first semester of a master's degree program that required a thesis based on collected data. She further explained that she was lost in this project and needed my help. And there was one other item to share: she had changed her entire research project, the one I had spent my weekend considering.

So much for my efforts to settle down! At this point, I was thinking that my weekend had been wasted and this session was going from bad to worse. I was puzzling over her new plan and resenting that she had made this change without consulting me.

There was conflict in my mind between my commitment to be helpful and my reaction of frustration at the surprises occurring before and during the first few minutes of the session. The conflict was further aggravated by my attitudes about her, her questions, and her new thesis topic. (These inner feelings were evident when I reviewed the video later. I appeared to be talking to myself and often talking *at* her rather than listening *to* her.)

At this point, I decided to spend some time clarifying the question Brenda hoped to study in her new thesis. Rapidly, it became apparent that her question was squarely in the middle of the set of questions that I did not regard as worthy of my time.

My struggle to clarify what she hoped to do in her thesis was exacerbated by my thinking that she required more statistical knowledge to do this project than she had. I thought that it was unacceptable for her to proceed without that knowledge because she would not be able to defend her work.

During this internal conflict, I looked at her and said, "I notice that you are in a course that will help you plan your research project. Have you taken a statistics class?" I was hoping that somehow, somewhere, she had taken a course that she had forgotten to list on her form.

"Hm mm." (Vigorously shaking her head—that is, "No!")

"Okay, are you planning to take a statistics class this year so that when—"

Brenda interrupted, looked me right in the eye, and emphatically stated, "No!"

I hauled myself up from the deep physical and mental slouch that I had been in since the start of the session, looked down upon her, and said disdainfully, "I would highly recommend that."

Unfazed by my attempt to pull rank and intimidate, she again looked me straight in the eye and asked, "But how do I test a theory in my thesis?" The conversation rapidly deteriorated after this exchange.

At the next consulting class meeting, I explained to the students that I had a video; however, it was dull, and the client did not want to learn statistics. Her thesis topic had been studied hundreds of times. I begged them, "Isn't there one of you who has a video that would be more useful to review?"

No one answered my plea. My own attitudes had me by the throat. I also was convinced that reviewing the video with the class would be a waste of time. I knew my consultation was another routine, unsatisfactory session with a bad client who had a bad question and a bad attitude.

After viewing the video, one student asked, "Why did you treat her so arrogantly?" I reacted quickly: "She was a bad client. You can ask anyone, and they'll agree." The class ended with me still convinced that the session went poorly because she was a bad client.

Suffice it to say that she met with me once more *with* her adviser present and never again. She completed her thesis by working with a statistics graduate student instead.

The Impetus

The anecdote above served as an incentive to change how I interacted with people thereafter. It prompted years of study and data collection that led to writing this book. The goal of this book is to share lessons learned and assist you in becoming a more effective professional. I hope that some part of my journey will be of use to you on your journey.

The Brenda case was a milestone in my career. Why? In *forty-five minutes*, I met a new client and laid the foundation for losing her (and everyone she knew) as a client forever. She had a basic question. I proposed a strategy for addressing it. She summarily rejected my advice. I treated her in a shabby way and did not recover from her rejection well enough to come up with another approach to her question. Rarely had I made so many mistakes in such a short time.

Her question was basic; the interpersonal and intrapersonal issues that I encountered in the session were not. Having my advice rejected outright by a young female client compromised my ability to access my technical expertise and answer her question in a respectful way.

I had met clients like Brenda several times in my career with similar results. What made this experience different was I videoed my meeting with her and showed it to my students. In addition, I showed it at a conference on how to teach statistical consulting using video. During this conference, I was confronted by a respected statistical consultant who said, "I don't see what the problem is here. I have clients like this all the time. I love to work with them and see how I can help them."

With this new input, continued study of this video confirmed that more than technical expertise is required to be an effective consultant. Brenda demonstrated to me that attitudes are not merely touchy-feely trivia that can be discounted. They are powerful enough to derail a consultation, even a consultation on a basic topic. *Both technical expertise and relational expertise are as necessary for success in consulting as is looking both left and right in crossing a street.* This idea is at the heart of this book.

As I became conscious of how I interacted with Brenda, I was not willing to once again pass the session off as worthy of only minor discomfort because, after all, she was a "bad client." I became aware of the unacceptable gap between my actual performance and my desired performance. This new awareness led to discovering important changes I had to make to improve the quality of my services.

The most important change was that I had to take responsibility for my attitudes and emotions, as well as learn to manage them during consultations. Brenda being in the wrong room, changing her mind, studying a project I regarded as unworthy, and rejecting my advice to take a statistics course produced enough upset to cloud my thinking, and I could not explain a basic point I had taught many times. *Watching the video opened my eyes to the power my attitudes and emotions have over my intentions.* My defensiveness made me information-proof: I was *unwilling* to incorporate new information that conflicted with my attitudes about all aspects of Brenda.

> **Stumbling Block: Information-Proof**
>
> Unwilling to incorporate new information when it conflicts with one's attitudes.

The source of this resistance was my attitude about attitudes. Though I had never expressed it, my actions in this case revealed that I held my attitudes as *truth*. This mind-set did not serve me or my clients. Eventually, I learned another point of view about attitudes: *my attitudes give information only about me and my willingness to be generous or petty.* Not surprisingly, I resisted this point of view for some time. Eventually, I had enough conversations with colleagues and students to see that my attitudes about Brenda were not universally shared as they would be if they were in fact truth. It became abundantly clear my attitudes revealed an embarrassing willingness to be petty with Brenda. This shift opened the door for me to see what had happened in the Brenda case.

Getting Started

Life is complex. It is increasingly necessary to involve other professionals in serving our clients. Learning to work together cooperatively requires identifying and addressing our individual areas of expertise as well as our attitudes and emotions.

Whatever path we choose to walk in life, we serve and are served every day at home and at work. We serve friends, family, clients, teachers, employers, and many others. In turn, they serve us.

At the core of any service event are a relationship and an interaction between two or more persons. Some of our relationships work; some don't. Some of our interactions are successful; some are not. Sometimes we are aware of what is happening, and sometimes we are not. My goal in this book is to assist you to improve both the service you give and the service you receive by providing an opportunity for you to improve both your relationships and interactions.

Is This Book for Me?

Yes, if you have these three characteristics:

- the desire to *improve* your relationships and interactions,
- the willingness to "look in the mirror" to *discover* your barriers to improving your relationships and interactions, and
- the commitment to the contributions you want to make in your lifetime to make the *changes* required. The cost is high. The benefits are higher.

Some changes are changes in you. Change is challenging. Some of these changes are changes in others. Enrolling others in making changes is more challenging. Whether to make the change is their choice. You may have influence; you don't have control.

Three Core Processes: POWER, RAPID, LEARN

Three fundamental procedures that will help you work collaboratively with your clients are POWER (*prepare, open, work, end, reflect*), RAPID (*recognize, address, pinpoint, identify, do it*), and LEARN (*listen, evaluate, act, review, next*). Each process is explained and applied in the following three parts of this book. Studying how to use them will give you strategies for

- facilitating an effective consultation,
- rapidly recovering from problems that occur, and
- using video to learn how these problems occurred, how you traditionally have reacted, and how you can *respond* more effectively.

These three core processes have the potential to help you to transform your problems from stumbling blocks into stepping stones, thus yielding a more satisfying career for both you and your clients.

Our success as consultants and collaborators depends in large part on how well we work with people. Here is how the absence of the core processes contributed to my mistakes with Brenda.

- Without the POWER process, I did not prepare for the meeting, did not know how much time was available, did not make sure that my client knew where to meet, did not identify what she wanted from the meeting, nor did I end with a clear plan of action. The POWER process is a strategy for producing an effective interaction.
- Without the RAPID process, I did not have a strategy for recovering from my upset when she rejected my advice to take a statistics course. Not recovering from this incident meant that I

was in an emotional cloud that affected the rest of the meeting. This cloud is a jumble of emotions that makes it hard to see anything clearly; it grows with every passing moment. Using the RAPID process, you will have a way to rapidly recover from your mistakes during the meeting rather than descending more deeply into your emotional cloud.

- The LEARN process can be used to create a role-play of the situation that stumped me with Brenda, which also may challenge you, namely having your advice rejected. Videoing such a role-play with a trusted partner yields much information in a safe arena about how to better deal with this situation in the future by helping you become aware of your blind spots. My experience with Brenda was the reason I created the LEARN process.

Relationships and Interactions

Every relationship consists of a series of interactions. I will use the term "interaction" to refer to any exchange of information, such as meetings, consultations, collaborations, and disciplinary sessions. Though this book will primarily discuss professional and business interactions, the content can also be applied to interactions in other areas of your life.

Interactions occur because one person thinks that someone else has information, advice, or expertise that will be helpful in their current project. Either person can assume the role of information provider at some point in an interaction because both parties have information essential to the success of their meeting. Making smooth transitions from provider to receiver is at the heart of effective interactions.

This book is designed to be useful to you as a consultant, collaborator, or client. It is intended to assist you to systematically increase the proportion of your interactions that are effective. Also available in this book are methods to assess your interactions as you experiment with new ways to be more effective.

An interaction is effective if it produces three results:

1. The interaction ends with a workable plan, a plan where both the client and the consultant know what each will do next, to what criteria and by when, and the plan is implemented.
2. The results of the plan stand up to external scrutiny.
3. The client regards the consultant as a valuable resource for future interactions.

Three Basic Questions

You are engaged in a variety of jobs in addition to your job description (i.e., teacher, supervisor, project team member or leader). Here are three basic questions to ask yourself and my thoughts on each:

1. What is my primary job?

> To be successful in any of your many jobs, effective interactions with your coworkers are essential. Effective interactions are the solid foundation for doing all aspects of your job successfully. Part 1 presents the POWER process for achieving this.

2. What if I make a mistake?

> After you know what your jobs are, the good news is that you know what to do. The rest of the story is that now you can make a mistake because defining your jobs gives you and others specific standards by which to assess your performance.
>
> At some point, you realize this, and a question darkens your brow: "What if I make a mistake?" To be blunt, you will, and your client will too. Other surprises will occur as well. All mistakes and surprises will affect how you work with others to accomplish a job and correct mistakes that will inevitably arise.

On reflection, the question, "What if I make a mistake?" rapidly evolves into, "What do I do *when* I make a mistake? What do I do when my client makes a mistake or when other surprises occur? How do I recover?" Part 2 presents the RAPID process for recovering from mistakes and surprises.

3. How can I improve?

A key step here is learning how to analyze video data. Part 3 is an exploration of the LEARN process, a strategy for systematically improving your interactions. Video is used in this process to enhance your effectiveness and efficiency. LEARN, as well as POWER and RAPID, can be applied to your interactions with someone else and to your interactions with yourself as well.

Parts 1, 2, and 3 contain "broad-spectrum antibiotics" to improve interactions and relationships that are not functioning well. I invite you on a journey to learn how to interact in ways that you may have never attempted before.

This book is the result of examining many interactions. Some went well; others did not. After the pivotal experience with Brenda, I became curious about how it happens that some meetings don't go well and about the active ingredients in those that do. These inquiries have led to the observations and thoughts presented here.

What's in It for You?

By implementing the ideas in this book, you will have the opportunity to discover the following:

• Relationship is the most critical ingredient of an effective interaction.

In many situations, your technical expertise may not be available to your client unless you have strong interpersonal skills. For example, if a client fears your wrath when she tells you that she has failed to follow any of your instructions, she may withhold that information.

- How to produce effective interactions. This is explained in detail in part 1, "Exploring the POWER Process."

  1. Prepare for success
  2. Opening steps
  3. Working smarter
  4. End play
  5. Reflect prudently

- How to rapidly recover when things are not going well. This is explained in detail in part 2, "Exploring the RAPID Process."

  1. Recognize your emotional cloud.
  2. Address your emotional cloud.
  3. Pinpoint the breakdown.
  4. Identify how to get back on track.
  5. Do it.

- How to use video to systematically improve your interactions. This is explained in detail in part 3, "Exploring the LEARN Process."

  1. Listen to your interactions.
  2. Evaluate one of your interactions.
  3. Act out a role-play of this interaction.
  4. Review the video of the role-play.
  5. Next?

- Attitudes that enhance your effectiveness:

  For example, a useful mind-set in any interaction is that it is important to stay in the conversation. Continuing a conversation, even when it becomes uncomfortable, allows one to sort out confusion, distress, and disagreements. Prematurely abandoning a conversation forfeits these insights and sabotages the potential success of the interaction.

- Attitudes that interfere with your effectiveness:

   Believing that clients, colleagues, managers, or any age group or any profession could not possibly know anything about the topic of conversation works with uncanny speed to derail a conversation. Attitudes can keep you from even the slightest consideration of their input. To see this in action, pick a group, choose a topic, and identify your attitude about this group's inability to contribute to a discussion of this topic. Everyone has attitudes that make it difficult to deal with certain people and in certain situations.

A Working Partner and Video-Based Coaching

Improving the quality of your meetings requires practice and a working partner. Some improvement is possible working alone. For instance, you can become more aware of how you use gestures by practicing in front of a mirror.

However, there is an old saying, "It takes two logs to keep a fire burning." Similarly, the encouragement and assessment of a working partner are essential to achieving success while implementing the activities described in this book. Since videoing and analyzing role-plays with your partner are central to these activities, select a working partner carefully. Verify that both of you look at the world through different lenses. If you are to add value to each other, this is necessary.

Consistently keep the promises you make to each other to become predictable and trustworthy. Patiently create a relationship in which each of you

- is honest,

- has goals that are aligned with the other's (not necessarily identical and definitely not at odds with each another), and
- treats the other with respect.

Though the task may be daunting, the strength of such a relationship will serve you both well, especially when your partner is explaining weaknesses of one of your favorite strategies. The return on your investment will be much greater than its cost.

Your working partner does not have to be a professionally trained coach or counselor. Both of you can support and coach each other as you improve your interactions.

If the only data you have on a meeting that went badly are memories, use the memories. How you start this journey toward improvement isn't nearly as important as starting it. Several of the cases in this book are based on memory because that was all that was available. However, keep in mind that we all remember selectively. Holiday dinners where siblings share their memories of childhood incidents regularly demonstrate this phenomenon.

Video can become your best friend in making a change in your life! As Barbara Kingsolver (1990) wrote, "Memory is a complicated thing, a relative to truth, but not its twin." Video is perhaps its cousin. Combining video with your memory will give you an additional perspective and enhance your ability to produce change.

Reservations

Either you or your partner may have some reservations about being videoed in a role-play. I encourage you to mutually identify and explore these reservations. Here are a few objections I have encountered and my responses:

I don't want anyone other than you and me to see the video.

Okay. Let's video the session on your cell phone. Then we can watch it at a mutually agreeable time. I will respect your confidentiality and not discuss anything on the video with anyone other than you. Will this work for you?

I'd be embarrassed to see myself on a video.

That's a natural reaction. I find it useful to remember that everything I see on my video is news to me and not to anyone else. Watching your video can help you and me be more aware of our actions and reactions in meetings. I, too, am embarrassed at times by what I see, and I'm grateful also to know what I do naturally so that I can change unwanted behavior intentionally in the future.

I don't see any benefits for me that will come from our video when I'm playing the role of client.

Based on my experience, I can assure you that there is a wealth of information you can learn by being a client in a role-play. For example, you will find that you become more aware of the value of clarity and the barriers formed from using professional jargon. The more you adhere to the character you are playing, the more you will learn.

Courage

Courage is defined as "the attitude of facing and dealing with anything recognized as dangerous, difficult, or painful, instead of withdrawing from it" (*Webster's New World Dictionary* 1980).

Courage has three parts: recognition, choice, and action.

The first component is *recognition* of an interaction as dangerous, difficult, or painful. Challenging interactions normally happen in our daily lives. One may occur when you encounter an unfamiliar airport, a new tax form, or an unexpected performance review. For your client, the triggers may include a new computer system, more responsibility, or a conference with a boss. The interactions you recognize as dangerous, difficult, or painful are a result of events that have occurred in your life. Thus, interactions that are challenging to you may not be challenging to your client and vice versa.

Second, after recognizing a troublesome situation, you now have a *choice*. Will you adopt the attitude of facing and dealing with it, or will you adopt the attitude of withdrawing from it? While we all face and deal with many of the troublesome events we encounter, most of us have certain issues we routinely avoid. Problems will arise if an important issue is on the "avoidance" list for both of you.

Third, the attitude you adopt will determine the *action* you take. If you choose to deal with the issue you regard as dangerous, difficult, or painful, a step into the unknown is required. This is the heart of courage.

You will be required to call on your courage when it comes to following the advice in this book in several situations, including: asking questions that expose you to uncertainty; saying "I don't know"; being honest; speaking your truth to a superior who may disagree with you; terminating a relationship; working with clients you regard as difficult; cleaning up mistakes you have made.

Developing courage takes time and attention. The benefits you derive will pay off when you stay the course.

A Call to Action

You *can* systematically improve the quality of your consulting practice. What are the most challenging aspects of your practice? Where are the biggest gaps between your actual and your desired interactions? Do you have any clients like Brenda? Do you suspect you may have some unproductive attitudes? Have you made statements in a heated interaction that you wish you had not? Have you had any clients who mysteriously disappeared in the middle of a project? If your answer to any of these questions is yes, read on and you will find tools to address challenges like these.

We mortals can do this! Formal training isn't required. Discipline is. You can learn lessons from your stumbling blocks, as I did. Yes, this journey will require courage. It will also cost you time, expose you to risk, and reveal aspects of your practice that will require change on your part. The more you invest, the greater will be your return. As you enhance your effectiveness, your clients will be more successful, make the contributions they wish to make, and be more satisfied with their careers. Successful clients provide future clients, enhance the reputation of your profession, and improve the quality of life on the planet.

Today there are increasing complaints about the decline in the quality of services provided by professionals. A prerequisite to improving our effectiveness is to change ourselves and stop blaming others for not being perfect. A courageous step toward rigorous self-examination is required.

PART I

Exploring the POWER Process

At work and in life, we engage in a variety of activities that involve interactions with other people. Effective interactions with your coworkers and clients are an essential element for being successful. Thus, whatever your activity, whatever your job, and whatever your role, your primary goal is to make these exchanges beneficial for all parties. Part 1 presents the POWER process, a systematic way to plan and execute effective interactions. Let's begin with an overview of the POWER process to give you a context for the rest of part 1.

There are five steps of the POWER process:

Prepare for success

Opening steps

Working smarter

End play

Reflect prudently

CHAPTER 1

The POWER Process Revealed

The Brenda case led me to see the value of having a process for intentionally creating effective interactions. At several points in that exchange, I was baffled and did not know which way to turn. The desire to have a process for addressing confusion *as it arises* led to the creation of the five-step POWER process.

Let us consider each of the five steps of POWER—*prepare, open, work, end,* and *reflect*—and how to apply them effectively.

POWER

"Power" in this context does not imply controlling, dominating, or manipulating your client; instead, POWER is an acronym for steps to achieve desired results.

Prepare

Your preparation for an interaction begins during the scheduling of the meeting. Be sure that you are both clear on when and where you are meeting, as well as the estimated length of time allotted for this meeting. Develop an agenda if possible. Ask your client if there is any background information that would be useful for you to review prior to meeting.

If you are planning to video this session, and I hope you are, now is the time to make your request. Explain that videoing this meeting is a part of your continuing effort to systematically improve your services.

To prepare for focusing your full attention on this client during the upcoming meeting, plan ahead to follow these steps:

- Manage your sleep and diet to be physically alert.
- Address any mental, physical, or emotional issues that could potentially interfere with your concentration.
- If your client has given you information on the content to be discussed, refresh your memory of it and be prepared for changes.

Interactions that begin poorly generally end poorly. Here are some preparation pitfalls to avoid:

- Poor preparation includes underestimating the value of a break between adjacent meetings. Scheduling interactions back-to-back arises from the belief that you can instantly make the transition from one client to another. I suggest having a full ten minutes between clients.
- Physical unpreparedness can result from lack of sleep, an unhealthy diet, or ignoring time management in a way that habitually leaves you running from one meeting to the next, day in and day out.
- Being emotionally upset in your personal or professional life can also interfere with being able to serve your client. Learn and practice disciplines to set aside personal matters until you can devote your full attention to them at another time. If a matter is urgent, you may need to contact your client and reschedule. Knowing yourself and the conditions under which you can be fully focused is part of your responsibility to your client.

Open

Getting prepared for a conversation is one thing. Opening the conversation effectively is another. The *open* step is comprised of four distinct conversations: time, wanted, willing, and able.

To begin, ask your client how much time is available for this interaction. Make any adjustments required after considering any changes requested by your client or you. Do this even if both of you have agreed on a time frame for this meeting in the preparation step. This is the *time conversation*.

Here's an example to help us see how the pieces of *open* work:

> Carl is flying at 7:00 p.m. tomorrow to a meeting. Steven is his favorite clothing salesman.
>
> Steven: When we scheduled this meeting, we both had one hour available for it. This still works for me. Does it work for you?
>
> Carl: Actually, no. A conflict just showed up, and I have only half an hour now. Could we at least get started?
>
> Steven: Sure and maybe we will finish in half an hour. If not, we can schedule a continuation.
>
> Carl: Great!

Ask what your client wants to receive from this interaction to learn their list of today's requests. For each request, obtain a complete description of the product or service requested, *including* by when it is to be accomplished. This is the *wanted conversation*.

> Steven: What brings you in today?
>
> Carl: I'm looking for a new suit.

Steven: Okay. Can you narrow that down a bit?

Carl: Sure. I'm attending an important sales conference, so I'd like to look at suits that would tastefully set me apart from the crowd.

Steven: Okay. Is there anything else?

Carl: I'm also searching for shoes to go with the suit.

Steven: Okay. Anything else?

Carl: Not today.

Ask yourself if you are willing to work on this project, based on your moral, ethical, and professional standards and personal preferences. This is the *willing conversation.*

(Steven to himself: *These are standard requests. I'm willing to work with him. However, I'm concerned about finding both items in thirty minutes. I'm not willing to rush the selection process.*)

Steven: I'm happy to start searching for these with you. I don't want to rush you.

Carl: Okay.

Steven: Do you have any more shopping time before the conference? *(Note the return to the time conversation.)*

Carl: I have another hour tomorrow morning, and I fly out at 7:00 p.m. tomorrow.

Ask yourself if you are able to produce the products or services, given your resources. This is the *able conversation.*

(Steven to himself: *With his additional hour tomorrow, I will be able to help him find both the suit and shoes, since I know he is generally a decisive shopper.*)

Steven: Great. That will give us time to tailor your suit before your flight.

Both the willing and able conversations consider time constraints. The number of client requests, the priority of those requests, and the estimated time required for each will directly affect your response.

Work

Address what is wanted from the interaction.

Providing complete, accurate, technical expertise is crucial for serving your client; however, it isn't enough. For example, an explanation that isn't understood is useless. Periodically assess whether your client is following you. However, if you ask, "Do you understand?" most people will say, "Yes." A better approach is to ask for an explanation of what you have been discussing. It is important that your interaction be cooperative in nature and not an interrogation. A question such as "How do you see this working with your plan?" could provide the confirmation you seek.

Be sure that your explanations address all aspects of information critical to your client's project. Take the time to do this. Be concise. During the preparation step, spend time and effort on organization and pacing of information you plan to present, as both assist comprehension. Finally, though stories may be entertaining, facts embedded in a long story have a good chance of being missed. So, attend to your client's stories, listening for facts that relate to what is wanted today, and limit the length of *your* stories.

End

Develop a workable plan and end the interaction on time.

A plan is workable if both your client and you agree on three questions: who will do what; to what standards; and by when. Assessing this requires reviewing each of the tasks to be completed and verifying your agreement.

Here, at the end, your client and you are trading a series of requests and promises. This concluding step is the last chance in this interaction to ensure that the requests and promises include all the required characteristics of the tasks to be completed as well as the time frame.

Reflect

As soon as possible following the interaction, consider what worked and what did not work, what you learned, and how this information can be useful for future interactions. Preserve these answers. Later, watch the video and discuss the session with your client, if possible.

Chapters 2–7 examine the five steps in the POWER process in detail.

As you become familiar with the five steps of the POWER process, you will become more confident and agile in revisiting the steps when required. It is important to address each of the five POWER steps at some point in the meeting.

Rarely does anyone progress linearly through POWER, RAPID, or LEARN. For example, in POWER, you may have a complete opening conversation. While you are addressing what your client wants from this interaction in the *work* step, you discover that they have additional wants. I encourage you to go back to the open conversation and clarify what these wants are, who the stakeholders are, and how the results of achieving these wants will be scrutinized and used. Considering whether you are willing and able to address these additional wants is also essential, as is reassessing the priorities for this interaction in light of the additional wants.

Table 1. The POWER process

Step	Essential Activities
Prepare	Identify and handle essential matters to be prepared for this interaction, including getting the okay to video. Allow enough time for transition from your previous activity to this interaction.
Open	Have the four *open* conversations: Agree on a *time* frame for the interaction. Identify what your client *wants* from the interaction. Assess the priority of each want. Assess whether you are *willing* to produce your client's wants. Assess whether you are *able* to produce your client's wants.
Work	Address the wants in priority order. When offering explanations, stop frequently to give your client a chance to rephrase either what they have said or what they heard you say. A request to rephrase provides an opportunity to compare what was said to what was intended. The more complex the material, the more frequently you check for comprehension.

End	Allow enough time to verify that both of you agree on what was decided today, what to do, to what standards, and by when. Close the interaction on time.
Reflect	Consider what worked and what did not work in the interaction, how this happened, and how this information can be used to improve future interactions. Take the time to do this step in writing as soon as possible. Later, watch the video and, if possible, review the session with your client. *Do not skip this step.*

Foundations of the POWER Process

There are three foundations of the POWER process: relationship, listening, and speaking. We will consider the quality of these three and how each contributes to an effective interaction. Let's begin with relationships.

There are many different degrees of relationships, which you readily recognize in your daily life. For our purposes, we will examine casual, working, and synergistic relationships.

A Casual Relationship

Let us begin with a *casual relationship*: casual—without definite or serious intention; relationship—a connection, association, or involvement. This relationship is without thoughtful intent.

> Chuck goes to the gym every week before running errands. He frequently sees another male near his age and often says "hello" or "have a good day" if they are leaving at the same time, but they have never engaged in a personal conversation.

A Working Relationship

In a working relationship, the parties

- have aligned goals,
- tell each other the truth as they see it, and
- do what is necessary to clean up incidents in which they have not stated their truth.

Chuck continues around the corner into his dry cleaner's shop and discovers that the man at the gym is Darrell, the new owner of the shop.

Now their relationship is no longer casual. It has a definite intention: Darrell provides the service of dry cleaning for Chuck, who compensates Darrell for his service. Chuck and Darrell now have a connection as customer and dry cleaner.

As long as the clothes are Chuck's, they are cleaned to his satisfaction, and he pays what Darrell asks, the interaction is successfully completed.

If, however, issues arise, such as a shirt is missing, a spot on a suit coat was not removed, and Chuck arrived at 2:00 p.m. when Darrell had promised the clothes for 6:00 p.m., their relationship is facing greater challenges than in the smooth-sailing scenario. The next step is to evolve into something more intentional than a casual relationship—namely, *a working relationship.*

At the *heart of telling the truth* as you see it is *a commitment to provide full disclosure of your intentions and keep any promises you make.* Both parties must be committed to staying in the conversation until each issue is sorted out in a mutually satisfactory manner. This is tough because many of us prefer to leave a difficult conversation rather than sort out the misunderstandings. A possibility in this scenario is for Chuck to return at 6:00 p.m., giving Darrell time to hopefully find the shirt and remove the spot.

While no expectations are present in a casual relationship, specific expectations are at the heart of a working relationship where parties have aligned goals and will keep their word. They will clean up breaks in integrity and their consequences whenever they occur. Meeting these expectations will result in the relationship consistently producing effective interactions. This is a cooperative way to work together. Trust will grow between both parties with each promise that's kept.

A Synergistic Relationship

In a synergistic relationship, the parties

- have a working relationship;
- treat each other with respect, avoid abusing each other, overtly or covertly; and
- do what is necessary to repair incidents in which they have been abusive, overtly or covertly.

If Chuck and Darrell resolve these three issues to each other's satisfaction, they have begun to build a working relationship that each of them can count on. If Chuck continues to frequent Darrell's shop and they have additional effective interactions, they will grow a stronger, more resilient relationship.

Steps along this journey will involve addressing and resolving bigger problems—the lost suit, the burn marks on an heirloom dress, and so on. If they continue to treat each other with respect, to resist denigrating each other when mistakes occur, and to stay in the difficult conversations until they are resolved, they will gradually develop a *synergistic relationship*, one in which their combined efforts produce a total effect that is greater than either could have produced alone. Each is trustworthy in the eyes of the other.

Treating each other with respect also produces a relationship that's cooperative rather than adversarial. Neither is in competition with the other. The synergistic relationship is also collaborative rather than hierarchical. Decisions are made on the basis of conversations that reach consensus. Neither tries to dominate the decision-making process by dictating what will be done.

Even in consultations where one person is the other's boss, a collaborative relationship is still possible. What this requires is that the boss does not use positional power in the organization to resolve disagreements.

> **Positional Power**
>
> The power that a person has in an organization due to rank.

A synergistic relationship is stronger than a working relationship by virtue of producing higher-quality results because of the trust developed in each other. When each realizes that they can make a mistake without being put down by the other, they are free to take risks and be more creative. They no longer have to take the safest path through each situation they encounter.

Two of the most important consequences of a synergistic relationship are that both parties are confident that

- they can disagree with the other without being abused in any manner, overtly or covertly, and
- they can speak up when their goals conflict or their integrity is challenged.

A disagreement is resolved in a respectful conversation that both stay in until it is complete to the satisfaction of both. Neither is a yes-man. They value this perhaps more than any other aspect of the relationship, as the more successful each is in their career, the harder it will be for them to find someone they can count on for the truth. This is the kind of relationship I referred to in the introduction while describing the characteristics I recommend for your partner who will work through this book with you.

> Returning to our example, Chuck is the manager of a marketing firm. He and Darrell have sons on the same soccer team that could use new uniforms. They live in a small town with plenty of civic spirit and not much money for extra school expenses. As his relationship with Darrell deepens, he begins to see possibilities for working with Darrell to develop a fundraising project for the team: 10 percent of the money spent during soccer weeks at team-sponsoring stores will be contributed by the stores to the team for new uniforms. Possibilities like this evolve naturally in synergistic relationships as each party is encouraged to look beyond the original reasons they had for working together.

In summary, an effective interaction builds trust between your client and you, which strengthens your relationship. Building a strong relationship with your client allows both of you to deal with increasingly difficult challenges and have effective interactions in an ever-widening set of circumstances.

Conversational Roles: Speaking and Listening

Volumes have been written on "the art of conversation" and for good reason: thoughtful conversation is the foundation of successful communication. The *art* portion of the phrase refers to the relative ease with which we begin and end the exchange, how smoothly we switch between the role of speaker and the role of listener and vice versa, how efficiently we present our message, and how carefully we respect and share the space and time allotted. When done well, conversation is like a dance; when done poorly, it becomes a duel!

The Role of Speaker

Before you say anything, be clear about what you *intend* to communicate. Concentrate on your message and your choice of words, sequence, and length that will best convey a clear message. Consider your vocabulary and how it will be interpreted. Everyone has certain words that trigger personal reactions, but you will not have this information for each individual you encounter, especially unfamiliar persons, so pay attention to your listener's reactions.

Be attentive to your use of slang—words that are specific to your profession, culture, or generation. Different interpretations of certain words among various groups may surprise you and confuse the other person or worse. My years working in the UK provided this experience regularly. Being clear and true to your message is your major goal.

After you have spoken, consider what you said and compare it to your intention. If your words don't match your intention, immediately retract your statement and try again.

As a speaker who has delivered a message that reflects your intention, you have one more step to consider: has the listener interpreted the message in a way that reflects your intention? To assume that your listener has understood your message could be a major miscalculation. You can avoid this misstep by saying something similar to, "Would you please rephrase what you just heard so I can check to see if I have omitted anything you will need?" Be certain your listener understands that you are evaluating your delivery and not their comprehension. The more important the message, the more critical it is that you engage in checking for mutual comprehension.

> **Stumbling Block**
>
> Often what you hear isn't what your client intended to say, and vice versa.

The Role of Listener

In a successful conversation, the roles of speaker and listener are fluid, and exchanges between the conversational partners are relaxed and respectful. If you find yourself in the role of the speaker vastly more than listener, that is called a lecture, and listeners are often offended, so learn to be a great listener. It is a skill that will serve you well.

As a speaker only moments before, you now assume the role of listener, hopefully with as much resolve and attention as when you spoke. Many people find listening more difficult than speaking, often because we are likely to be planning our next comment rather than paying attention to the speaker. Instead, listen as if you have never been presented with any of the material before, especially if you have heard it a hundred times! Your attentiveness often pays off in discovering information that you missed or that was added or revised.

In the role of listener, to assume that you understand the speaker is just as dangerous as it was when you were the speaker. As listener, you can approach this stumbling block by saying, "This is a complex topic. May I confirm that I have correctly interpreted what you said?"

Listening is a learned behavior. Ask any parent! And careful listening will serve you for a lifetime.

Body Language

Many books have been written about body language. Most people are familiar with the rudiments of what they say. For example, a popular interpretation of body language is to view someone sitting with their arms crossed as resistant to input, perhaps even impervious to outside information. The problem is that sometimes people sit with their arms crossed because they are cold. A good approach to body language is to attend to the hypothesis that this posture suggests and check it out. For example, in the crossed-arms situation, you could ask, "I'm sorry I forgot to ask. Is the room temperature comfortable for you?" There is so much information in what your client says that my usual advice is to attend to the spoken words and sort out any confusion you encounter there.

However, useful information about nonverbal communication that goes well beyond that found in books on body language is presented in a TED talk (Cuddy 2012) entitled "Your Body Language Shapes Who You Are."

Speaking

There are four broad categories of statements that are useful in interactions:

> requests,

> demands,

> promises, and

> assertions.

These statements differ in their forms. Understanding these differences will enhance your ability to communicate effectively. Each is explored in detail below.

Requests

A complete request has two components: a detailed description of the task requested and a statement of by when the task is to be completed. To omit either component can easily derail an interaction. Sometimes when we are reluctant to make a request, we leave out the detailed description or the "by when."

The three possible responses to a legitimate request are to accept, deny, or deny with a counteroffer. When making a request, be honest with yourself: Are you willing to consider all three of the responses to a legitimate request? Or is "accept" the only tolerable response? If so, you have not made a legitimate request; you have made a demand. People often try to camouflage a demand as a request.

When denying a request, a denial with a counteroffer gives the other person more information and may facilitate finding a mutually satisfactory way forward.

> "What kind of graph will you use in the final report?"

> "I'm not sure. I can give you a simple example of what's possible. Would that work for you for now?"

> "Sure."

Demands

In contrast to a request, the only acceptable response to a demand is yes. Calling a demand a request will damage your relationship with your client. The distinction between a request and a demand is important. Polite terms will not transform a demand into a request. Most anyone will see through such an attempt at camouflage.

Rarely does someone say, "I demand that you do this." More frequently, you become aware that a request is in fact a demand when all counteroffers that you make are declined. Eventually you realize that the only acceptable response is yes. You may wish to clarify matters by asking, "Is this really a request, or is this a demand?"

When your boss makes a demand of you, learn what the consequences of denying it are before you do so. If the price of denial is high, you may wish to reconsider your denial.

Promises

A complete promise, like a request, has two components: a detailed description of the task promised and a statement of by when the promise will be fulfilled. Both components are required. Sometimes when we are reluctant to make a promise, we leave out the detailed description or the by-when date.

Whenever you make a promise to your client, you have three options: keep it, break it, or revoke it. The first two are obvious. The third is less so.

As the by-when date draws near and you realize that you don't have the necessary resources to complete the promised task on time, revoke your promise. Likewise, when you realize that any part of your promise is in jeopardy, revoke or replace it with one you can fulfill.

This action is distinctly superior to breaking your promise. Your client will still be upset that you are not delivering on your original promise but will probably be less upset than if you break your promise without warning. The sooner you choose to revoke your promise, the less upset your client will be. Revoking your promise at the last minute will be interpreted as a broken promise.

A friend regularly borrows my lawnmower. His skillful use of requests and promises, coupled with his generosity, makes these interactions effective.

> "It's time for me to mow my yard again. When will your mower be available next week?"

> "Tuesday through Friday."

> "Okay. I will pick it up on Wednesday and return it on Friday with a full gas tank and with the oil checked."

He picks it up on Wednesday and always returns it by Friday evening, with the gas tank full and additional oil, if necessary.

Over the past two years, we have created a synergistic relationship based on these effective interactions. Our conversations have expanded to include discussions of many challenging professional or personal situations, leading to a good neighbor relationship.

Assertions

An assertion is a statement that you can prove. "I have read two books in preparation for this meeting" is a valid assertion if, indeed, you have read two books and can show their application to the topics in this meeting.

Rigorous Listening and Speaking

Clients also make requests, demands, promises, and assertions. An important part of working with your clients is to find out "by when" and "conditions for satisfaction" for each request and promise they make. For critical assertions, it is also important to find out what evidence your client has for them. These conversations can be challenging when your client is your boss or anyone with authority in your world, such as a parent, teacher, doctor, or police officer.

During an interaction, your client will have questions about your statements. You may have noticed that your responses to these questions vary. One response is a willingness to consider any and all questions about your statements. On the other hand, you may get defensive if you discover that your statement under scrutiny has been rejected. Think carefully about your requests, promises, and assertions before making them. Calmly explaining statements when they are questioned reflects your integrity and accountability. Staying present, focusing on your intent while speaking, will improve the quality of any interaction.

Recap

The POWER process consists of five steps that you can use to produce effective interactions: *prepare, open, work, end,* and *reflect.* The results of using the power process depend on the strength of the relationship you have with your client, how well you listen, and how rigorously you speak.

Frequently Asked Questions

1. What can I do when I've explained everything and my client still insists on a different solution than the one I recommend? I feel a responsibility to deliver the best solution, but I see conflict arising.

    To resolve this conflict collaboratively, the template I use goes like this: "I favor doing Action A for several strong reasons, and you have indicated a strong preference for doing Action B. Please help me understand your reasoning to see if there is something that you are considering that I'm not and vice versa." I prefer invitations to force. Seeking to force your client to do anything will have a negative impact on your relationship.

2. A physician said, "I don't have enough time with each patient to be as complete as you suggest in the *work* step. Rules exist for how much time I can spend with each patient. What can I do when today's time is up and my patient is upset because questions remain unanswered?"

    This issue is growing larger every day as insurance companies, hospitals, HMOs, and private practices construct guidelines and rules for how much time a doctor may spend on a particular procedure or conversation. This situation can create problems for both doctors and patients; however, your heart is in the right place. Although it may not be optimal for all situations, I suggest considering the following:

    Take advantage of the intake appointment. Most physicians are granted more time and leeway for this initial meeting. Allot a portion of time to acquaint new patients with the constraints you have within your practice.

    Provide written material that clarifies procedural information, such as what to do in an emergency, how to access an after-hours physician, how missed appointments and late arrivals are managed, and what to expect when the day's schedule is running behind.

Inquire if your practice is able to offer telephone or digital access to a qualified person who will handle most questions and requests for information. If not, direct the message to your nurse. I have found that this access addresses the majority of my reasons for contacting my physician's office after a visit.

It is helpful to talk with other physicians dealing with time constraints. Most of them will have similar issues and may have solutions you could incorporate.

3.   I have been reading about "active listening." How does that method relate to the conversational roles discussion earlier in this chapter?

It is my understanding that the purpose of active listening is to verify what you have heard by rephrasing the speaker's input. During a typical conversation, *both* consultant and client will assume the roles of speaker and listener. In each role, one has the responsibility to be understood. This is often accomplished by restating the speaker's message in one's own words. The speaker's job is to verify that their intention has been accurately interpreted by the listener. The listener's job is to verify that their interpretation accurately reflects the intention of the speaker.

4.   Have you ever watched a video with your client?

Yes, I have. Watching the video and comparing notes with the client in the video was very informative. I have not done this often, and in hindsight, I regret that decision. Using and watching video are easier now with the advent of smartphones. I encourage you to experiment with video as often as possible. In my experience, clients are eager to contribute to improving the effectiveness of their consultants. This became apparent when virtually all our clients in the FSU Statistical Consulting Center agreed to be videoed when we instituted that aspect of our program.

CHAPTER 2

Preparing for Success

Now that we have taken a brief look at the major steps of the POWER process, let's examine each step on its own. As you recall, the first step in this process involves preparing for a client meeting. We will cover each of the three components in this step as we continue:

1. Review the POWER process.
2. Prepare for the content.
3. Get focused.

These actions improve your chances of having an effective interaction with your client, the start of developing a working relationship.

Review the POWER Process

Begin your preparation by rereading table 1 (the POWER process), which is presented in chapter 1.

Jot down a few words to help you stay on track during the meeting. My favorites are "focus, time, wants, clarity, end, respect." They are reminders to

- focus on my client before, during, and at the close of our interaction;
- agree on how much time is available;

- have a wanted conversation at the beginning of the session and return to it when either of us seems lost, confused, or unclear;
- frequently check to be sure that both my client and I are clear about what is being discussed;
- agree on who will do what, by when, and to what standards at the end of the session; and
- attend to whether I'm respecting my client by their standards rather than mine.

This activity can serve to prepare you for the interaction and help you get back on track when the conversation strays.

If this is the first interaction you have had with this client, it may well be on the phone or by email. Its purposes may be to identify when and where you will meet, as well to agree on a proposed agenda for the interaction and an ending time.

Another part of preparation for a meeting is to plan how you will deal with any sexist, racist, or ageist comments that may be made. Use your plan the first time such a comment is made because this is the most effective time to address it. If you have not yet developed such a plan, now is the time to do so.

Still other questions may show up and can be considered in your preparation, such as:

- Are you willing and able to work after hours or on weekends? For free? For regular pay? For overtime pay?
- Are you willing and able to expend the time and energy required to expand your technical expertise?
- Are there some actions that you are unwilling to engage in for moral, ethical, or personal reasons?

Thoughtfully consider these matters during a quiet, calm time well before the interaction begins. Attempting to address them thoughtfully in a heated interaction is virtually impossible.

If you have met with this client before, mentally review previous meetings to see if issues remain that you did not address before and you do want to address now before any more time passes. Perhaps your client made comments that you found offensive and did not address. You may have agreed to work on a weekend as a one-time exception. How will you deal with a request that you work on a weekend "just one more time"? Did your client speak faster than you could understand or with an accent you had trouble comprehending?

Just because you did not deal well with these issues in the past does not mean you can't deal effectively with them today. If you don't, they will be even more difficult to deal with in future meetings.

This conversation goes both ways: Are you treating your client with respect? Does your client have issues with you from previous meetings? Unless you are a mind reader, the only way to find out is to ask. Concentrating when unresolved issues are present is like trying to concentrate with the proverbial elephant in the middle of the room.

Prepare for the Content

Examine the boundaries on your ability and willingness to address this client's requests. First, candidly self-assess your technical expertise in areas that you think may be relevant to your client's presenting problem. In addition, examine your ability to expand your technical expertise as needed and review your prior commitments.

Since the Brenda case, I have been reluctant to spend time preparing for *potential* technical topics that *may* relate to my client's problem. In my experience, time spent on technical topics yields higher returns after having clarified in our first interaction what my client's specific technical questions are. If a client sends a description of their problem, read it before the interaction. However, the best preparation for the content of an interaction is to go into it with a commitment to serve your client, whatever comes up, including surprises.

If you have agreed to complete certain tasks that will be discussed in this meeting, do that! If circumstances have arisen so that you have not done this, let your client know as soon as it becomes apparent to you that you won't have the tasks done before the meeting. Then alternative plans can be made. A barrier to having this conversation is a form of optimism many of us experience: somehow in the last day before the meeting, we will get three days' work done, just in time! Once in a while, this magical thinking works, just often enough to keep us using it! Don't count on it!

Being prepared does not mean that you will be able to answer all questions that may arise, because you have no control over what your client will ask. When you have no idea how to answer a question or when either of you becomes distressed, stay in the conversation to resolve the discomfort by clarifying the question and identifying your resources to address it. By bringing flexibility to the interaction in this way, you can best serve your client and maintain calm as you sort through options.

One way to begin this process is to summon the courage to say, "I don't know." Stay in the conversation until you have identified exactly what question has stumped you. Promise to investigate the matter and report your findings by a specific time. Don't pretend you have the answer; clients are remarkably adept at detecting this ruse. In my experience, faking it will jeopardize your relationship.

Assemble an ever-growing list of resources, including people and websites, to turn to when you encounter an unexpected question that baffles you. Intentionally gathering this list is an efficient way to enhance your effectiveness.

Realize that asking questions is a sign of strength rather than weakness. We are no longer in school; the rules have changed. No one

Stepping Stone

Compile a list of print and internet references as well as people you know who can help when you are baffled. Be prepared!

expects you to be able to answer all their questions immediately. You may have just said, "Wrong! I expect myself to have all the answers!" If so, you have an attitude that will not serve you well, as it is a barrier to being honest with your client when you are perplexed or confused. Identifying dysfunctional attitudes is an important segment of preparing for the meeting.

Get Focused

Focusing includes assessing whether this is still a good time for you to meet, reflecting on the purpose of this interaction, and considering how you may be of service to your client. Today may no longer be a good time for you to meet. If it isn't, reschedule as soon as you discover the need to change this.

The purpose of today's interaction may be clear from an agenda your client has sent you. However, your client may now have additional questions for you. Remind yourself to start the meeting with a wanted conversation so that you are working on your client's current top-priority question.

As you consider how you can be of service to your client, reflect on the many ways in which you serve, such as listening, recommending actions, identifying potential sources of information, and reformulating your client's question in a way that more accurately addresses your client's long-term goal.

Emotions can be challenging right before a meeting. Anxiety is a frequent stumbling block. Two strategies for managing the effects of anxiety are as follows:

- Stay in the present. The only way you can be of support to your client today is to keep your mind in the present; don't wander off into either the past or the future.
- Focus on being client-centered rather than self-centered. How can you contribute to your client today?

You can use these strategies whenever anxiety arises during a meeting. After such a meeting, write a note to yourself about what triggered your anxiety as best you can recall. In time, you will see a pattern from which you can develop a plan for how to deal with your anxiety triggers. Add to your premeeting focus activities any plans you develop that help you deal with your anxiety whenever a trigger occurs.

> **Stumbling Block**
>
> Anxiety: the anticipation of pain.

These focusing strategies require time between meetings. Schedule your meetings with enough time to transition mentally from one client or activity to the next. Also allow enough travel time between meetings. Putting these margins into your life will do wonders to reduce the level of stress you encounter.

Prepare for all aspects of your interactions by using each step of the POWER process in conversations you have with a friend in which you are asking for help or someone is asking you for help. The more times you practice using the POWER process, the more proficient you will become.

A great way to build in practice time is to agree with your partner that you will have a wanted conversation at the start of each of your interactions. Suppose you are meeting to decide where to go to lunch. Your partner wants to go to a new place. Sit at their desk and video the interaction with your phone. Even when the interaction is short, it will provide useful information if you video it. Later in the day, watch the video together. How did it go for each of you?

Increase Your Courage

Inventory the situations you recognize as dangerous, difficult, or painful so that you are not blindsided when one occurs. Make notes about each of these as you encounter them. As you become more aware, you will be able to recognize the scenario early on. This will make it easier to identify and address the fear or anxiety attached to each one as it happens.

Realize that you have a choice when encountering a dangerous situation. You can face and deal with it, or you can withdraw from it. Remember that discretion is often the better part of valor. It is okay to withdraw from the situation and make notes about it. Eventually, as you practice, you will become better equipped to adopt the attitude of facing and dealing with what you recognize as a threat because you have learned how to defuse the fear and anxiety that arise when you face a difficult situation.

When you have successfully used different ways to defuse situations, you will take the step into the unknown and deal with your fear. If you are not comfortable in an interaction, withdrawing is not failure; it gives you a chance to analyze the situation and deal with it another day when you are ready.

The Prepare Checklist

1. Review the POWER process.
2. Prepare for the content.
3. Focus.

Construct an Effective Role-Play

The current widespread availability of video removes technical barriers to videoing a role-play or an actual meeting. However, interpersonal and intrapersonal barriers to video still remain.

Participants in courses and workshops often resist performing role-plays because they have found the experience embarrassing or difficult, resulting in little or no useful information. The steps below are tried-and-true actions designed to create role-play experiences that will be of value to both you and your working partner.

1. Address each person's attitudes toward role-plays. Move ahead only when each sees value in this activity.

2. Identify a situation that you would like to resolve more effectively in the future. Assuming the role of the consultant, describe this situation to your partner, who will assume the role of the client.

3. The consultant lists the desired learning outcomes from the role-play.

4. Your partner, in the role of the client, is responsible for creating dialogue that will target one or more of the desired outcomes. Engaging in role-play does *not* require formal training as an actor. Respond as you would if it were a situation arising in your daily life. Though this is a practice session, your ability to be authentic will provide the best results. As in all practice sessions, in the arts or in sports, the benefit you receive will be directly proportional to the effort you give.

5. Agree on who will own the video and when it will be deleted.

6. Practice with your partner using the video owner's smartphone to video the role-play, verifying that you are getting a clear picture and sound with both individuals in the frame.

7. During the role-play, either of you may start laughing. Recover as soon as possible and return to the point of interruption. Know that nervous or self-conscious feelings during role-play are natural.

8. When one is assuming the role of the client, respond with plausible answers. This will add to the authentic feeling of the exercise.

9. When the role-play is complete, turn off the camera and briefly discuss the role-play in general. Watch the video. Then explore in depth the outcome for the consultant—namely, were the desired learning outcomes achieved? If not, repeat the role-play with any changes that will address the outcomes not achieved.

Chapter 2 Activity

Now that we've explored the *prepare* step of the POWER process, it's time to practice with your role-play partner. Using a smartphone, digital camera, or video device of your preference, have your partner set a five-minute alarm and start videoing both of you when you are ready to start your role-play.

Sometimes clients say they are meeting with me because they have been assured by their boss that I will be able to help them prove that they are right in some dispute. My response is that I supply consultation, not agreement. I promise to carefully consider their situation and give them my honest assessment of it, which may not be the answer they want.

Role-Play

Generate a videoed role-play in which your partner plays such a client—one who continues to look for agreement with their point of view.

Throughout this book, I will suggest role-plays in a text box as above.

Tips for you:

Have a willing conversation with the new client.
Have an able conversation with the new client.

Tips for the new client (your partner):

Begin with the following sentences: "I'm so happy to catch you. My boss assures me that you will be able to help me prove that I'm right in a dispute that has arisen in our department. Can we get together this afternoon? My time line for resolving this dispute is tight." Make up a plausible dispute and be passionate about why your position is right and your colleagues' position is wrong. Think back to the last dispute that has arisen in your life.

Following your role-play exercise, explore the chapter 2 debriefing questions at the end of this chapter. Please look at these questions with your partner *after* having completed this activity, as you will learn more from the role-play experience this way.

Brenda's Case—The Prepare Checklist

To see how the *prepare* checklist works, let's apply it to Brenda's case.

1. Review the POWER process.

    > My intention was to explain the plan I had designed for Brenda over the weekend and tell her what she had to do to successfully complete it. The meeting would be a one-way flow of information, punctuated only by her agreeing to take all the steps I recommended.

    > To be better prepared, I could have held the plan I developed lightly, not being certain that it would solve all her problems. I also would have been better prepared by reminding myself to engage in a dialogue rather than deliver a lecture.

2. Prepare for the content.

    > Paradoxically, the preparation I did for this interaction was not helpful. My attachment to it served as a barrier to considering the content (in this case, a change from her prior information) that Brenda wanted to discuss with me.

    > Holding my preparation lightly would have served both Brenda and me by making it easier for me to address the content she was interested in discussing, rather than the content that I was prepared to discuss.

3. Focus.

Focusing was not on my mental agenda when I entered the videotaping room. In fact, I was fragmented: I was late and upset when she was not where I expected her to be.

Client-centered preparation was also missing. My preparation consisted entirely of working to create a bulletproof way to explain my plan to this client who had not taken a statistics course. At the time, my preparation seemed to me sufficient. I did not discuss it with anyone else.

I confidently entered the session committed to delivering my prepared material. The thought never entered my mind that Brenda's goals for the meeting may have changed in the five days since she filled out her New Client Information Form. In my mind, unconsciously, she was obligated to follow her original plan. This point of view left me upset when she did not.

At the time of the meeting, I was unaware of my negative attitudes toward young clients, certain research questions, and clients who are unwilling to follow my advice. I was also unaware of how strongly these attitudes negatively impacted my professional practice.

Addressing all these issues required many conversations and repeated viewings of the video of our meeting to identify the issues. Addressing them then required several personal policy shifts that were challenging and took time, sometimes years, to complete.

Consultants at all stages in their careers make similar mistakes, with similar dire consequences. To avoid this,

- have a *flexible strategy* for your interaction,
- be *ready for the content* of the meeting without falling into the trap of thinking you already know exactly what will happen, and
- *focus* yourself on serving your client immediately before your interaction.

These are essential steps to take regardless of how many times you have been in a similar interaction.

Be prepared!

Recap

Prepare for every meeting, even those with drop-in clients. Review the POWER process. Prepare for the content. Focus. Set aside distractions.

Frequently Asked Questions

Below are questions that come up in discussions about the *prepare* step of the POWER process. I hope my answers are helpful.

1. Lots of people recommend, "Fake it till you make it." Why don't you?

   Faking anything is risky to the relationship. Underneath the "faking" is a lie since you are not telling the truth about what you know and don't know. This lack of integrity is damaging when your client discovers the lie. The persistent question that remains in the relationship is, "What can you be counted on knowing, *really* knowing?"

2. What if your boss calls right before you are to have a meeting with your client?

   Tell your boss the truth: you are to meet with your client now. Ask your boss what to do: reschedule your client or call back as soon as the meeting is over. In my experience, trying to have even "just a short phone conversation" with your boss under these circumstances isn't a good idea. You already have committed this time to your client. Honoring that commitment is also in your boss's best interest.

Role-Play

Create a videoed role-play of this situation, with your partner playing the part of your boss.

Remember that this is the person who does your annual review.

3. I have no quiet place to focus myself before my interactions. What can I do?

    Keep searching. How about climbing stairs, taking a walk outside, or sitting in the corner of an office of a colleague who won't disturb you?

4. Sometimes someone drops into my office and starts asking me a question. I don't have time to prepare. What can I do?

    First, look at your calendar and tell the truth. Do you have time to meet right now? If not, say so and offer to schedule a later time. If you can meet right now, consider how long it will take you to transition your brain from what you were doing to being able to have an effective meeting with the person who dropped in. Also, look at how long you have available for this meeting. See if that works. If it does not, offer to schedule a later time. Remember: nothing takes "just a moment." How long will it realistically take for both of you to have an effective interaction on the matter at hand? (Note: all these activities are preparation!)

Role-Play

Drop-ins are great interactions to practice because they occur so frequently.

After you do the video coaching session with your partner, pay attention to how well you deal with this type of interaction in your day-to-day work environment. If problems persist, return to your partner and redo the role-play, concentrating on those problems you encounter in your life.

5. I'm scheduled to meet my first client next week. I know that I don't have the complete collection of tools that experienced consultants possess. How can I prepare?

> Begin your preparation by doing all tasks and answering all questions in this chapter with your partner. Pay special attention to the paragraphs at the end of "Step 2. Prepare for the Content" about "I don't know" and asking questions. These *do* apply to you (as well as to all experienced consultants)!
>
> Even though this is your first meeting with a client, that client will still expect the interaction to produce these results:

   i. The interaction ends with a workable plan, a plan where both your client and you know what to do next, to what criteria and by when, and the plan is implemented.

  ii. The results of the plan stand up to external scrutiny.

 iii. Your client regards you as a valuable resource for future interactions.

> Which of these three results would you not expect if you were the client? Prepare accordingly.

Role-Play

Practice an interaction with your partner similar to your best guess as to what the interaction with your first client will be like.

Video it. Review the video with your partner. If you are able to do additional videoed practice interactions with persons similar to your first client, great! The time and energy you spend on these role-plays will pay big dividends. The more realistically challenging the role-plays are, the better.

> Meet with your client alone only when your self-assessment is that you are capable of having an effective interaction. If you

are not at that point, arrange for a more experienced consultant to also be present with you in the meeting.

Contact your client before the session and ask for permission to video it as a part of your professional development program. Invite your client to review this video with you after the session as another part of your professional development program.

These two tasks are challenging, even for seasoned professionals. If you are not ready to do them now, that's normal. Keep looking for situations in which you are ready to do them. These situations will appear! Hang in there.

Chapter 2 Debriefing Questions

Watch the video.

What did you notice? How effectively did you deal with the situation? Did you do it without damaging your relationship with the client?

You may be surprised at what you see! Unclear language. Your voice may be too soft or too loud. The point is to watch the video to find out. Constantly reassess yourself as a professional. Continuing education takes work, time, and motivation to pursue and complete!

Did you agree that you could help the client? What did you say you were willing to do? Able to do?

Did you keep looking for alternatives that would work for both of you?

CHAPTER 3

Open with Intention

The *open* step begins, as you might expect, by introducing yourself. This courtesy serves as an affirmation for your client that they are talking to the person they came to see. In addition, it is an invitation for your client to respond in kind, which assures that you are talking to the right person as well. This confirmation is especially important when you are meeting each other for the first time.

In the *open* step are four conversations: time, wanted, willing, and able. Mastering these will give you a running start toward having an effective interaction.

The Time Conversation

The purpose of the time conversation is for you and your client to explicitly agree on how much time is available for today's interaction. Knowing this benefits both of you, as it avoids surprises at the end of the interaction, such as one of you standing up to leave when the other thinks twenty minutes are left.

Stepping Stone

Agree with your client on how much time is available at the start of the interaction. If you forget, stop your conversation as soon as possible and return to this task before proceeding.

A simple beginning is "It's good to see you. Is this still a good time for you to meet?" and, if so, "How much time do you have available?"

Your client may not, in fact, have a whole hour you agreed to yesterday, for a variety of reasons. For instance, their group may be understaffed today due to an unexpected absence. If now isn't a good time to meet, reschedule!

Confirm the time available at each meeting. Life brings constant changes.

On the other hand, if you are the one whose schedule for today has suddenly changed, call your client as soon as possible to revisit the time conversation.

Role-Play

Design a videoed role-play of a first meeting with a client who does not have as much time as they thought they would yesterday when you set up this meeting.

Did you come to an agreement on how long this meeting will last?

Agreeing on the time available for a meeting may sound simple, but it is not easy. It is difficult for a variety of reasons. Here are a few.

I have worked with many professionals on this material. The biggest pushback has been that they did not want to tell their supervisor that they had a prior commitment and could not participate in a meeting the boss had just called. Not revealing this information to their boss is an example of not fully disclosing their situation and will eventually undermine their relationship. Courage is required to tell the truth about how much time you have available for a last-minute meeting, especially when your boss is asking.

Some people think asking about time is inappropriate, especially if the client is their boss. They are afraid that they will be judged as disrespectful. To avoid this risk, explain to your boss that knowing how much time they have available for this interaction will allow you to better use their time by prioritizing your activities according to the amount of time available.

Discussing a time frame for an interaction reveals other thorny issues relating to personal work styles and attitudes about boundaries around time. Some believe that they should always be available to their clients regardless of prior commitments. However, setting and keeping priorities requires setting boundaries around time.

Boundaries around your time are also necessary to manage your well-being so that you can continue to serve your clients without burning out. Some believe that it is inappropriate to protect personal time for themselves "just" for relaxation. Recall that every flight attendant instructs us, "Put on your own oxygen mask first before assisting others."

There are cultural challenges relating to the time conversation. In many cultures, it is considered rude to initiate business without first engaging in small talk. The term "small talk" is a misnomer. These initial discussions are, in fact, anything but small. Your client and you form your initial impressions of each other during this time. These impressions set the tone for conversations in this and future meetings. Through them, your client senses whether this is a safe space. They are forming opinions about your level of respect for them from clues such as your willingness to share the floor. These preliminaries are important to the success of all your interactions—present and future.

Having the time conversation in the first meeting is difficult in large part because it is so rarely done. It is especially difficult in a first meeting with a client from another culture. I prefer to start the conversation with an invitation: "It's good to see you today. Would you like a cup of coffee or tea before we begin?" After serving the beverage, pick your favorite small talk starter. Possibilities include "How are you doing today?" and "Did you have any trouble finding a parking place?" Avoid questions like "How was your weekend?" because they may lead to long digressions. The challenge is to have enough preliminary conversation to set your client at ease and not so much as to seriously compromise the time available for work. If you are meeting your client for the first time, the small talk may be extended.

When you sense there is a break in the preliminary conversation, you might ask, "What would you like to do in the time we have today?" or "How can I help you today?"

At least *two major exceptions* to the use of small talk exist. Here is a possible way for you to handle each. For clients who have an urgent need to begin, follow your client. Read the following and imagine yourself in this situation.

> Client: I need to get right to work. I have a major deadline on Friday.
>
> You: Okay. How much time do you have for our meeting today?
>
> Client: Two hours.
>
> You: All right. What are your top priority items for today's agenda?

A second exception:

> Client: I'm so upset. My daughter was in a car accident last night.
>
> You: I'm so sorry to hear that. How do you feel about working today?
>
> Client: I had planned to reschedule. As the day has gone on, I can see that it's important to meet with you today. I think I can handle it.

You: Okay. Tell me if something changes. How much time do we have?

Another challenge occurs in the time conversation when your client asks you to work under a time constraint that you can see will cause the project to fail. This situation can arise if your client insists a problem be solved in less time than is required in your experience and says, "I have only thirty minutes to solve this," or assumes you have unlimited time available and says, "I have as much time as it takes."

Whatever the situation, don't agree to a time plan that you know will fail. Amazingly, many smart people agree to plans they know are likely to crash and burn. Here are three attitudes I have seen precede this course of action:

- I want to please my paying client by saying yes to all their requests.
- I don't want to rock the boat in any way, regardless of the consequences.
- My annual review is next month, and I will look bad if I say no.

Weak interpersonal skills can negate even the strongest technical skills. If you know you have a strong tendency to be a people pleaser, whenever you are feeling pressured to work on a project, one possibility is to stop and say, "This project is intriguing. Please give me a day to consider if I can rearrange my existing commitments to work on it."

A possible response to your client who has "as much time as it takes" is to offer an alternative, such as, "For a problem of this complexity, I prefer to work in ninety-minute sessions. I propose that we try this. Will this work for you?" If the answer is no, explore whether your client would like you to assist in finding another consultant who is willing to work in the way your client desires. Boundaries are a potential issue in every interaction. Stay alert for situations that can sabotage your ability to continue to serve your other clients. Keep yourself healthy in every way.

Agreeing on a time line with a drop-in client who begins with the infamous question, "Do you have a minute?" is also challenging. Look at your schedule, decide how much time you *do* have, and be clear. "I have ten minutes right now. Is that enough, or shall we meet when we will have more time to consider your question in detail?"

Sometimes this person will say, "That's enough," and sometimes it is. On other occasions, at the eight-minute point, it will be obvious that you won't finish in the next two minutes. Then you can say, "It looks like we won't finish within our ten minutes. Would you like to schedule another time to continue? I do have to stop momentarily."

Agreeing on a time frame isn't enough; honoring it is also required. A consultant may assume that, even if a client says they want to finish by 2:00 p.m., when this same client seems so interested in the gems being dispensed by the consultant, they are actually available until 2:20 p.m. This conjecture results in the message that there is nothing in the client's life as important as continuing to listen to the consultant. Not honoring a client's time line will reduce the chances of repeat business from this client.

> **Stumbling Block**
>
> Assuming that an agreed-upon time line may be ignored is dangerous and disrespectful.

Role-Play

Pick one of the challenging situations mentioned above in this section. Construct a videoed role-play of it with your partner.

What did you each learn from the video?

> **Role-Play**
>
> Generate a videoed role-play with a client who has found you at the water fountain and asked, "Do you have a second? I've got a simple question for you."
>
> How long did it take you to deal with the simple question?

Often there are *two time lines* to consider: the time line for today's meeting and the time line for a larger project of which today's work is part. Addressing these two distinct time lines is illustrated in the following example.

Sarah has hired John to help her complete a two-month landscaping project. The first part of the plan has been completed, a preliminary blueprint for a three-acre plot of land. They are meeting at his nursery today to begin picking out the foliage. Read the following and imagine yourself in this situation.

>Sarah: Hi, John. Are you ready to get started? (John nods.) Great! I'd like to order all the plants today. I know that will be fun because you work with so many different suppliers in other states.

>John: I'm eager to get to that part too. First we have to determine the condition of the soil and how much sun different parts of the plot will get as the seasons change. The sooner we accomplish that, the sooner we can order plants. Before we start, may I check on our time lines?

>Sarah: Okay.

>John: As I recall, we agreed to meet for one hour today, and our goal is to complete the entire project in two months.

Sarah: Right. Can't we order just a few plants to test the colors? I'd like to see how they will mix in the different beds.

John: I'm afraid if we order now, we'll end up with some plants that won't grow well because we don't have enough time today to address both the soil and sun questions.

Sarah: Okay, but you know I want to order plants as soon as possible.

John: Oh, yes! I'm keenly aware of that. Could we start with the soil sampling? We do have enough time to get this done today.

Sarah: Sure.

The Wanted Conversation

If you were considering a trip with someone, you would probably first agree on a destination. The planning would continue with how each person views this trip. For instance, if one of you has a distinct itinerary in mind with specific stops along the way and the other does not like to be on a schedule, at least one of you will be disappointed. Yet many interactions begin in this manner without benefit of a complete wanted conversation.

Asking a client what results they want from an interaction and then making sure you understand the details may be unusual. In fact, the question is rarely considered. Yet everyone goes into an interaction wanting something, though that "something" may not have been explicitly identified. However, everyone will easily recognize what was missing *after* the fact when the results are clear. Then, in the midst of collective disappointment, the rework begins. How much better to specify the desired results in advance!

Courage is required to ask your client what they want from a meeting. Asking this question is risky because it will expose you to uncertainty. For example, you may not be able to provide what your client wants. They may not be able to state what they want. Your client may not have considered the question and may feel embarrassed when asked to formulate a response. Despite these difficulties, it is far riskier to enter the *work* step of a consultation not knowing what your client expects.

Another risk is that your client may think that you already should know want they want. At some point in the past, they may have made a comment that they thought clearly answered this question. Possibly, you missed the comment or forgot it. In any case, no one has a perfect memory or mind reading capability.

Another reason many interactions start without a complete wanted conversation is that often both consultant and client are more comfortable discussing some concrete topic, anything safe that both are confident they can handle. Unfortunately, this approach does not yield information about why the client has come and whether the consultant is willing and able to provide the requested service.

After you have agreed with your client on the time available for an interaction, summon up the courage to get through the above barriers to learn what results your client wants. Often this interaction is part of a larger project that will require multiple meetings. Thus, your client may have wants related to this interaction and others related to the project as a whole. Your task now is to determine which of these your client desires to address today and what their respective priorities are.

If an agenda has been created for this interaction in a previous meeting or in the *prepare* step, check whether any changes have occurred since the agenda was created and make the necessary modifications.

If there is no agenda, now is the time to ask, "What do you want to get out of this interaction?" Other versions of this question are "What brings you in today?" or "What do you want us to accomplish in our time together?" In any case, ignoring this question or addressing it incompletely will at least sidetrack the progress of your meeting—and at worst derail it. This conversation is so critical that it has a name: *the wanted conversation*.

The wanted conversation is an important conversation, especially when you are confident you know what your client *should* want. Consultants often refer to this outcome as "This is what my client *needs* to do." Generally, you don't know what your client wants until you are told.

The purpose of the wanted conversation is to *identify all your client's wants for this session* before you begin to filter out those that you are unwilling or unable to address. This process requires patience to keep asking, "Is there anything else you want from this meeting?" until your client answers, "No."

Persisting in the wanted conversation is important because often there is an item that's important to your client that has not yet been named. Your client may be reluctant to make another request. They may be concerned about your response to it.

An essential component of the early part of your interaction with any client is that you treat your client with respect, *respect as defined by your client*. This step is required to start the slow process of building trust and, thus, eventually creating a synergistic relationship. After some trust has been built by allowing your client to reveal what they want, acknowledging the value of their goals, and noting your alignment with them, they may feel safe enough to bring up unnamed wants.

For each of your client's wants, identify all the conditions to be met, including a due date (by when) for your client to be satisfied that this want has been successfully addressed. I will refer to this set of conditions as your client's "conditions for satisfaction" for that

> **Stepping Stone**
>
> Conditions for satisfaction: if these results occur in the session, your client will be completely satisfied.

particular want. Not knowing the conditions for satisfaction means you are shooting in the dark.

Continue the wanted conversation until both of you agree that you know what your client wants from this interaction (including "by when"). To discover if this has occurred, summarize what you think your client wants and when it is due, and verify that your client agrees with your summary. Agreement is *not* determined by saying, "Yes, I understand what you want." Stating explicitly what you think your client wants in your own words may well save you from future misunderstandings since what you heard isn't always what your client intended to say. The following example illustrates this.

After his second meeting with a client, Art was enraged and met with his consulting class instructor. Read the following and imagine yourself in this situation.

> Art: I spent hours doing the task we had discussed in our first meeting. At the start of our second meeting, my client looked at my results and said he was not interested in them.

> Instructor: Why did you do this task?

> Art: It seemed exactly like what would address the questions we discussed in our first meeting.

> Instructor: Did he ask you to do this at the end of the first meeting?

> Art: No.

> Instructor: So, you gambled and lost?

> Art: Yes. Does this relate to having a complete wanted conversation?

> Instructor: Yes.

Role-Play

Create a videoed role-play with your partner in which they want you to complete one complex task with several conditions for satisfaction.

Did you stay in the conversation with them about conditions for satisfaction until they said that you had identified all their conditions for satisfaction?

The most frequent mistake in the *open* step is to move to the *work* step of the interaction prematurely (POWER: prepare, open, work, end, reflect). Often you are so eager to start working that you don't have a complete wanted conversation in which you come to a mutual understanding with your client of all the tasks your client wants done today. Not knowing all of your clients wants will create mischief when five minutes remain in the session and your client's top-priority want emerges.

Stepping Stone

Clients are not required to name their wants in priority order.

Some clients enter your office and immediately begin to discuss the questions and goals for their overall project. Read the following and imagine yourself in this situation.

> Client: I'm so excited about this project. (Then follows a rapid-fire monologue about his entire project.)

> You: *(What does he want from this meeting? How much time is available? I must say something.)* May I interrupt?

> Client: *(Isn't she interested in my project? There are two more critical points.)* (Then follows two more monologue minutes.)

> You: *(How can I stop him gracefully?)* Excuse me, I'm getting lost.

Client: (*Okay. I guess that was a lot of material.*) Sorry.

You: I appreciate this overview of your project. However, I can serve you best if I know how much time you have for this meeting and what you want to accomplish *today*.

The purpose of this conversation is to assist your client in separating the work to be done today from the work involved in the entire project. These two often get entangled in clients' minds.

The Expanded Wanted Conversation

To expand your wanted conversation, look beyond the results required to meet your client's present requests to how your client plans to use those results. Questions to explore together at this point are:

- Who are the stakeholders and what are their ultimate criteria for success?
- How will the results of this study be used?

Addressing these questions with your client will provide information that will be valuable in the *work* step.

Having a complete expanded wanted conversation for each want identified in the wanted conversation allows you to be well prepared to address each want. These conversations will reduce the number of unpleasant surprises waiting for you and your client in the course of the project. The more carefully these two questions are addressed, the greater chance of avoiding rework.

Another benefit of the expanded wanted conversation is to help you see the value in your client's question by addressing your unasked question, "So what?" This insight is important if you see many clients with similar questions. Exasperation can set in for you, as it did for me with Brenda.

The expanded wanted conversation may reveal areas of interest that fall beyond your client's immediate wants. Here is an example:

> A client is meeting with you today to collect technical information to include in a presentation she is making to an executive committee tomorrow. Her basic want is this technical information. In an expanded wanted conversation, you could offer her an opportunity to practice her entire presentation with you today. If she accepts your offer, your interaction will go beyond just giving her the technical information. It will give her an opportunity to practice her presentation of the initially requested technical information. Then your client will have a better chance of delivering a successful presentation tomorrow. This practice session will be most useful if you and your client know the criteria the committee members will use to assess her presentation.

You may be thinking, *Good grief! We will never complete the wanted conversation and the expanded wanted conversation!* These two conversations are demanding work, and they do require time and discipline. Yet consider the alternative: agreeing to do something when you are not sure what that something is or how it will be used. Identifying your client's *and* your client's stakeholders' conditions for satisfaction will improve the chances that your work is on target the first time you do it. Proceeding without knowing *both* sets of conditions for satisfaction is folly.

> **Stumbling Block**
>
> Why is it that there is never enough time to do a project right the first time, as if there will always be enough time to do it over?

A frequent complaint is "These wanted conversations take too long." This begs the question, "Why is it that there is never enough time to do a project right the first time, as if there will always be enough time to do it over?"

When faced with an imminent deadline on your boss's favorite project, it is easy to cave in to pressure and start doing *something*, agree to an unrealistic time line, or get to work doing the *something* that looks like it may be of use. In the fullness of time, this strategy can prove worthless, and the project is reworked or scrapped.

Unfortunately, managers in levels above you may be unaware of how much work will be required to meet their requests. Stay in the conversation as you seek to clarify all their conditions for satisfaction and the resources and work required to meet each request. The whole open conversation is about counting the cost—becoming aware of the project's scope and cost in time, energy, expertise, and money *before* you start. Courage is required to say, "I certainly can begin this task, and if you want a superior product, I must take the time to understand the task clearly and develop a workable plan. I have found that, in the end, this takes less time with fewer revisions." A complete expanded wanted conversation is a way to avoid putting yourself in situations where you ask yourself, "How much longer will I continue to agree to do tasks that I don't understand within a time frame that initially seems impossible and often proves to be?"

> **Stepping Stone**
>
> The open conversation is about becoming aware of the project's scope and cost in time, energy, personnel, and money before you start.

Wanted Conversations in Challenging Situations

In some situations, it is difficult to initiate a wanted conversation. A common thread in many of these situations is that the relationship between the consultant and client is either hierarchical or adversarial or both.

The Annual Review Meeting

The annual review meeting is one such situation. The relationship between supervisor and employee is always hierarchical by nature because of their positions in the company; it can often be adversarial as well.

However, the supervisor does have a choice between being domineering or collaborative. Both persons have a choice between being adversarial or cooperative. Every annual review occurs within the context of the relationship between the supervisor and employee. The more domineering and adversarial the relationship has been in previous years, the more difficult it will be to initiate a wanted conversation in an annual review meeting. Read the following and imagine yourself in this situation.

> Sheila (supervisor): My impression is that your three previous annual reviews have been too much of a one-way street, which has not been as helpful as it could be. I'd like your help in making a significant change. I want to work with you in a more collaborative way. Are you interested in exploring this possibility?

> Elaine: (*cautiously*) I guess so.

> Sheila: (*That's not the response I had hoped for, and I have finally opened this conversation. I think it's worth the risk to continue.*) I know that in the past I have been too focused on failures and who was at fault. Starting now, I want to concentrate on what we can learn from failures that will make us more effective next year. I'm committed to becoming a better listener.

> Elaine: (*Sounds good, but I've endured three years of offering solutions, and it always ends with some version of, "My way is the way it will be. I'm the boss."*)

> Sheila: (*That's a long pause, but I will continue in good faith.*) I have been thinking about this review for some time and came up with three items I hope we can discuss together. The first is to review what each of us thinks the other did well last year. The second is to explore where each of us sees an opportunity to improve how we can work

together throughout this coming year. The third is to mutually decide how often to meet when problems arise on projects. I also want to know what items and questions you would like to discuss today.

Elaine: Well, I'd like to acknowledge that you have obviously put much thought into this new process. I definitely have several ideas about how to better cooperate. Do you think we can cover all this ground by the end of this meeting today?

Sheila: We are scheduled to end at 3:00 p.m. Does that still work for you?

Elaine: Yes.

Sheila: Good. I doubt that we can cover everything by 3:00 p.m. If we don't, I'm happy to schedule a continuation at a time that works for both of us.

Elaine: Okay.

Sheila: What are your highest priority items to discuss today?

The Messenger

Another example of a reluctant client is the messenger. In this situation, there may be no prior relationship between the messenger and the consultant. A common barrier to an effective meeting of this kind is an often shared point of view, "Messengers should never be sent to a meeting," where both parties think the messenger's boss should be at the meeting, rather than the messenger.

Marshall has been sent by his boss to get Christine's answer to a specific question. Marshall is upset at being in the role of messenger; he thinks that his boss should be meeting with Christine rather than sending him.

Sometimes consultants have a policy of not working with messengers. If Christine had this policy, Marshall would be in a difficult position. Such a policy could be interpreted as a rejection of the messenger's boss. After all, if Marshall's boss wanted to be in the meeting, he would have been there. Happily for Marshall, Christine does not have this policy. Read the following and imagine yourself in this situation.

> Christine: Hi, Marshall. I understand from your phone call that you have a short question for me. Do you think fifteen minutes will be enough time for us?

> Marshall: Yes. I'm here to find out whether you think it is time to update our accounting software. My boss wants a yes or no answer today.

> Christine: That's a complex question. Before I can responsibly answer it, I require more information. For example: When was your last update? How long will the current version be supported?

> Marshall: My boss really gets upset when you guys don't answer the question he asks when it is a simple question.

> Christine: Yes, his question is a simple one, and it isn't easy. If we don't consider all the issues, we will risk major losses in the next few years. For example, here are more questions whose answers are required before I can respond to your boss's question:
>
> Are there changes anticipated in our operations that will require the new software? What training resources does your boss have available to support the transition? Who will be making the final decision on installing an update?

> Marshall: Christine, you know my boss. You're putting me in a bind here.

Christine: Yes, I know. I'm willing to have a meeting with you and your boss to discuss these questions. Would that be helpful?

Marshall: Helpful? Yes. Possible? I doubt it. At least, I don't know how to make that happen.

Christine: How about if we work together to develop a plan for how to present this idea to him so that he can see the benefit to everyone of getting this information first before making the decision?

Marshall: Can't hurt. Where do we start?

Often messengers think they do not personally want anything out of the conversation other than a message to deliver to their boss. Here the wanted conversation involved an exploration of what Marshall initially wanted, "just a yes or no answer." This conversation continued until Marshall realized that he did want more from the meeting, namely a strategy for dealing effectively with his boss's upset when Marshall reports to him that he won't immediately get what he wanted from the meeting Marshall had with Christine.

The Willing Conversation

After reaching agreement on what your client wants from this session, consider whether you are *willing* and *able* to do what it takes to address these wants. There are *two* conversations here, the first about what you are willing to do and the second about what you are able to do. Do not homogenize them.

What you are *willing* to do is determined by your standards: morals, ethics, and matters of personal preference. What you are *able* to do is determined by your resources: time, energy, expertise, knowledge base, speed at which you learn, and the network of consultants available to you. Both conversations are also affected by your client's standards and resources that relate to their wants (i.e., by what they are willing and able to do). Wants, willing, and able are three separate conversations.

First, assess whether you are willing to work with your client. Ignoring this step with Brenda led to serious problems. What are your standards that determine whether you are willing to work with a client? What are your boundaries? For instance, when you treat your client with respect, you expect the same in return.

What do you do when your client says something that you regard as disrespectful? For example, if your client uses language you find to be offensive, address this the first time it occurs: "The language you just used is offensive to me. I request that you not use it in the future. Are you willing to refrain from using this type of language?"

Second, assess whether you are willing to address your client's wants. Some of these may be at odds with your personal standards, such as working on weekends. If so, now is the time to address this directly. You may choose to offer assistance in finding a consultant who is willing to address these wants and who is willing to work on weekends; first check to see if this help is wanted by your client.

The time to prepare for the willing conversation is well before the interaction begins. When you are alone and under no time constraints is the ideal time for you to clarify your morals, ethics, and matters of personal preference. What requests from your client would conflict with your moral standards or personal code of ethics or the code of ethics of your profession? What request would conflict with your personal preferences? Obvious examples for most people include requests such as destroying or falsifying evidence or presenting deliberately misleading advice. In addition to moral issues, your unwillingness could include working thirty hours on each of the next eight weekends.

Late in my career, I was not willing to address the wants of two potential clients. The first one wanted me to work with her on her dissertation.

It was unlikely that she would complete it before my retirement date. Unwilling to delay my retirement date, I declined this request.

The second one also wanted me to work on a dissertation. To do so would have required learning complex technical material, an activity I was not willing to do at that point in my career. I also declined this request. By declining these requests, I honored my boundaries, and each student accepted my assistance in finding other professors to assist them.

Clients like these appreciate the integrity required to say that you are not willing to do a task. If you combine this statement with an offer to search for someone who is willing to do the task, there is a good chance that you have gained an advocate and a future client on another problem that will fit you both.

Willing as It Relates to Consultant Wants

Though previously we have discussed only *wants* of the *client*, you as the *consultant* also have *wants* that must be met for you to be *willing* to work with this client, such as:

- agreement on how and when you are to be paid;
- clear and all-inclusive description of the results your client expects from you (also called the client's *conditions for satisfaction*);
- timely delivery to you of all inputs from the client you require to complete your tasks; and
- agreed-on processes for negotiating changes to any of the client's or consultant's conditions for satisfaction. (Changes occur and conflicts arise in the course of any project. Coming to an agreement on how to address such conflicts in advance is a valuable practice.)

Role-Play

Construct a role-play in which your partner is asking you to do a task that you regard as unethical.

Video the role-play and watch it. Were you able to clearly say that you are not willing to do this task?

Consultation or Collaboration?

Often consultations involve a payment from the client to the consultant for services rendered, and the client is the sole owner of the results of the consultation. However, many consultations are done in environments in which both the client and the consultant share ownership of the results, using a formula developed during the *open* conversation before the project starts. This conversation can feel awkward because the two of you are discussing how to share the fruits of your labors before any work has been done on the project. If you choose to delay this conversation, agree with each other when you will have it.

In environments such as academic research involving coauthors or industrial research resulting in a new product, a fixed salary is often not adequate compensation for either the client or the consultant. For these consultations, often called collaborations, all ownership details must be sorted out before the project begins in order to eliminate or at least reduce the chances of complex litigation at the end of the project.

If you and your client have agreed to work together and share the fruits of your labor, your next meeting will be a collaboration. If you have not already done so, now is the time to identify in writing how you will share the fruits of your labor. This agreement is essential to the success of your collaboration. Be sure that you make complete requests and promises to each other. Verify that what each of you intends to communicate is accurately interpreted by the other. Depending on the magnitude of your collaboration project, your agreement may well be a legal contract.

This book addresses one-on-one meetings, activities that both consultants and collaborators employ. When you are functioning as a collaborator, you will express your wants in the wanted conversation in addition to listening to the wants of your collaborator.

The Able Conversation

For the wants you are willing to address, now is the first time to examine whether you are able to address them. As you consider your client's top-priority item for this interaction, consider your resources that will determine whether you are able to address it today.

A seductive trap some consultants fall into is restructuring a client's want into one that fits the consultant's existing skill set. Here the goal is to covertly avoid having to say, "I don't know." This consultant-centered strategy reduces the chances of a productive interaction. Filtering out approaches to your client's wants that require skills, knowledge, and abilities that you don't currently possess may result in providing inferior service. Eventually, this deceit will damage your relationship.

If your client wants information that you don't have, speak to this matter directly. For example, "I don't know the answer to your question right now. I can investigate it and get back to you tomorrow. Will that work for you?" If it does not, check to see if an offer of assistance in finding a consultant who is able to address this question today would be helpful.

Not Able—The Courage to Say, "I Don't Know"

Dealing with "not able" situations brings us back to courage. Many people are reluctant to say they don't know. Why? Many factors contribute to this. We have all survived many years in educational systems where "I don't know" was rarely an acceptable answer. Actually, it's worse than that. Not only was this answer unacceptable, it often produced chiding, ridicule, or worse from both our teachers and our peers. These childhood wounds often cast long shadows.

Fear of financial loss is another contributor to this reluctance. Many are concerned that telling a client, "I don't know" will result in the client seeking another consultant. However, your client may be well aware that their question is genuinely difficult, requiring expertise that they have been unsuccessfully seeking for many months. Saying, "I don't know" may be a breath of fresh air, as they now realize you are a consultant who is willing to be honest about the difficulties posed by their question. This interaction could open up the door for both of you to explore the problem. Even if this does not happen, they now know that you have the courage to be honest when you don't know. Your client may return with other questions, knowing that you will tell the truth about your abilities rather than sending up a smoke screen, hiding a lack of knowledge and resulting in wasted time and energy.

Considering Control

Control is another issue relating to the not-able conversation. Clients come to us for advice. While this does not necessarily put the client in a less powerful position, interesting power dynamics are at work between the parties. Some consultants fear that telling a client, "I don't know" will cost them control of the session. This attitude is dangerous. Such a consultant may think that they *should* be in control of the session. They likely have a hierarchical attitude about the structure of consulting sessions. Their reluctance to reveal what they do not know serves as a barrier to being honest about what they do know. If they persist in this charade, their relationships with clients will be short-lived.

There are alternatives to covering up what the consultant does not know. For example: a consultant can cooperatively explore with a client how long it would take the consultant to learn what is required to answer the client's question; or they can search for someone else who has this knowledge; or they can explore the client's question further to see if an alternative, acceptable solution exists that the consultant *does* know.

Estimating Time

A tough part of the able conversation is *assessing* whether you have *enough time to address what your client wants today.* A related challenge is estimating how long it will take to do the entire project. Experience can be a great teacher here if you are willing to gather data on this process. Estimate and record how long you think it will take you to do each of your professional tasks, before you do them. When you complete the task, record how much time it took. Record also any surprises that occurred during the task that caused it to take more or less time than you estimated.

Eventually you will learn to estimate with confidence how long it will take you to do frequently occurring tasks and how often surprises occur. A related discipline is to contact your client as soon as you become aware that the project time will exceed your initial estimate.

Whenever your client has more than one want for the interaction, assess priorities. There is a good chance that you won't be able to address all of them in one meeting. Ending the willing and able conversations by agreeing on priorities assures that you are addressing your client's most important issues first.

Distinguishing between Not Willing and Not Able

Many people are more comfortable saying that they are not able to do a task rather than they are not willing. If you say you are not willing to do a task, this may open up a conversation about your moral, ethical, or professional standards and preferences. Doing so requires a willingness on your part to deal with the vulnerability that can surface around topics that are often not discussed.

> **Stepping Stone**
>
> Contact your client as soon as possible after you realize that you will not be able to keep your promise to complete a task by the agreed-on deadline.

Seeking to hide "not willing" behind "not able" can create mischief and do harm to the relationship. Clients in these situations may press hard to find out why you are not able. They can be creative in locating alternatives that you are able to do. Once cornered in the interaction, you may find that your only option is to admit the real barrier, which is that you are not willing.

Stepping Stone

An old adage is helpful here: when in doubt, tell the truth; when not in doubt, tell the truth.

Admitting your unwillingness invites the question of "why?" which, in turn, invites a conversation to determine the worthiness of your reasons. You might say, "I'm unwilling to work on this project for personal reasons." Your client may press with questions about why precisely you don't want to work on this project, so that they can decide if your reasons meet their criteria for a valid rejection. What to do? Explore the purpose of their questions to determine what your client wants.

Does your client think that their project does not conflict with your personal reasons? Or is your client seeking to find a way to persuade you to work on this project regardless of your personal objections? Careful conversation with your client will reveal the answer.

The *open* step consists of a series of conversations, each addressing different issues. For each conversation in which a decision is made, make sure you are recording it in some form so that you have the information for future reference.

Able as It Relates to Consultant Wants

Each of the four *consultant wants* at the end of the *willing* section also necessitates an able conversation in which your client assesses their willingness and ability to address the consultant wants.

The Open Checklist

1. Agree on the amount of time available for this interaction.

2. Determine what your client wants and how these results will be used.
3. Have a complete willing conversation.
4. Have a complete able conversation.
5. Treat your client with respect, by your client's standards, not yours.

Role-Play

Each of the conversations on the *open* checklist is a source of additional role-plays for you and your partner. For starters, you might focus on a situation that recurs in your workplace.

Chapter 3 Activity

Now that we've explored the *open* aspect of the POWER process, it's time to practice with your role-play partner. Using a smartphone, have your partner set a five-minute alarm and start videoing both of you when you both are ready to start your role-play.

Role-Play

You are sitting at your desk preparing for a meeting in thirty minutes. A colleague appears at the door to request your assistance.

Suggestions for Role-Play

Tips for you:

- How much time will be required?
- What does your colleague want from the conversation?
- Are you willing to interrupt your meeting preparation?
- Are you able to provide what your colleague wants?

Tips for colleague:

> *Begin with the following sentences:* "I'm so happy to catch you. I've been working on this all night, and I need you to look at it with me. I'm sure it will only take a few minutes." (Make up a problem that's currently troubling you or has troubled you in the past. You might remind your colleague how helpful you were last week when the tables were turned.)

Following your role-play exercise, refer to the chapter 3 debriefing questions at the end of this chapter. Please look at these questions with your partner *after* having completed this activity, as you will learn more from the role-play experience this way.

Brenda's Case—The Open Checklist

I will illustrate use of the *open* checklist by applying it to my interaction with Brenda.

1. Agree on the amount of time available for this interaction.

   I did not ask about this.

2. Determine what your client wants and how these results will be used.

   When I discovered that what Brenda wanted from the interaction was not what I thought she wanted, I did nothing to clarify her wants before going into the *work* part of the session. Instead I addressed what I thought she *should* want from the meeting without confirming that belief. This strategy wasted time and damaged the relationship.

   I did not engage her in an expanded wanted conversation in which we could have explored together whether her plan would meet the expectations of the professors she would have to satisfy in the future.

Here was another missed opportunity. We could have explored the fact that ultimately she would have to defend her thesis by answering statistical questions from her major professor and other faculty members on her thesis committee. Then she *might* have been willing to explore how to increase her statistical competence.

If I'd been willing to drop my demand that she take a statistics course, we might have been able to develop another strategy for her learning what was required for her to be successful.

3. Have a complete willing conversation.

> There was a conflict relative to whether Brenda would take a statistics course. The conflict was not addressed directly. I attempted to resolve it hierarchically by "highly" recommending that she take a class; she immediately rejected my recommendation. That was the end of the discussion.

> We carried on in the session, not addressing this unresolved conflict directly, leaving it on the table. I found myself doing something that I was not willing to do and yet not willing to say so.

> Certainly what was at issue (unknown to me in the session) was whether I was willing to work with her. I did not pause to look at whether I was willing to work with her after she declined my request/demand that she take a statistics course.

> After the second session, she did not return. It was then clear that she was not willing to work with me.

4.   Have a complete able conversation.

I was confident that I was able to answer her questions.

5.   Treat your client with respect, by your client's standards, not yours.

The above paragraphs reveal numerous examples of my not treating Brenda with respect, including my confusion about where to meet her before the session, being unprepared for the changes she had made at the start of it, and my attitudes toward her thesis topic, her area of study, and her commitment to not take a statistics course. Also disrespectful was my being only weakly engaged in the session until I rose to make my pronouncement that she should take a statistics course.

Recap

Intentionally open every interaction. Agree with your client on how long the meeting will be. Identify your client's wants and verify that you understand them accurately. Discuss how the results of these wants will be used if they are achieved. Discuss what you are willing to do and able to do relative to meeting the identified wants.

Frequently Asked Questions

1.   Do you ask all these questions in every consultation you have?

No, and not always in the order presented in this chapter. Sometimes I get distracted and forget one. If a question is critical (e.g., How much time do we have today?), I will realize my mistake at some point and correct it at that time.

The more stressful the consultation is as it unfolds, the more I need to pay attention so that I ask all the applicable questions.

2. What if your client has no idea what they want from this consultation?

> If they have no idea what they want from today's meeting, ask them what prompted them to come see you. Perhaps they are following an order from their boss. If so, ask what the boss wants them to get from today's consultation. If they do not know, suggest that either they or both of you visit their boss as soon as possible to find out what their expectations are for the consultation.
>
> If they have only a vague idea of what they or their boss wants, your job right now is to make sure that the wanted conversation stays focused on clarifying what your client wants. In this sort of conundrum, exasperation may cause you to move the discussion along by inserting your best guess as to what your client *might* want. If you proceed then to accept that guess as *the* want to be addressed, you are headed for confusion at best and considerable loss of resources at worse. This practice is also known as mind reading, which rarely works out well. Instead, start with the vague idea and patiently ask questions that will help your client to make it specific so that both of you know what your job is today.

3. How long should the *open* step of an interaction take?

> The short answer is "as long as it takes." Stay in the *open* conversation until all the crucial questions have been addressed. Leaving any unaddressed is a recipe for an ineffective interaction, begging for rework. For large projects, the *open* conversation may take a day, a week, or longer. The sooner you understand the time frame for a project, the easier it will be to plan for a successful completion. In addition to becoming effective in your consulting practice, learning to become more efficient, as well, will serve you in the long run.

4. Whose job is it to identify and agree on the time line and wants?

    The answer to your question depends upon the role you choose. The traditional role tends to view these decisions as the consultant's job and may even reject the idea of agreeing on these matters. If you choose to follow the traditional hierarchical structure by excluding the client from decisions, you risk alienation and deterioration of your rapport. Alternatively, to engage your client in decision-making increases your chance of fostering a cooperative working relationship.

5. What do you do when a client makes it clear that they have a position they expect you to endorse?

    This client's attitude raises an ethical question: do I provide consultation, or do I provide agreement? If I provide consultation, I cannot guarantee that I will endorse any particular position. If they insist on this guarantee, I would be risking my integrity and would not accept the person as a client.

6. How does the *open* step of the interaction change when it is a collaboration?

    "Collaboration" is used in two ways relative to interactions. It describes the cooperative relationship between consultant and client when both parties have equal power in the decisions they make as they work together, either because of the organizational chart or because of an agreement between them. This relationship is the opposite of a hierarchical relationship in which one party has the positional power to overrule the other and uses this power.

    A hierarchical relationship can be collaborative if the party with more positional power agrees not to use that power when a decision is to be made.

The second use of "collaboration" relates to the division of the fruits of the labor that the parties do together. The reward is shared according to a formula that both parties have agreed upon during the wanted conversation at the *beginning* of the project.

The Open Rubric

My colleagues Eric Vance and Heather Smith and I have developed rubrics to aid consultants in assessing how well they are executing the *open*, *work*, and *end* steps of an interaction (Vance, Smith, and Zahn 2014). These rubrics may be used to measure adherence to the steps during consultations. They also may be used by an instructor or coach to assist in providing feedback to students or clients.

Table 2 is the open rubric. Table 3 presents the results of applying the open rubric to the Brenda interaction. This table reveals at a glance which aspects of the open conversation were omitted. It also illustrates how the client was mistreated.

Table 2. The open rubric

Strength	Okay for Now	Opportunity for Improvement
1. Agree on the amount of time available for this interaction.		
Consultant asks the client about time available.	Consultant tells the client time available and asks if this works for the client.	Consultant tells the client time available, or consultant does not mention anything about time.
Both agree on session time frame.		
2. Have a complete wanted conversation.		
Consultant asks what result the client wants from this session.	Consultant tells the client what consultant thinks should be done in the session and asks the client if that's okay.	Consultant tells client what is to be done in the session, or consultant skips the wanted conversation and immediately starts *work*.
Consultant and client clarify this want.		
Consultant asks if the client has any more wants. Both clarify each want.		
Both continue this process until the client agrees that the consultant understands all client wants.		

3. Have a complete willing conversation.

Consultant *clearly* states which of the client's wants they are or aren't willing to address.	Consultant *vaguely* states which of the client's wants they are or aren't willing to address.	Consultant skips this conversation.

4. Have a complete able conversation.

Consultant *clearly* states being able or not able to do the work required to address the client's wants.	Consultant *vaguely* states being able or not able to do the work required to address the client's wants.	Consultant skips this conversation.

5. Agree that your client's wants and your willingness and ability match.

Consultant and client intentionally verify that wants match with willingness and ability.	Consultant tells client that everything looks promising.	Consultant skips this conversation.

6. Consultant treats the client with respect, by the client's standards, not the consultant's.

Consultant is on time.	Consultant is one to five minutes late.	Consultant is more than six minutes late.
Consultant does not talk over or interrupt the client.	Consultant interrupts one to three times.	Consultant interrupts more than three times.

Table 3. The open rubric—Brenda's case

Strength	Okay for Now	Opportunity for Improvement
1. Agree on the amount of time available for this interaction.		
		Time available was not discussed.
2. Have a complete wanted conversation.		
		I skipped the wanted conversation and immediately started *work*.
3. Have a complete willing conversation.		
		I skipped this.
4. Have a complete able conversation.		
		I skipped this.
5. Agree that your client's wants and your willingness and ability match.		
		I skipped this.
6. Consultant treats the client with respect, by the client's standards, not the consultant's.		
	There were a few interruptions and talk-overs.	
	I was five minutes late.	

Chapter 3 Debriefing Questions

Watch the video. What did you notice?

Did you agree on the amount of time available for this interaction?

Did you determine what your client wants and how these results will be used?

Did you have a complete willing conversation?

Did you have a complete able conversation?

Watch the video a second time. What did you notice that you missed the first time?

CHAPTER 4

Open Your Mind

Now that we've put the four open conversations in context, let's take a closer look at how to apply what we've learned so far. To apply the open concept in a real-life consulting situation requires opening your mind to the possibility of changing how you currently begin consultations. You will find examples below, as well as a table, activity, and frequently asked questions related to how the *open* concept works when applied to the real world.

Let's start out with a brief discussion regarding the nature of respect. Everyone deserves consideration, to be treated respectfully. That may be obvious. Less obvious, perhaps, is that the respect should correspond with the client's standards, not yours. As discussed earlier, the relationship between consultant and client is often hierarchical but that need not imply adversarial or abusive.

Sometimes consultants will say, "But I didn't mean to be disrespectful" or "That client is overly sensitive." It does not matter what you think about the situation; it only matters how your client evaluates it. It is critical that your client feels respected. You can be cooperative and collaborative with your client even if you outrank them in the organization.

Though you, too, expect to be treated with respect by your client, no one can force this to occur. What you can do is behave in a way that models the way you wish to be treated.

Here are two examples of sorting out the *open* step of an interaction, the first in a recreational setting and the second in an office setting.

The Novice Kayaker

Greg is a kayak trip guide in the mountains of North Carolina. Tracy recalled that her best friend who now lives in North Carolina recommended Greg for offering outstanding kayaking tours. She finds his office, knocks, and enters. Read the following and imagine yourself in this situation.

> Tracy: Excuse me, are you Greg?
>
> Greg: Yes. How can I help you?
>
> Tracy: My friend Joan went on a trip with you last month. She had a great time and recommended that I look you up.
>
> Greg: My thanks to Joan for her recommendation. (Greg glances at his calendar and his watch.) I have half an hour free before my next client. Does that work for you?
>
> Tracy: Sure.
>
> Greg: Please have a seat. Now, what kind of kayak trip are you interested in?
>
> Tracy: I'd be thrilled to go on the same trip that Joan took. The spectacular scenery, the whitewater—it all sounded so exciting. I've never done anything like that, and it's about time that I started!

Greg: You've come to the right place! Let me check my records to see which trip Joan was on. Ah, yes! That's one of my favorite trips. Before we make any specific plans, how well can you maneuver a kayak?

Tracy: Oh, dear! Not well.

Greg: Joan's was on a class 4 river. That's code for a dangerous river requiring expert kayakers; however, there are many other possibilities I think you would enjoy. Several rivers are equally scenic and safe enough for someone learning to kayak. Are you able to tread water for twenty minutes and swim thirty yards?

Tracy: Yes, I can do that.

Greg: Would you be willing to come in for a two-hour lesson in basic kayak skills this afternoon?

Tracy: Absolutely.

Greg: Great. I have found that people who master a basic set of skills, like righting a capsized kayak, are able to handle a class 1 river. After you are comfortable executing the basic skills, I'm willing to be your guide for a half-day kayak trip on a class 1 river. We could kayak two hours in the morning, take a break, and then kayak two hours in the afternoon. Are there other things you would like to include in the trip?

Tracy: Well, I'd like to have lunch and to return in one piece!

Greg: I can certainly provide lunch, and my highest priority is your safety and mine! Do you have a particular date in mind?

Tracy: How about tomorrow?

Greg: That works for my schedule.

Tracy: Terrific! When will I be able to do Joan's river?

Greg: We can plan for that in the future as your kayaking and swimming skills increase.

Tracy: Fair enough. I'll see you this afternoon for my beginner's lesson. How long will it last?

Greg: About two hours.

Tracy: Okay. See you this afternoon.

Let's look at what happened here using the first two steps of the POWER process, *prepare* and *open*.

Prepare

Preparation includes all the actions Greg has taken before the start of the conversation with Tracy. The most relevant part of Greg's preparation is the sum of his experiences as a kayak guide: his knowledge of various rivers and of working with clients with differing skill levels. His attitude of soliciting exactly what his client wants from a kayak trip has earned him frequent recommendations.

For you, your immediate preparation might include clearing your desk, making certain your business cards are within reach, or taking five minutes to clear your thoughts and become focused. Of course, full preparation can't happen for a drop-in client like Tracy. One of Greg's challenges was to rapidly shift from whatever he was doing to being focused on Tracy and what she was saying.

Open

Time: Before Greg engages Tracy in conversation, he checks his calendar and his watch to discover how much time he can offer. Once half an hour has been agreed upon, he can prioritize his questions with the time limit in mind.

Wanted: Greg identifies what Tracy wants from the trip. Her conditions for satisfaction are to take the same trip that Joan did, with the spectacular scenery, whitewater, and excitement. He also learns when she wants to take the trip: tomorrow.

Able: The determination of whether Greg is able to meet Tracy's wants is made within the consultation. Unless Greg is clairvoyant, he can't know exactly what Tracy will ask of him. He is able to do the class 4 river trip with an experienced kayaker; he is unwilling (rather than unable) to take Tracy on that trip because she has no kayaking experience and little swimming expertise. His integrity dictates that he is obligated to consider her safety first. By declining her initial request, he realizes that he could lose this client.

Willing: Greg rapidly shifts to a conversation about what he is willing to do with Tracy based on her current skills: guide her on a four-hour, class 1 river trip. He also notes that he is willing to guide her on more challenging rivers in the future as her skills increase.

How does all this relate to interactions in an office situation? Let's explore this now.

The Required Course

Alice is a trainer for a consulting firm that is assisting Wilkes Tools to implement a quality management program. Warren is a middle manager who will be affected by this project, as it will require him to collect data on his own performance using a new computer system. Implementing the new system will involve many interactions between individuals such as Alice and Warren.

Warren has been told by his supervisor, Stephen, that he is required to attend the course that Alice is teaching because she will show him how to collect and enter the required data.

Alice has spent years earning various certifications from the American Society for Quality and has worked continuously to develop her understanding of the various stages of the quality improvement process. She was told by Stephen that Warren wants to be excused from the course because he does not understand why attendance is required.

Stephen's instruction was clear: "I want Warren to be in your course."

Force

Let's consider one way Alice could approach this: using force to address resistance.

Scenario 1

> After receiving Stephen's instruction, Alice sends Warren a notice to come see her about the course. She is blinded by her zeal to impart all her expertise to Warren and is convinced that the course will be of value to him.
>
> When Warren arrives, Alice states, "I have heard from your supervisor that you don't want to take my course. What you should remember is that Stephen wants *everyone* to take this course. I've also seen other quality movements come and go. I can assure you that this one is different. I look forward to seeing you Monday."

Warren nods, leaves her office, and begins immediately to plan how to avoid this class. Given his savvy, the smart money is on his not being in the course on Monday, having figured out a way to make this happen without jeopardizing his annual performance review. He does not see the benefits of the course and won't take it, even though his supervisor expects him to do so.

The thought cycling through his mind is, *I won't do it, and you can't make me.*

Another thought is beginning to take hold of his emotions: *Alice's presumptiveness is the last straw. Stephen has been pushing me around for months, telling me to do this or study that. Yet when he hired me, he said I was well qualified for the job. If I can't get out of this course, I may well quit.*

Stumbling Block
Warren has upsetting thoughts resulting from the pressure that Stephen and Alice are applying.

Small repeater issues like this one can add up to a loss of talent in companies.

An alternative to not showing up that also has nasty consequences is that Warren shows up for the course, makes the minimal effort required to complete it, and regards the exercise as one more example of management force-feeding its idea of the month. This experience would color all his future interactions with the corporate quality program as a whole, as well as adding one more reason to quit.

Stepping Stone
Staying in the conversation is essential for an effective interaction and requires managing your impulse to end the conversation abruptly and prematurely.

Stay in the Conversation

To stay in the conversation with Warren, rather than resorting to force, Alice has to manage several internal urges. One is her urge to be an expert and provide Warren with what *she thinks he should want.*

Another is pulling rank and forcing him to do what she wants "or else ..." This is an example of a self-styled expert thinking, *I know what this client should do, and it's my job to make sure that happens.* Alice pulled rank in scenario 1. Using positional power is a tempting strategy to employ when someone has openly said they will not abide by company policy.

Another example of how this strategy works can be seen in one aspect of police work in which many uniformed police officers are killed or seriously wounded—that is, intervening in domestic violence. Here, police officers and society at large agree that a violently quarreling couple requires external help before someone gets hurt. Unfortunately, the couple often does not want anyone else's "help." When it is provided, tragically the contesting parties often unite and turn their anger onto the officer, now perceived as an interloper.

Reactance

Providing what is needed (from the perspective of the expert) and not wanted (from the perspective of the client) is also a dangerous activity for consultants. Though physical violence fortunately is rare here, there is a phenomenon called "reactance" that's likely to occur when the consultant tells the client what to do.

Reactance is a psychological phenomenon that occurs when your clients think you are infringing on their behavioral freedoms, choices, or alternatives. Your clients will take steps to regain their choices, even though these steps may be counterproductive.

> **Stumbling Block**
>
> "**Reactance** is a motivational reaction to offers, persons, rules, or regulations that threaten or eliminate specific behavioral freedoms. **Reactance** occurs when a person feels that someone or something is taking away his or her choices or limiting the range of alternatives."
>
> Wikipedia (accessed June 2, 2017)

Alice produced reactance in Warren in scenario 1. There was a direct conflict between what

Warren wanted (not to take the course) and what Alice thought he needed (to take the course). Alice sought to resolve the conflict by trying to force him to do what she wanted him to do, implying, "Trust me, this is for your own good." Warren responded with reactance by beginning to think about how to avoid this class: *I won't do it, and you can't make me. If I can't get out of this course, I may well quit.*

To avoid reactance in this conversation, Alice would have to shift from force to engagement. If she hears herself saying, "But you also need to take the course so that your data will meet the system's requirements," this is an indicator that she has put on her "expert hat" and is resorting to force. Engaging Warren in the course requires Alice to identify aspects of the course that may lead Warren to *want* to participate.

Invitation to Engage

Let us now consider a different approach to Alice's meeting with Warren: invitation.

Notice that Alice has called this meeting at the insistence of Stephen, Warren's supervisor; it isn't Warren's idea. In our kayak example, the meeting between Greg and Tracy was Tracy's idea. Thus Alice and Greg are dealing with two different types of clients. We can refer to Tracy as an "eager" client and Warren as a "reluctant" client.

With a reluctant client, Alice's first job is to set the context for the meeting and then identify what Warren wants from it. Her task is complicated by the fact that she has been ordered to meet with Warren about a course that he has already told Stephen will be a waste of his time. Her primary task in this conversation is to avoid escalating the level of reactance that Warren already is experiencing.

Scenario 2

After receiving Stephen's instructions, she starts the meeting in an invitational manner. Read the following and imagine yourself in this situation.

> Alice: (After receiving Stephen's instruction, she calls Warren.) Hi, Warren. This is Alice, the trainer for the course about the company's new quality management program. I heard from your supervisor, Stephen, that you have asked to be excused from this course even though he is requiring everyone to be there. Would you be willing to meet with me to see if we can develop a plan to sort this out—one that works for both you and Stephen?

> Warren: I appreciate your call, but I think this meeting would be a waste of your time and mine.

> Alice: I understand your skepticism. I'm optimistic we can agree on a way forward that would serve you if we could work together for about an hour tomorrow. I want this to be a course that you are looking forward to rather than one you feel forced to attend. Are you willing to give it a chance?

> Warren: Well, I suppose so. I know Stephen will be upset if I don't take the course.

> Alice: Thanks. How about eleven to noon tomorrow?

> Warren: Okay.

The next day, they meet as planned.

Alice: Yesterday, we agreed to take a shot at looking forward to see how we can work together to satisfy both you and Stephen.

Are you still willing to do this?

Warren: Yes.

Alice: Can you still meet until noon?

Warren: Yes.

Alice: What would have to happen in the course that would support you in your job?

Warren: Well, if it turns out that I have to take the course, I want to know if there is some way the course can help me get my promotion.

Alice: Okay. Anything else?

Warren: Not that I can think of right now.

Alice: All right. I'm willing to address that possibility. Let's start by looking at your concerns about the course.

Warren: Okay. At least two things are upsetting me. I have seen many quality improvement programs come and go in my twenty-three years with the company. What makes this one different? What I think is that I'm being told to go to a course to learn how to fill out forms. To be frank, this is an insult. Furthermore, this course is scheduled near the end of the fiscal year. I usually have to work fifty-five-hour weeks just to manage my existing responsibilities during that time of the year.

Alice summarizes Warren's concerns; he agrees that she understands what he intended to say.

Alice: I've been teaching quality improvement courses for about twenty years. I understand your concerns. One promising thing about this new program is that Stephen told me that I have flexibility in selecting dates for the course so that I can respond to the work schedules of participants.

Warren: That's a major change! If you can change the dates, I'm willing to talk with you about how you see this program as an improvement on the others.

Happily, the date change is approved. Alice and Warren schedule a meeting for Alice to explain how this course involves more than learning to fill out forms. She also points out how the additional performance information that will be documented by the new program can help him make a stronger case for his next promotion.

The Rest of the Story

Forging ahead after the scenario 1 meeting that required Warren to gather data on his performance without addressing his concerns is folly. Children regularly teach parents the challenges of forcing anyone to do anything they don't want to do. One of the consequences that using force may produce is a subordinate saying yes with the sole intention of sabotage.

A graphic reminder of the many meanings of *yes* is table 4, Levels of Commitment, produced by Watkins (2001), expanding the work of Senge (1990). This list shows what Warren may actually mean if he says yes to Alice's request. Warren's level of commitment to his yes can determine if he will attend, participate, and implement the training.

In summary, the first scenario ends with Warren at a level of passive noncompliance, with even his attendance in the course in doubt. In the second scenario, Alice is doing her best to engage Warren in being at a level of genuine compliance, if not enrollment. If both of them are able to agree on the potential benefits of the course to Warren, we can count on him being a positive contributor in the course. If the course delivers on Alice's promises, he will be looking for ways to effectively implement what he has learned in his workplace. Further, the value he finds in these implementation activities will likely lead to his future participation in such programs, especially if Alice is providing them. He may even recommend them to his staff.

Stay in the willing and able conversations until your client's wants from this interaction match what you are willing and able to do. When you tell your client what you are willing to do and what you are able to do relative to each request, you are making a series of promises. Verify that each is a complete promise with a detailed description of the task you are promising to do, including by when you will complete it. Then move into the work phase of the interaction.

Table 4. Levels of Commitment

Commitment		Wants to be in the course. Will make it successful. Creates whatever laws (structures, rules, and regulations) required for it to be successful.
Enrollment		Wants to be in the course. Will do whatever can be done for it to be successful within the spirit of the existing laws.
Compliance		
	Genuine	Willing to be in the course. Sees the benefits of the course. Does everything expected and more. Follows the letter of the law. A good soldier.

	Formal	On the whole, sees the benefits of the course. Does what is expected and *no* more. A pretty good soldier.
	Grudging	Does not see benefits of the course. Also does not want to lose his job. Does enough of what is expected because he has to and also lets it be known that he isn't really on board.
Noncompliance		
	Active	Does not see benefits of the course and won't do what is expected. Overt noncooperation. "I won't do it; you can't make me" is the attitude he exhibits throughout the course.
	Passive	Does not see benefits of the course and won't do what is expected. Covert noncooperation. "I'm against it, and you won't know that I'm against it."
Sabotage		Destructive or obstructive actions, overt or covert. "I won't receive value from the course, and neither will anyone else."
Apathy		Neither for nor against the course. No interest. "Whatever. I don't care. Is it five o'clock yet?"

Based on Senge (1990) and Watkins (2001).

Chapter 4 Activity

Now that we've further explored the *open* aspect of the POWER process, it's time to practice with your role-play partner. Using a smartphone, have your partner set a five-minute alarm and video both of you during the role-play.

Role-Play

This is a role-play about a power struggle between Carolyn and Margaret, with Howard in the middle. Carolyn, a new member of Howard's staff, wants him to support her 100 percent in her disagreement with his boss, Margaret. What he wants to do is set up a meeting and be there, but he isn't willing to unconditionally support her. Play the role of Howard with your partner, playing Carolyn.

Here's the setup for the role-play:

Carolyn arrives at Howard's office for a meeting she has scheduled with him to discuss a conversation she had with Margaret yesterday.

> Howard: Good afternoon, Carolyn. Ah, yes, it's time for our meeting. We agreed on thirty minutes. Does that still work for you?

> Carolyn: Yes.

> Howard: I understand you want to discuss the conversation you had with Margaret yesterday. What do you want to get out of our discussion?

> Carolyn: Yesterday, Margaret told me what to do on her project. There was no room for my input. I'm in an awkward position because I have a better strategy for completing her project than she does. I need you to arrange a meeting with the three of us so that I can show her the strength of my approach. She's not listening to me, so I need your unqualified support so she will realize the merit of my approach.

Howard: (Your turn to respond.)

Suggestions for Role-Play

Tips for Carolyn: You want Howard to support your proposals without qualification. Be confident about your strengths. Develop at least three reasons to support your approach. Be dismissive of Margaret's. Appeal to his tradition of supporting his staff members.

Tips for Howard: Carolyn is requesting two items: set up a meeting and support her ideas. Focus on what you are *willing* to do relative to her requests. Also focus on how much you are willing to commit without knowledge of Carolyn's proposal or Margaret's orders to Carolyn. Keep in mind that you are not *able* to force Margaret to meet with both of you.

Following your role-play exercise, refer to the chapter 4 debriefing questions at the end of this chapter. Please look at these questions with your partner *after* having completed this activity, as you will learn more from the role-play experience this way.

Recap

Open your mind to new strategies for dealing with difficult interactions. Do not use force to address resistance; this will only produce reactance and further difficulty. Stay in the conversation.

Frequently Asked Questions

1. My client William regularly insists on an impossible time line. How can I deal with him?

    First, establish the parameters of his request. Estimate how much of your time would be required and compare this to the amount of time you have available. If he insists on more time than is available, tell him, in a nonconfrontational manner, that you are unwilling to break a promise to another client to meet his deadline. If, however, you discover that with additional personnel, resources, and increased cost you could meet the deadline *without* disturbing the priority of your other clients, then William has the option of paying for his demands.

2. When I meet with my boss, he often extends the length of time for our meeting without notice. How do I work with him to get to an agreement on how long the meeting will last?

> Clearly, you don't have the positional power to force him to make this agreement with you. Rather, it is a matter of enrolling him in a conversation that will lead to this agreement. To have this conversation intentionally, schedule a time with your boss when no other conversations are scheduled and apply the following scenario to your own situation.

> You: Yesterday, we scheduled a one-hour meeting at 2:00 p.m. At the start of our meeting, you told me it would last two to three hours. I made the mistake of not mentioning that I had scheduled a client at 3:00 p.m. I panicked about potentially being an hour late for my meeting and lost focus during our conversation. I wish I had said something at the time. Fortunately, our meeting ended before 3:00 p.m.

> Afterward, I thought about how often this level of uncertainty shows up in our interactions and decided that it was an important topic for us to address. Could we develop a system that will allow me to manage my appointments with both you and my clients so that I can completely focus on our conversations and avoid being late or missing client appointments? I believe that

knowing we have a solid time limit on our scheduled meetings will help address the current ambiguity.

Your boss: I don't think we have to go to all this trouble. Incidents like yesterday hardly ever happen.

You: I recall a similar problem two days ago and another last Wednesday.

Your boss: I still think you're making a mountain out of a molehill.

You: Perhaps, and being significantly late for client appointments matters to me, and I'll bet it matters to you.

Your boss: Of course it does. I just don't want to waste a lot of time setting up a complex strategy for something that rarely happens.

You: Yes, I agree. Would it work for you to give me a five-minute break to reschedule a client when one of our scheduled meetings threatens to run overtime?

Your boss: All right. I'm willing to do that. But I don't think this will happen very often.

You: Maybe not. I appreciate your agreeing to this plan for our future work together. Knowing this, I can concentrate on our conversations rather than worrying about being late for my clients.

Having this conversation probably will be uncomfortable. However, not doing so will perpetuate the status quo and leave you more frustrated. If your boss returns to his former behavior, revisit this conversation if you want the status quo to change.

One strategy often recommended in situations like this is "wait for a good time to raise this issue with the boss." The problem with postponing is that there may never be a perfect time to raise the issue. You will always be able to find something wrong with every opportunity to raise the issue. Though procrastination is the path of least resistance, it does not solve the problem. To solve it will ultimately require you to have the courage to engage in a conversation like the one above.

3. If you are an independent consultant, you can perhaps afford to say you are unwilling to do a certain task. But if you work for someone or don't have many clients, you will have to take on something undesirable as a part of your job. You make it sound like everyone lives in an ideal world of consulting only on those projects you feel good about.

    Whatever situation you are in, assess whether you are willing to do your client's task. If you are not willing to do it, assess the consequences of declining your client's request. To complicate matters further, it may even be a demand. In the short term, you may be willing to compromise some aspect of your ethics, morals, standards, or personal preferences, depending on how large a compromise is being requested. The danger here is that larger compromises may be requested in the future. Eventually the question will become whether you are willing to continue working for someone who continues to place you in uncomfortable or questionable situations.

Chapter 4 Debriefing Questions

Watch the video. What did you notice?

You may be surprised at what you see! You might resort to using your more senior status. The point is to observe the video to learn how you are reacting. Only with awareness can you make appropriate changes.

How did the session go for Howard? Are there any parts of the role-play that he would do differently, given a chance?

Did Howard determine Carolyn's multiple wants and how the results of achieving these wants will be used?

Did Howard have a complete willing conversation, considering each of the wants individually?

Did Howard have a complete able conversation?

Did Howard consider that he did not know Margaret's side of this dispute?

Did Howard realize that he did not know whether Margaret would want Carolyn or even him to be in a discussion about this project?

Did Howard suggest alternative ways to sort out the disagreement between Carolyn and Margaret?

Did Howard delay any discussion of the details of Margaret's project or Carolyn's approach to the *work* step of the meeting?

CHAPTER 5

Work Smarter

The *prepare* and *open* elements of an interaction are intended to develop a collaborative context in which two parties work by agreement with honesty and aligned goals, rather than force, fear, or intimidation. Plans made by agreement have a much higher chance of being implemented than do those built through manipulation. Agreement reduces the chances of reactance occurring.

If the *prepare* and *open* steps in the POWER process are truncated or skipped entirely, there is a high risk that the *work* done won't produce a satisfactory outcome, and rework becomes unavoidable. Many rush to begin doing work in which they bring all their experience and expertise to bear on the problem at hand before they are clear about exactly what that problem entails. This tactic is like starting on a trip without knowing the destination, let alone having a map.

To those who enjoy answering their client's technical questions in their interactions, who want to focus only on task and content without bothering with (or, as some might say, "wasting time on") relationship, here is my invitation: "Think of *prepare* and *open* as intrapersonal and interpersonal dues you pay so that you can give technical answers that your client *will understand and implement.* Then you have a chance at making your contribution." There is no escaping the intrapersonal and interpersonal work to be done!

The characteristics of an effective *work* conversation are as follows:

- Clear: deliver clear content, by both your client's standards and yours.
- Complete: answer all your client's questions comprehensively, by both your client's standards and yours.
- Concise: use the explanation time well, by both your client's standards and yours.
- Accurate: present precise content that will stand up to scrutiny by your client's stakeholders.
- Respect: treat your client with respect, by both your client's standards and yours.

As an example of a *work* conversation, consider the following situation I encountered after agreeing to give a presentation on "What Is a Good Colloquium?" I realized that I could improve my chances of being relevant by asking this question to a regular colloquium attendee. Perhaps since professors are not known for frequently seeking advice from their students, the student I approached (whom I will call "Rob") seemed surprised and pleased by the question. He asked for time to reflect and then get back together. We agreed on a time and place to meet.

During our meeting, Rob gave me several suggestions, including that professors "respect" the colloquium participants. Rather than agreeing to what seemed an obvious statement, I asked for clarification. He replied, "Professors often use this situation to show their expertise rather than create an environment in which those of us on the lower end of the power ladder feel free or even encouraged to speak. Colloquia would be more helpful if they were a place for exchanging ideas and responding to questions rather than preparing for an exam."

Though I thought I knew what he said, I pressed him for more examples. During our conversation, we shared ideas and constantly checked for being on the same page. It was stimulating, helpful, and produced a high level of response from the audience.

Clear Content

It is rare that your client will have your level of expertise in your discipline; therefore, it is critical that the content you deliver be clear to your client. This is an essential part of communication in the *open* step. It is equally important in the *work* step.

To learn what a client understands about your explanations, you could extend this invitation: "I understand that you may be explaining the results of this meeting to your boss. Would you like me to pause periodically to give you an opportunity to practice your presentation of the content? My goal here is to help you prepare a clear explanation for your boss." The more complicated the content, the more frequently you check on your client's level of understanding.

Cultivate your ability to explain complex concepts in simple terms so that they will be useful to your clients. This requires rethinking complex concepts so that you can explain them without jargon. Practice explaining a complex concept in a role-play until your partner can clearly explain the idea to you. Another option is to practice this conversation with your mother or your brother using an example that's related to technical material relevant to them, such as how to use the newest feature on their cell phones.

Difficulties with missed communications or different interpretations of events can be seen in the fallibility of eyewitness testimony. After an accident, witnesses often report contradictory observations. The same thing happens when we are in the midst of a complicated meeting. We interpret comments in ways that are skewed, based on our own biases. We interpret what we hear on any given day depending on whether we are tired and anxious or have just received a glowing performance review. The fact that people are imperfect observers is a fundamental reason why it is important to double-check how your client is actually interpreting and processing information during a meeting.

It is equally critical that you understand what your client is saying. To accomplish this, do the following:

- Stay focused in the conversation. Don't let your mind wander.
- Listen carefully to what your client says.
- Check your interpretation of what your client says by rephrasing, not repeating.
- Ask your client to check their interpretation of what you say in the same way.

These tasks require *all* your attention.

Complete Answers

Some consultants are tempted to address their client's concerns using only approaches that are familiar, not even mentioning the existence of other methodologies of which they may be aware but are unaccustomed to using. Intentionally omitting unfamiliar methods is a dangerous strategy. Yet we all do it. Why? Probably because it is more comfortable in the short run (though risky in the long run).

This strategy may eventually put your client in a difficult situation when one of the project stakeholders asks why a widely accepted approach was not used. Lacking any rationale for the superiority of the technique you used over the alternative puts your client in an awkward spot.

If there is any risk of your client being challenged on the technique you used, prepare your client to address the challenge *or* offer to accompany your client and be ready to assist by answering difficult questions.

An alternative strategy is to outline the approaches that are familiar to you and then to identify other reasonable candidates. Ask your client if they are aware of a strategy typically used to address their concerns in their discipline. If you are not familiar with the approach, estimate how long it will take you to become familiar with it, if you are willing and able to do this.

It is your client's choice to wait for you to learn the approach or to talk with someone who already knows. If you hold the point of view that clients are scarce and you think that this approach risks losing the current client, you may want to revisit the scenario in the previous chapter involving Alice and Warren and the required course. Take a long-term point of view on your client base. Clients are abundant if you deal honestly and generously with the ones you have.

Stay in the conversation as Rob and I did, even after there was one answer. I kept asking for more examples to identify more criteria for a good colloquium. This conversation involved continuing to look for criteria that were uncomfortable for Rob to state or for me to decipher.

Maintaining an open and collaborative mind-set is critical to ensure a clear and complete conversation. Though giving up prematurely may be more comfortable in the short run, the long-term success that comes from perseverance will more than compensate for your time spent and discomfort encountered in being clear and complete. Once again, courage is necessary.

Concise Answers

A concise answer isn't necessarily a short answer. To give detailed advice that's necessary to address a complex point clearly and completely may require the entire session. Conciseness is measured in comprehension, not in time. It becomes an issue when you explain a complex point in multiple ways *without* checking to see if your first explanation was clear. Not a good idea. Such repetition wastes your client's time and damages your rapport. Some clients will find needless repetition enormously annoying and rude.

Accuracy

Project stakeholders will eventually scrutinize the results of the plan you develop with your client. The importance of this scrutiny is reflected in the second characteristic of an effective interaction: *the results of the plan stand up to external scrutiny.* Anticipation of and preparation for this scrutiny are essential parts of an interaction.

Your task includes working with your client to identify the essential stakeholders in your client's project and their conditions for satisfaction. With this information, you will be in a position to be most helpful in assisting your client to achieve success. These conversations are often omitted from interactions, which exposes both you and your client to unnecessary risk.

The utility of the information I gathered from Rob and other graduate students and faculty before my colloquium was verified after it was over. A number of students said that they had learned material that would be useful to them as they prepared presentations for any purpose.

Respect

One way to determine how well you show respect to another is to apply an expanded golden rule to everything that you say or do in an interaction: treat your client as you want to be treated *and* as your client wants to be treated. Following this rule will help the interaction to remain cooperative rather than becoming adversarial.

Barriers to respect and cooperation often occur during the *work* step. When there is a disagreement, there is a natural tendency to get defensive and begin to attack, which may well lead to an escalation of the disagreement. Hence, a strategy for dealing with a disagreement in which you are feeling attacked is to ask yourself, "What have I recently said or done that my client may be interpreting as an attack?"

Disagreement will occur when your client rejects a plan that you are convinced will handle their problem. Emotions can run high on both sides of this challenging situation. My experience is that disagreements like this result when there is something that my client knows or believes and I don't know or believe, or vice versa. My strategy for sorting this out is to stay in the conversation until we clearly identify the differences in our knowledge bases or belief systems and either sort them out or agree to disagree.

Here is an example of staying in the conversation. Read the following and imagine yourself in this situation.

>Conrad: I worked late last night to sort out the difficulty we had yesterday. My resolution of the problems is summarized on this page.

>Jean (after reading and considering what Conrad has written): You've only rearranged the arguments you presented yesterday. That does not help! Talking more about this will be a waste of time.

>Conrad: I can see that the changes are too small to have addressed your major concerns, and it's my understanding that we are obligated to resolve this difficulty. Do you agree?

>Jean: Yes, but we keep going around in the same circle, and that doesn't help anything.

>Conrad: I agree that we are stuck; maybe we could use some outside help. I recall that our Tulsa plant engineers encountered this problem last year. Would you be willing to join me in a conversation with them to see if they can help us?

>Jean: Yes. I think that's a better idea than both of us staying on this merry-go-round.

>Conrad: I agree. Let's do it.

Conrad noted that the problem was a shared problem and had to be addressed at some point. Jean stayed in the conversation long enough to hear a proposal that had promise. Even if the outside help fails to solve their problem, they will have begun to consider out-of-the-box thinking and will keep looking for resolution.

Disrespect

A consultant can communicate disrespect to a client in many ways. Assume that your client is sensitive to them all. Each one has devastating consequences on the interaction. For example, if the consultant makes it clear by words or actions that the client's question was "dumb," this may well lead the client to refrain from asking any more questions. What matters here is whether the client thinks they were treated with respect by *their* standards, not whether the consultant thinks they treated the client with respect, or at least intended to do so. Other ways to show disrespect include: being late for an interaction, interrupting, talking over or finishing your client's questions or answers. A subtler error is to reply with

> **Stumbling Block**
>
> It doesn't matter what you say; it only matters what your client hears.

an "okay" to your client's statement before you have considered whether or not you understand the implications of the proposed action, let alone agree with it. When you talk so fast or so softly that you can't be heard or understood, you may create confusion for your client. There are many other characteristic patterns of interacting that each of us displays and of which we remain blissfully unaware. This is another reason for utilizing video in your practice. Like it or not, we all exhibit some of these behaviors some of the time, and the more often they occur, the more agitated your client becomes.

Listen for these and other such comments you make that may have an unwanted reaction and treat them as red flags, warning you to stop (or at least pause). You want to check with your client to see what effect you are having before proceeding.

Sometimes an action is viewed as acceptable by some individuals and disrespectful by others. For example, often consultants from large families, accustomed to struggling to get their point across, will begin their question or comment as soon as the client pauses for breath. Clients from large families often have no problem with this, while others from small families may take offense, thinking their consultant has not even considered their comments before speaking.

Role-Play

Pick one of the above disrespectful ways of treating a client that you recognize as your trademark. If you cannot identify one, ask your partner! Construct a videoed role-play with your partner of a situation in which this action occurs.

Watch the video to see how you treated your client. Where do you see opportunities for improvement on your video? Construct an alternative approach and video a follow-up role-play.

A similar discrepancy can arise in the volume of a conversation. Some families speak loudly all the time, while in other families a raised voice is interpreted as a sign of anger and is rarely used. Clearly, the background of both the consultant and client has a major impact on their definition of respect and disrespect. In either case, my recommendation is to stay present and alert to how your client is responding to you. Avoiding fast talk and loud volume in any interaction gives you a better chance of being heard.

Sometime later, Rob told me that he felt respected because I had asked for his opinion. He also felt respected when I displayed an authentic interest in his input by questioning him to verify that I understood precisely what he was intending to say.

The *work* step consists of a series of conversations, each addressing one of your client's wants for today. These conversations will yield a series of decisions and action steps. Make sure that you and perhaps even your client are recording these decisions as they are made. Compare notes to verify that they agree. This is a remarkably difficult result to achieve, especially as the number of people in the meeting increases and the meeting gets longer.

The Work Checklist

1. Deliver clear content.
2. Answer your client's questions completely.
3. Use the time well.
4. Present accurate content that will stand up to scrutiny by your client's stakeholders.
5. Treat your client with respect, by your client's standards, not yours.

Chapter 5 Activity

Now that we've explored the *work* aspect of the POWER process, it's time to practice with your role-play partner. Using a smartphone, have your partner set a five-minute alarm and video both of you during the role-play.

Role-Play

Present technical information to your partner and have your partner ask you questions. Some questions can be naive, at least in your view. Answer your partner's questions concisely and with respect.

Following your role-play exercise, explore the chapter 5 debriefing questions at the end of this chapter. Please look at these questions with your partner *after* having completed this activity, as you will learn more from the role-play experience this way.

Brenda's Case—The Work Checklist

Brenda's case offers an example of how a checklist can be used to dissect an interaction and identify specific steps to take in the future.

1. Deliver clear content.

    Early in the *work* step of the session, I made mistakes by using technical terms without checking whether Brenda understood what I was saying. Similarly, as in the *open* part, I assumed incorrectly that I understood how *she* was using technical terms without checking with her.

2. Answer your client's questions completely.

    I did not give Brenda complete answers to several of her questions. At the time, this was not intentional, as I was still lost in the surprise and upset resulting from her refusal to take a statistics course. Some of my answers were incomplete enough that I doubt she could have implemented anything I was telling her to do.

3. Use the time well.

    Time was not well used, as I explained several basic statistical concepts, something that I thought she needed to consider and that she already had told me that she did not want to consider. I never verified with Brenda whether what I was doing in the session was useful to her.

4. Present accurate content that will stand up to external scrutiny by your client's stakeholders.

    Though the technical statistical material I presented was accurate, it did not address the task her professors had given her. I put her into a difficult situation by essentially requiring her to take a statistics course, a task they had not assigned to her. Unfortunately, I did not recognize this at the time and did not help her to sort out the conflicting advice she received.

5. Treat your client with respect, by your client's standards, not yours.

    Brenda was not treated with respect when I responded to her denial of my order to take a statistics course. I went into command mode and fully expected her to say, "Yes, sir!" I was infringing on her freedoms, and reactance immediately showed up in her response.

    Disrespect also occurred in the *work* phase as I agreed with her criticisms of her instructors when I had no evidence supporting those criticisms.

Recap

Address the wants in priority order. Consider all approaches to your client's questions, not just those that are familiar to you. When explaining material, stop frequently to give your client a chance to explain to you what they have heard. At the same time, verify that what your client has interpreted is what you intended to say. The more complex the material, the more frequently you check for comprehension. Use the time well. Stay on topic. Ask your client if the subject matter and questions being considered are useful and if the time is being well spent. Give accurate answers that will stand up to external scrutiny. Respect your client.

Frequently Asked Questions

1. What if my client does not understand the technical material that we are dealing with as well as I expected she would?

    Here is a possibility for dealing with this situation. Read the following and imagine yourself in this situation.

Consultant: This material gets complicated fast, doesn't it?

Client: And how!

Consultant (*smiling, leans back in the chair, looking and sounding relaxed, even if he isn't*): I know how how complex this can be! What points do we need to clarify?

(Note to reader: Avoid telling your client "it's easy." That will not put the person at ease; nor will it make you another friend.)

Client: Uh, everything!

Consultant: Okay, then. Thanks for being honest. I'd like to suggest a way to help us both get where we need to be so I can better assist you with this project.

Client (*nodding*): That would be great!

Consultant: I have some written material that addresses the main points in a nutshell. We can cover the rest of what you want in a broad sense today and then meet later for a more detailed exploration of what you want after you've taken a look at the material. Sound good?

Client: Better, yes, though it does sound a lot like homework!

Consultant: Well, yes. But would you be willing to do it?

Client: Sure, if it will give us more time to discuss the difficult points.

Consultant: It will.

2. Why did you insist on Brenda taking the course?

    I insisted she take the course because I made a judgment that she should understand the theoretical foundations of her work.

She was interested only in the part she considered relevant: the calculations to be done. It was an affront to me and my profession that she wanted a tool without understanding the entire machine. It was a consultant-centered session, which I now regret.

3. What if my client's goals can't be met?

Be aware that this is *your* assessment based on the assumptions you are making. Explain to your client the grounds for your assessment.

Do this in the spirit of exploring whether there is some assumption that you are making that is not accurate or whether there may be some aspect of the situation that you have not considered. Your client may also have made similar assumptions.

Collaboratively search for a way to meet these goals rather than arguing that your assessment is correct. Remember that forcing your client to do something, in this case take a statistics course, will elicit reactance, which will compromise the quality of your relationship.

4. Suppose my client isn't satisfied with my answer to his question. What then?

Stay in the conversation. Identify the source of his dissatisfaction.

- Does he think that you made an error in your work? Review your work with him to see if you did.
- Is he dissatisfied because your answer does not match the answer he was looking for?
- Compare the basis for your answer and his. Is the difference between them trivial, or does it relate to your professional, ethical, or moral standards? If it relates to your standards, resolving the difference to the satisfaction of both of you will determine whether you can continue to work together with integrity.

The Work Rubric

Table 5 presents the work rubric. Table 6 presents the results of applying the work rubric to the Brenda interaction. The work rubric reveals that the consultant did not attend to key aspects of the *work* step in the POWER process and continued treating his client with disrespect.

Table 5. The work rubric

Strength	Okay for Now	Opportunity for Improvement
1. The client understands the content that the consultant delivers.		
Consultant asks the client to explain in client's words what consultant has just explained. Consultant checks every ten minutes, more frequently if content is difficult.	Consultant checks if the client understands content. Consultant checks at least every twenty minutes.	Consultant does not check if the client understands content.
2. Consultant's answers to the client's questions are complete.		
Consultant gives what consultant considers to be complete answers and then asks if the client has follow-up questions.	Consultant gives what consultant considers to be complete answers, not checking them out.	Consultant gives incomplete answers to the client's questions.
3. Consultant uses the time well and verifies with the client that what is being done is useful.		
Consultant occasionally asks if the time is being used well, relative to what the client now wants from the session.	Consultant is guided by the results of the original wanted conversation.	Consultant skips this conversation.

4. Consultant presents accurate content that will stand up to external scrutiny.		
Consultant asks who will be reviewing the results of this session and by what criteria. Consultant and the client assess whether the criteria are being met.	Consultant asks if the client is satisfied with the content of the session.	Consultant skips this conversation.
5. Consultant treats the client with respect, by the client's standards, not the consultant's.		
Consultant does not talk over or interrupt the client.	Consultant interrupts one to three times.	Consultant interrupts more than three times.

Table 6. The work rubric—Brenda's case

Strength	Okay for Now	Opportunity for Improvement
1. The client understands the content that the consultant delivers.		
		I did not check if client understood content.
2. Consultant's answers to the client's questions are complete.		
I gave what I considered to be complete answers.		

3. Consultant uses the time well and verifies with the client that what is being done is useful.		
		I skipped this conversation.
4. Consultant presents accurate content that will stand up to external scrutiny.		
		I skipped this conversation.
5. Consultant treats the client with respect, by the client's standards, not the consultant's.		
	There were a few interruptions and talk-overs.	

Chapter 5 Debriefing Questions

Watch the video. What did you notice?

Did you verify that you understood your partner's question?

Did you verify that your partner understood your answer?

Did you ask if you had answered your partner's question?

Explore these questions for each of your partner's questions.

CHAPTER 6

End Play

Many interactions are brilliant until the last five minutes. Often these closing minutes are rushed and full of incomplete conversations. After a confusing closing, people tend to make up a version of the action plan and then do nothing because of their well-founded uncertainty about what they are to do. Consequently, action is at least delayed and may be derailed until all tasks have been clearly defined.

To avoid rework, allow sufficient time to end the interaction effectively. My suggestion is to reserve between 15 and 25 percent of the total length of the meeting for a complete *end conversation*. This one action will enhance the chances that the plans made in the interaction are indeed implemented following the meeting.

An End Play Gone Wrong

Early in his career, Mark had a consultation with a new client, John. They discussed several potential analyses that had potential for addressing John's questions. They did not take time at the end of the session to review who would do what and by when before their next meeting.

After the session, Mark reviewed the possibilities in his mind and decided that there was one that clearly had more potential than the others. He proceeded to invest several hours in doing this analysis.

A week later, Mark and John met again. Mark was pleased to present his complete analysis to John and looked forward to his response.

Read the following dialogue and imagine yourself in this situation.

> John replied, "Thanks for doing that, but there were several analyses we discussed. I thought we had not decided on which one to do. In fact, my problem has changed slightly so that this analysis is no longer relevant."
>
> Later that day, Mark met with his supervisor, Darrell. "I can't believe how inconsiderate clients are! I did several hours of work for my new client, who came in this morning and said he wasn't interested in it. I can't believe it."
>
> Darrell replied, "How do you think that happened?"
>
> "I don't have a clue!" Mark said. "I thought we had a good session last week, and then today—*bam*—he tosses out all my work, saying, 'My problem has changed slightly'!"
>
> "How did you leave things at the end of your session last week?" asked Darrell.
>
> "We talked about what a good session we had and agreed to meet this week."
>
> "Did you explicitly discuss what analyses you were to do before today's meeting?"
>
> "Well, no," Mark said. "But it was clear to me then that the analysis I did was the best one by far."

Decisions

Mark's troubles began because he did not do the first part of a complete *end play*: review and agree on any decisions made during the interaction.

Pausing at the end of an interaction to review all decisions made is essential. The "eyewitness syndrome" also occurs in consultations. People who were in the same room, in the same interaction may have different versions of what was decided during the interaction. In fact, sometimes they end up disagreeing on "agreed decisions" that were "agreed on" minutes ago!

Before anyone leaves the room, take the time to review every decision that's important to at least one person in the room and make sure there is agreement on it. The more people in the interaction, the more critical it is to identify a scribe before the interaction starts. Then the scribe can be recording all the decisions as they are being made. Even with a scribe, review the decisions made before anyone leaves because someone may disagree with the scribe's version of a decision.

Sometimes a meeting consists of a series of short segments, each addressing a different topic. Reviewing decisions after each completed section is effective, especially when the scribe records each decision as it is made.

This process can be tedious and will take time. The resources saved are dramatically larger than the cost of the review. As you practice this process of recording decisions, and experience success, the process itself becomes second nature.

The end conversation is the last chance in a meeting for all parties to address any concerns that came up as each decision was made. Such concerns may require:

- identifying barriers to implementing the plan developed;
- assessing whether the results of this plan are likely to stand up to scrutiny by stakeholders, and if not, identifying the weak points; and
- agreeing on when and where to address the barriers and weak points.

The first meeting between Mark and John ended without a review of the potential analyses and an assessment of whether they had agreed on which one to do. Mark then leapt to a conclusion and decided that he knew which analysis would be best for John. Unfortunately, he was wrong, and judging from his language, his attitude likely created a fracture in their relationship.

Tasks, Time Frames, and Standards

The process of addressing each decision discussed in any interaction takes time because each task identified includes who will do what, by when, and to what criteria. Each part of this agreement is critical.

Who will do what by when is often not made clear in the *work* step. "By when" is often omitted or specified vaguely, such as "sometime soon" or "maybe next week."

The standards to which the work is to be completed depend on the stakeholders and their criteria. Ideally, the stakeholders' conditions for satisfaction have been identified in the *open* step. Be aware that new wants may have been uncovered during the *work* step, requiring the identification of the stakeholders' corresponding criteria. If you skip this process of continually clarifying criteria, especially in the rush that often occurs at the end of interactions, you may find yourself in the all too familiar place of rework—wasting resources you can ill afford to lose.

Allocating enough time to the *end* step can be problematic in that there is a tendency to regard the *end* step as not "real work." It is then shortchanged by this attitude, as are the *prepare* and *open* steps.

Stumbling Block

If any aspect of what is to be done after the interaction is left to chance, someone will be engaged in work *based on a guess* of what is wanted by when and to what criteria. Guessing is risky at best and can lead to a disaster.

The interaction between Mark and John is a small and clear example of what can happen.

Stepping Stone

Following each meeting, record your understanding of the agreements made and send it to your client for confirmation or correction. You may also want to call by the end of the week to clarify any changes either of you wants to make.

Client Satisfaction

Ask your client, "Did you get what you wanted from this interaction? Is there anything else that you can see now for us to address relative to this project, either today or in the future?"

These can be uncomfortable questions, especially if you think the interaction did not go well. At the heart of dealing with discomfort is the question, "When do you want to receive the news that your client was disappointed with the session?" The sooner you get it, the sooner you can address it. Another benefit is that your client has less time to stew.

Do not ask the question about whether your client's wants were met unless you are willing to accept "No!" as an answer and respond with patience and respect. If you do accept "No!" clarify exactly what is missing before you attempt to address it. Stay in the conversation until you are clear about everything that was missing.

A temptation is to try to immediately fix everything that was missing. This isn't a good idea, especially if you are at the end of the agreed-on time for this interaction. In this situation, schedule another interaction either in person or by phone to address the missing pieces.

Role-Play

Construct a role-play in which you ask your partner if they are satisfied with the interaction you just had, and they aren't.

Watch the video. How effectively did you address their dissatisfaction?

How completely and accurately your client answers these questions about the quality of the interaction depends on the quality of the relationship you have developed with each other during your time together. (Incidentally, this is also true for any question you ask during the interaction.) You may receive a thoughtful answer, or you may get a quick, "It's okay," even though your client thinks the interaction was useless.

How do you get complete and accurate answers to any of your questions? The answer lies in the process of intentionally attending to your client's questions and concerns with respect. When you take the time to create a safe place, your relationship grows. Trust is built by treating each and every one of your client's questions and answers with honesty and sincerity.

You may find it useful to say, "I want to improve the quality of my services. Are there parts of this meeting that could have gone better for you?" For the ensuing conversation to be successful, you must have enough time available at the end of the session to complete it in an unhurried manner.

You also have to be honestly interested in receiving your client's feedback, be it positive or negative. In fact, I find negative feedback from my clients to be more helpful than positive, as it tells me where I can improve my services. Do I like hearing the negative feedback? No, not in the moment. I pause, take a couple of deep breaths, and then begin to explore possibilities for addressing the parts of the interaction that did not go well for my client.

An alternative to asking your client for feedback face-to-face after the interaction is to design an evaluation form for your clients to complete and return to you. Such forms have become a regular part of all sorts of interactions, face-to-face, on the phone, and on the internet. I encourage you to collect these forms and utilize their questions to design your own questionnaire to help you improve the quality of your service. Possibilities include the following:

- Did you get what you wanted from our meeting today? If not, what was missing?
- What was the most confusing point remaining after our meeting was over?
- What aspects of how your consultant worked today were effective? Were not effective?
- Do you have any other comments or suggestions?

Clients are more likely to return this form if their feedback is more positive than negative. I suggest addressing this directly by prefacing your request to fill out the form with, "Your feedback gives me information that I cannot get from any other source. Please give me your thoughts on the session, both positive and negative."

Neither Mark nor John checked at the end their first meeting if one another's wants for the meeting were met. No one had clarity on what tasks were to be done before their next meeting. Mark chose to guess, select a task that he thought would be useful, and do it. Unfortunately, his guess was wrong, and this produced upset. A wiser choice would have been for either of them to take a moment as their first meeting was ending and say, "Let's not do any specific tasks before next week

> **Stepping Stone**
>
> When in a meeting with a client, as soon as you realize you will not be able to complete everything you hoped to, immediately tell your client.

because we have just gotten started talking about the problem. I think actions taken prematurely might turn out to be wasted."

End on Time

I well recall how surprised I was the first time I learned that a client was not grateful for my running overtime and giving her more pearls of wisdom, whether she wanted them or not. It had never occurred to me that a client might have a prior commitment more important than continuing our discussion.

I noticed that, when I ran overtime, I was often trying to clarify something I thought I should have explained better in the meeting. I was more attentive to appearing competent than to respecting my client's time and priorities. If you discover a mistake late in the meeting, identify it and ask for an extension of the meeting time to address it. If the extension is granted, clean up the mistake. If it isn't, schedule another meeting or phone call to clean it up.

If a client has listed several wants for a meeting, you may not be able to address all of them within one meeting, even though you thought you could. An important part of treating your client with respect is having the courage to discuss this miscalculation *as soon as you realize it*. Then another meeting can be scheduled, allowing today's meeting to close at the agreed-on time. Don't try to do twenty minutes of work in the last five minutes of the current meeting. This is impossible! I know; I have tried and failed each time!

Sometimes it is possible for both of you to extend the meeting by as much as thirty minutes. If so, do this intentionally and well before the wrap-up begins by verbally agreeing on the extension rather than cruising past the scheduled ending time. Helping both of you to stay conscious about time is part of respecting each other's boundaries. You don't want to lose track of time and suddenly hear your client exclaim, "Oh, no! I was to be in a staff meeting forty-five minutes ago!" Clients appreciate support in honoring time limitations.

Stumbling Block

As a meeting approaches its agreed-on ending time, a client's mind tends to move toward their next meeting. Thus, unilaterally extending the meeting not only annoys your client; they don't absorb anything you say anyway, even if it could have been helpful.

The End Checklist

1. Allow enough time at the end of the session for completing the following closing tasks:

    a. Review and agree on any decisions made during the interaction.
    b. Review and agree on who will do what, by when, to what standards.
    c. If further meetings would be helpful, agree on the purpose, time, and place of the next meeting.

2. Ask whether your client's wants for the interaction were met.
3. Close the interaction at the mutually agreed-on time.
4. As soon as possible after the meeting, communicate with your client to verify that you both agreed on the same path forward.
5. Treat your client with respect, by your client's standards, not yours.

Chapter 6 Activity

It's time to practice with your role-play partner.

Role-Play

Video a replay of the ending of the first session between Mark and John, which is described at the beginning of this chapter. Apply what you now know to their situation.

Following your role-play exercise, refer to the chapter 6 debriefing questions at the end of this chapter. Please look at these questions with your partner *after* having completed this activity, as you will learn more from the role-play experience this way.

Brenda's Case—The End Checklist

1. Allow enough time at the end of the session for your client and you to do the following:

    a. Review and agree on any decisions made during the interaction.

      There was no provision to write down agreements Brenda and I had made and what would happen next. We did no review. Time ran out; that is, time was mismanaged, and the session ending time was ignored. In fact, the next person scheduled to use the room knocked on the door before we were done.

    b. Review and agree on who will do what, by when, to what standards.

      The session ended without an agreement on any of these.

    c. Agree on the time, place, and purpose of the next meeting.

      We only agreed on a time and place to meet in the next week. No purpose was discussed.

2. Ask if your client's wants for the interaction were met. If they were not met, develop a plan for how and when to address this.

      I did not ask her if she had received what she wanted from this interaction. I had a good idea that she had not, and I did not want to discuss the matter further! Commitment to my comfort was stronger than my commitment to serve her.

3. Close the interaction on time.

> I did not do this. We did not agree on the time available at the start. Also, I was distracted by the number of aspects of the session that went poorly.

4. As soon as possible, communicate with your client to verify that you both agree on the way forward.

> This was not done. I was not routinely doing this with any of my clients when Brenda and I met. Even if I had been routinely doing this, I suspect that I would not have communicated with her after the session, given the set of attitudes I had about her and her topic.

5. Treat your client with respect, by your client's standards, not yours.

> Disrespect of Brenda showed up often:
>
> a. by neglecting to check when the next person was scheduled for the video room before the session began;
> b. by neglecting to reserve time for ending our session;
> c. by not reviewing decisions made and tasks to be done;
> d. by failing to discuss, let alone agree on, our time line in the *open* step.
>
> Another aspect of disrespect was that I ignored Brenda's decision to decline my recommendation to take a statistics course. Instead, I tried manipulation to get compliance, and you have seen how well that worked!

Recap

Review and agree on all decisions made. For all tasks agreed on, verify who is doing what, by when, and to what criteria.

Frequently Asked Questions

1. My boss called me out of a consulting session just before we started the end conversation. What could I have done?

    Before you leave the session, agree with your client when you can schedule the end conversation. Then schedule a meeting with your boss on how this happened and how better to handle such incidents in the future.

2. Sometimes I'm meeting with several consultants discussing my problem. Their plans to address it get more and more elaborate until I'm not sure I'm willing to implement them, *and* I doubt that my stakeholders will approve them. What to do?

    As soon as you notice your discomfort, request that the discussion return to your original concerns. Point out to your consultants that they have departed from what you wanted from this meeting. This may be a challenge if your consultants have already become invested in their new plan.

    In a case like this, my favorite request is: "Please help me understand what you see that I don't see, regarding how this plan addresses my original problem." This is an essential step when you are either client or consultant. Noncompliance can occur in both roles. In addition, before you complete the *end* step, revisit the willing and able conversations for both the client and consultant.

3. What if you do not want to meet with this consultant in the future?

    If you would prefer not to meet with this person again, and this may be difficult to achieve, you can schedule a separate meeting with this person to discuss your working relationship and how to heal it. Many people find this conversation uncomfortable, yet most consultants appreciate the opportunity to heal their relationship with you for the future, rather than have you mysteriously disappear.

4. Can an *end* conversation occur in the middle of the session?

Yes. This is an excellent idea, especially in a long, complex interaction involving several people and many agenda items. It is like pausing on a plateau when climbing a mountain: catch your breath, establish a new base camp, have a snack and a drink. Survey the surrounding terrain and assess what direction looks most promising for the next stage of your assent.

The End Rubric

Table 7 presents the end rubric. Table 8 presents the results of applying the end rubric to the Brenda interaction.

The end rubric reveals that the consultant continued to skip critical steps and treat his client with disrespect.

Table 7. The end rubric

Strength	Okay for Now	Opportunity for Improvement
1. Agree on actions to be taken, decisions made, and the next meeting.		
Actions, decisions, and the next meeting are reviewed and agreed on.	Actions to be taken are reviewed and agreed on.	Rushed. Not enough time to review and agree on these actions and decisions at the end of the session.
2. Raise any concerns about the plan developed.		
Consultant asks the client for concerns about: 1. The plan developed, 2. Key stakeholders' reaction to the plan, and 3. How to implement it.	Consultant declares that session was successful. Consultant gives client only a minimal chance to comment on the session or the plan developed.	Consultant skips this conversation.
3. Ask if the client's wants for the interaction were met. Address the unmet wants.		
Consultant reviews the wanted conversation results, addressing each desired result and asking if it was achieved.	Consultant asks if session produced what the client was looking for.	Consultant skips this conversation.

For those not achieved, consultant offers to plan with the client when to address them.		
4. Identify any barriers to implementation of the plan. Address them.		
Consultant asks if the client sees any problems in the implementation process and whether or not the stakeholders may have any problems with the implementation process. Consultant offers to work with the client on any problems client sees in these areas.	Consultant asserts that everything will go well and asks if client agrees.	Consultant makes a broad assertion about how smoothly the implementation of the plan will go, or consultant skips this conversation.
5. As soon as possible, verify in writing that the consultant and client agree on the way forward.		
The next day, the consultant emails the client the consultant's understanding of the next steps in the project. Consultant asks for confirmation or corrections.	Consultant calls the client the next day and asks if the client has any questions.	Consultant skips this conversation.

6. Treat the client with respect, by the client's standards, not the consultant's.

Consultant does not talk over or interrupt the client.	Consultant interrupts one to three times.	Consultant interrupts more than three times.

Table 8. The end rubric—Brenda's case

Strength	Okay for Now	Opportunity for Improvement
1. Agree on actions to be taken, decisions made, and the next meeting.		
		Rushed. Not enough time at the end of the session to review and agree on future actions and decisions made.
2. Raise any concerns about the plan developed.		
		I skipped this conversation.
3. Ask if the client's wants for the interaction were met. Address the unmet wants.		
		I skipped this conversation.
4. Identify any barriers to implementation of the plan. Address them.		
		I skipped this conversation.

5. As soon as possible, verify in writing that the consultant and client agree on the way forward.	
	I skipped this conversation.
6. Treat the client with respect, by the client's standards, not the consultant's.	
	I frequently began speaking before client was finished.

Chapter 6 Debriefing Questions

Watch the video. What did you notice?

Did either of you seek to clarify the tasks to be done after the meeting?

Did both of you make complete requests and promises to the other, including specific descriptions of the tasks to be done, by whom and by when?

Was there reluctance on either of your parts to acknowledge that you were not sure what was to be done next?

Pick one actual meeting that your partner and you had recently. Review the ending of it. How does it measure up to the criteria in the *end* checklist?

CHAPTER 7

Prudent Reflections

Reflecting on a completed interaction can provide valuable insights for both present and future actions. The *reflect* step is the final step in the POWER process. Now is the time to consider the effectiveness of your words and actions in the session just completed. You can do this by yourself or with your partner. The data you use for reflection can be your memories of what occurred during the interaction. Of course, if you have a video, you will have more complete and less biased data. In either case, the task you face is to analyze the available data to identify information that will help you improve the quality of your interactions. In addition, you may recall some promises you made in the meeting that must be addressed sooner than later.

Initially, I strenuously resisted using video for analyzing my practice. While introducing others to the benefits of video to improve their practice, I learned that resistance is common among professionals at every stage in their careers. Not surprisingly, students training to become professionals are no less challenged.

My theory about this internal struggle is that reflection is a self-evaluation activity. For most of us, evaluations have not been a positive experience in our lives, beginning with grade school. Our collective experience of those who evaluate our performance (parents, siblings, teachers, pastors, supervisors, and colleagues) is that few have done so in a way that was nourishing, encouraging, and affirming. Search your memory for those few who offered you not just positive feedback but critically honest yet compassionate correction. Find someone you can emulate.

One of the ways we resist reflection is creating schedules that don't allow the required time. The current plethora of electronic devices that encourages conversation with anyone, anywhere, and at any time further threatens reserving time for reflection. As competition for success in the marketplace grows more intense every day, there is an associated fear that grows correspondingly: the fear that if we set aside time to reflect, we may be seen as wasting time.

Competition also drives us to be evermore frenetic, increasing the chances that mistakes, even major mistakes, will be made with greater frequency.

Clearly, major barriers confront you if you wish to change and begin to intentionally reflect on your performance. To add in the reflect step will require change in

> **Stepping Stone**
>
> Time and patience are required to intentionally complete all steps of the POWER process and increase the chances of *both* effective and efficient interactions.

your habitual lack of reflection. While change is always challenging, this particular change is especially difficult. Your mind is clever enough to know that if you open the door to reflecting on your performance, you may discover an unending series of changes to be made if you are to systematically improve your performance. I choose the word "unending" intentionally, as my experience is that those who are passionate about their vision and their mission while on planet Earth will never exhaust the possibilities that they see for improving their performance.

The power of reflection underpins my promise that the POWER process is a way to systematically improve your practice.

> **Stepping Stone**
>
> The task at hand is to pick one improvement at a time, address it, stay in the present, and not get lost anticipating other challenges that will show up.

Addressing the above-mentioned long-standing barriers is a critical part of the reflection process. Treat yourself compassionately and start reflecting on small matters in safe relationships. This is one of the most important benefits that can result from working with a partner. As you begin to help each other develop the skill to give reflection-based feedback, each of you will be nourished and encouraged to practice this skill with others.

Reflect

The *reflect* step is more complete and accurate when you engage in it immediately following a meeting. Find a place where you can reflect privately before details begin to evaporate. Since most of us create schedules that don't allow gaps between our meetings, this will be the first change in your modus operandi. Occasionally we may schedule a gap for reflection after a particularly important meeting; this is a fine start toward routinely reflecting. Creating a new professional practice of reflection following every interaction is a challenge, especially when you are already pressed for time. A reflection period will take time to inaugurate and integrate; however, the benefits of reflection will, with practice, save you far *more* time in the long run.

If you judge your performance immediately following an interaction as anything short of stellar, you will be reluctant to revisit the experience. One is tempted to think, *Whew! That's over. I don't even want to think about that meeting again!* However, the more problems there were in an interaction, the more opportunities there are for you to learn and improve. Brenda's case convinced me of this!

When you have video of the interaction, this is an opportune time to review it. When we review our videos alone, often we are excessively critical of our part in the interaction, especially our idiosyncrasies. Include your partner in this review to help you calibrate your reactions to the event and to the resulting video.

To get the most information from reviewing your video of a session with a trusted client, invite this client to join you in the reflection process. You will get a unique perspective on identifying where you are effective or ineffective, especially if your review is done as soon as possible after the videoed session. You might say to your client, "I'm working on improving my interactions. One of the best ways to do this is to discuss them with clients like you. Would you be willing to review a videoed session with me?" In my experience, these requests have been granted, especially when given this invitation while setting the meeting date and time. Afterward, your client may even report learning as much or more than you from the video review.

The bottom line for any interaction is whether it was effective. The goal of this book is to assist you to systematically increase the proportion of your interactions that are successful. Recall that an effective interaction produces three results:

1.   The interaction ends with a workable plan, a plan in which both the client and the consultant know what each will do next, to what criteria, by when, and the plan is implemented.
2.   The results of the implemented plan stand up to external scrutiny.
3.   The client regards the consultant as a valuable resource for future interactions.

At the end of an interaction, we can only assess whether a workable plan has been established. Time must pass before we can assess whether the plan is implemented, whether it stands up to external scrutiny, and whether the client engages this consultant again.

The Reflect Checklist

In this section, we consider checklists from each step of the POWER process to address the *reflect* checklist:

1. What worked?

    Here you are looking for effective interactions so that you may learn to repeat them intentionally.

2. What did not work?

    Here you are looking for any mistakes that occurred so that you may learn where improvements can be made in the future.

3. What had to be present in the attitudes of the consultant and client for this interaction to have gone the way it did?

    This question differs from the above, which can be answered through direct video observation; whereas, now we are creating inferences about attitudes. Confirming these hypotheses requires conversations with the consultant and client involved.

4. How can this situation be better addressed in the future?

    The first three *reflect* questions examine an interaction that has already occurred. Now we are looking to the future and asking how to use the information from the present to improve one's future effectiveness. If possible, discuss this question with your client rather than trying to work alone. Your trusted partner is another unique resource in this investigation.

Use POWER Checklists to Reflect

The POWER checklists provide a systematic way to reflect on each part of the meeting. They will guide you through a complete review of the interaction.

Prepare Checklist

1. Review the POWER process.

   Do you recall what your strategy was for the interaction? Did you use it? Did it help you achieve your intention to produce a workable plan? If it was not helping you, did you recognize this during the session and change to another approach?

2. Prepare for the content.

   Were you aware of and prepared for the content of the interaction? Did surprises occur? If so, did you rapidly recover from these surprises? Did you develop a plan to learn any aspects of the content with which you were unfamiliar so that the session could end with a workable plan?

3. Focus.

   Were you focused on your client and the problem at hand *at the beginning* of the session? If not, how did that happen? How long did it take you to focus? What did you miss, and how did you recover that information?

   Did you lose your focus at any point *during the session*? Can you recall what happened in the minutes before you lost your focus? How long did it take you to recover your focus? As a part of your recovery, did you acknowledge to your client that you had lost your focus?

Open Checklist

1. Agree on the amount of time available for this interaction.

   Did you agree with your client at the beginning of the session on how much time was available, or did you tell your client the time frame? Or did you agree on the time frame later in the session when one or the other of you remembered to do this? Or did you not address the time available at all? If so, what impact did your choice have on the session?

2. Determine what your client wants and how these results will be used.

When you identified your client's first want, did you verify that both of you were talking about the same thing by reiterating the want in your own language? Did you ask how the results of achieving each want would be used? Did you continue asking if your client had any more wants until you heard, "No"? Did you identify all the conditions for satisfaction, including "by when," for each want?

3. Have a complete willing conversation.

Did you assess whether you were willing to work on each of your client's wants and communicate that to your client? Was this a considered assessment rather than an automatic "Sure, I could do that"?

4. Have a complete able conversation.

Did you assess whether you were able to work on each of your client's wants and communicate that assessment to your client? Were these assessments considered or automatic?

5. Treat your client with respect, by your client's standards, not yours.

Were you ready to start the session on time? Did you listen to your client's complete statements or questions throughout the session before responding to them, or did you talk over your client? Did you interrupt your client? If so, what led you to interrupt? Were you honest with your client? Did you treat your client's questions with respect, not ridiculing your client either overtly or covertly?

Work Checklist

1. Deliver clear content.

   Did you check with your client periodically on how well they understood the material you delivered? If so, how did you do this? By asking them to explain it to you in their own words? Did you describe your client's subject matter in your words? If not, why not?

2. Answer your client's questions completely.

   On reflection, were any of your answers incomplete, either unintentionally or intentionally? When and how do you plan to clean up these omissions?

3. Use the time well.

   Did you verify with your client that the time was used well? Were there wants that your client had that were not addressed in the session? Did any of these have higher priority than the ones that were addressed? If so, how did this happen? Is there a plan to address these wants at another time?

4. Present accurate content that will stand up to external scrutiny by your client's stakeholders.

   Do you have any doubts about how well the content you presented will stand up to scrutiny by your client's stakeholders? If you had doubts in the meeting, did you raise them? If not, what led you to avoid them? Who are experts with whom you can critique your content?

5. Treat your client with respect, by your client's standards, not yours.

Did you listen to your client's complete statements or questions before responding? Did you talk over your client? Did you interrupt your client? Were you honest with your client? Did you treat your client's questions with respect, not ridiculing your client either overtly or covertly?

End Checklist

1. Allow enough time at the end of the session for your client and you to do the following:

   a.) Review and agree on any decisions made during the interaction.
   b.) Review and agree on who will do what, by when, and to what standards.
   c.) Agree on the time, place, and purpose of the next meeting.

   Was there enough time to do each of the above tasks to the satisfaction of both your client and you?

2. As soon as possible, communicate with your client to verify that you both agree on the same way forward.

   When will you do this? How will you do this?

3. Ask whether your client's wants for the interaction were met. If they were not, develop a plan for addressing them.

   This is a challenging question for you to ask and a challenging question for your client to answer, especially if this is your

> **Stepping Stone**
>
> To obtain useful information from clients, you must encourage them to provide both accurate and complete responses and support them in doing so.

first meeting. To be useful, this question, like any you have asked in the consultation, requires that you ask in a way that enrolls your client in giving you an accurate and complete response.

First, address any and all reservations you have about making requests; most of us have many of these (e.g., *I can't ask for this feedback. What will she think of me? Will I look like an incompetent consultant if I ask? I'll bet no one has ever asked her this before.*).

Next, enroll your client in giving you an accurate and complete response. Assure your client that you are authentically interested in their opinion of how the session went. Their opinion matters to you. After all, they have information about this topic that it is impossible for you to learn from any other source. Keep in mind that you are committed to serving future clients more effectively, and your client is in a unique position to help you do this.

This request isn't intended to be covert or manipulative. On the contrary, you are asking for exactly what information you want. Of course, your client may say yes or no to your request; some enrollment efforts succeed, and some fail. Stay in the conversation with patience and respect as long as you can.

If you discover you did not meet your client's wants for this consultation, propose another meeting to address the unmet wants. Don't try to fix this error now unless you both agree there is sufficient time to do so.

4. Close the interaction on time.

   Did the interaction end at the time agreed on in the *open* step? If not, how did this happen?

5. Treat your client with respect, by your client's standards, not yours.

If you did not end the session on time, did both of you agree to extend it beyond the initial time frame? Did you listen to your client's complete statements or questions before responding, or did you talk over your client? Did you interrupt your client? If so, what led you to interrupt and how did you do so? Were you honest with your client? Did you treat your client's questions with respect, not ridiculing your client either overtly or covertly?

Chapter 7 Activity

Role-Play

With your partner, apply the *reflect* step to a recent interaction that did not go well—one with which you are displeased whenever it comes to mind.

Following this activity, refer to the chapter 7 debriefing questions at the end of this chapter. Please consider these questions with your partner *after* having completed this activity, as you will learn more from the role-play experience this way.

Brenda's Case—The Reflect Checklist

As I was writing this chapter, I was surprised by a humbling insight: I was not the source of the idea to review the Brenda consultation. In my initial self-assessments, I had written it off as a bad session with a bad client. This is another strategy for avoiding reflection.

Initially, I thought, *I did fine, the best that anyone could do with such a client.* This thought led to sharing the video with others. In the end, it was those others—students and colleagues—whose questions and comments led me to reexamine my attitudes.

No progress occurred until I was willing to grant the *possibility* that I could have done better. After that attitude shift, I have been able to learn from this video each time I have watched it.

1. What worked?

    Brenda received input on how to express her research plans in a more formal, statistical way. She also received input late in the consultation on questionnaire construction and obtaining a sample for her study. The key verb here is "received." These are topics that I explained quickly. What I don't know is what she understood from these explanations, as I did not ask her.

2. What did not work?

    I will discuss each breakdown below under *prepare, open, work,* and *end* to illustrate how *reflect* has become an essential part of my systematically improving the effectiveness of my interactions. (Some people call these mistakes "breakdowns"; others call them "opportunities for improvement." Use whatever language works for you. The important activity is to identify and investigate such anomalies.)

    The following is a review of tools and concepts covered in chapters 3–6 that relate to Brenda's case. My purpose here is to highlight how all steps of POWER relate to one another, with success in one step creating success in another and vice versa.

    Prepare

    The first mistake occurred before the session began when I realized that there was confusion about where we would meet. Hence, I was not focused before the session started. The second one followed immediately as the session began, when Brenda explained that she had changed her study from her earlier submission. I was instantly offended since I had prepared all weekend on her prior study. My mind was clouded with my upset, such that I could not hear what she was saying.

Another mistake: I did not verify before the session started how long the meeting room was available, which caused a problem at the end of the session.

You can see that multiple errors can occur in rapid succession as we continue to look at the rest of the story.

Open

I did not establish a time frame for the session, let alone seek her agreement with it.

When she disagreed with my advice to take a statistics course, I was dumbfounded. I don't think a student had ever openly rejected such a basic piece of my advice before. I did not address the disagreement between us.

Work

The rest of the session involved a discussion of how to formulate a theory to be tested by the study she was planning, select a sample of subjects, and create a questionnaire for those subjects.

I was not focused in the last two-thirds of the session. Repeatedly I engaged in unproductive activities, such as explaining concepts that I suspect were too complicated for her to follow, and then I never checked how well she had understood my explanations. Rather, I continued to state that the topics I was explaining would be covered in an introductory statistics course.

End

There was no agreement as to who would do what, by when, and to what standards before our next meeting.

3.   What had to be present in the attitudes of the consultant and client for this interaction to have turned out this way?

To illustrate this part of *reflect*, consider my confusion in the *prepare* step five minutes before the meeting was scheduled to start.

Brenda waiting in the reception area outside my office reveals her belief that the information my secretary gave her was accurate. Though a perfectly reasonable assumption, unfortunately, it was incorrect.

My waiting in the video recording room indicates my attitude that my client should be aware that this was where I met clients for videoed sessions, even though I had forgotten to tell her this.

Another assumption I made was that my new secretary would know that I met with clients in the video recording room, though I failed to inform her about this policy.

Over time, I gradually became aware of these attitudes and assumptions. I saw how mistaken I was to blame the pre-session confusion on Brenda or my secretary. They had no way of knowing where the meeting was to be held.

> **Stepping Stone**
>
> When responding to the question, "What had to be present in the attitudes of both participants in order for this breakdown to occur?" the critical shift is to refrain from asking, "Whose fault is this?" and focus on answering the question, "What had to be present for this to happen?"

"Whose fault is this?" reflects a culture of fault and blame in which the first response after a mistake is to search for someone to blame.

"What had to be present for this to happen?" reflects a culture of systematic improvement

> **Stepping Stone**
>
> To enhance your reflection process after critically important sessions, schedule fifteen to thirty minutes following each of these sessions to reflect while your memories are fresh.

that recognizes one's responsibility and coownership of processes. It gives both parties a chance to be a part of the solution to the problem.

The goal is to create an opportunity for as many people as possible to contribute to either preventing a mistake or catching it early enough to minimize the damage.

Sometimes a mistake reveals attitudes that have not been encountered previously in a relationship. If so, it is an opportunity for you to explore how collaborative you want to be. Are you willing to be responsible for the problem and not duck behind, "It's not my job" or "It wasn't my fault"?

> **Stepping Stone**
>
> Diagnosing rather than blaming is essential for building relationships.

Taking responsibility to diagnose rather than blame, both when you are the consultant and when you are the client, is vital to building relationships.

4. How can this situation be better addressed in the future?

    After I moved past blaming my secretary, I had a discussion with her, apologizing for the difficult situation I had put her in with Brenda. This discussion revealed other aspects of her job that I had also forgotten to tell her about. After that day, I did successfully meet my clients in the video recording room.

Recap

Resist your natural tendency to skip the *reflect* step. Reflecting on an interaction is essential if you are to stop making the same mistakes again. Refrain from your automatic response to omit the *reflect* step. This may be uncomfortable in the short run, but you will benefit in the long run. Review each of the five parts of POWER.

Frequently Asked Questions

1. The *reflect* checklist is longer than all the others. Can it be shortened? What are the most critical items on it to assess immediately after the session?

   Better to reflect on one step in the POWER process than to do no reflection at all. If you are planning to shorten the checklist, I suggest focusing on the step in POWER where you have the most difficulty in your interactions.

2. Is it worth doing this level of reflection for every interaction? Do you do that?

   The short answer is no. However, it is useful to practice this step frequently for low-stakes interactions to develop your ability to effectively reflect on high-stakes interactions that don't go well. I *now* reflect completely on high-stakes interactions that don't go well. And that is only after years of practice on many and various types of interactions.

3. Are there other tools I can use rather than video to execute the *reflect* step?

Other forms of reflection include journaling or meditating on the session itself and recording whatever insights come to you. Audio recordings are also much better than memory. Discuss the results of these processes with another person to expand the value and breadth of your reflections.

The video of the Brenda session was the initial key to my learning from this interaction. It proved to be invaluable for deeper lessons from repeated viewings. For me, the primary insights came from discussions with other colleagues. Prior to the session, Brenda gave us consent to video and discuss her session by signing our consent form.

To be rigorous in your reflections, video your interactions. Nothing can match the amount of information contained in a video. The presence of any recording device does alter the interaction—always a consideration. However, usually the participants' awareness of the recording process fades as time passes in the session.

4. What are the most important characteristics a consultant should possess?

> The primary attribute for a consultant is a commitment to serve clients well.
>
> Several characteristics will forward your intention to serve others, including the following:
>
> - Be patient.
> - Treat others with respect.
> - Make specific requests and promises.
> - Stay in the conversation.
> - Be honest and compassionate.
> - Be open to change.

When you learn to use the POWER process seamlessly, my hope is that all these attributes will become second nature.

Chapter 7 Debriefing Questions

What worked?

What did not work?

What had to be present in the attitudes of the consultant and client for this interaction to have gone the way it did?

How can this situation be better addressed in the future?

CHAPTER 8

On the Flip Side

The flip side is about how to use the POWER process when you are a client. Either the consultant or the client may use the POWER process at any point in an interaction. Either may ask how much time is available; what matters is that someone asks the question early in the session. Similarly, for any other step in the POWER process, either person can initiate it; what is critical is that at least one person does.

The more proactive a client is in assuring that all POWER process steps are taken, the better. A proactive client makes it possible to have a truly cooperative, collaborative interaction. When working with a subordinate or superior, either as the consultant or client, you can use the POWER process, no matter which role you have.

Let's first look at a real-life example I call "Growing Pansies Successfully." At the heart of this series of events is my upset when I decided that I had received poor service from a usually reliable source. I did not use the POWER process during these interactions. However, I did use it after the fact to examine each interaction, learn what happened, and discover how to improve future interactions.

Growing Pansies Successfully

As an avid amateur gardener with a vegetable garden and several flower beds, I was drawn to a workshop on how to grow plants from seed.

The workshop was presented by my favorite nursery and led by one of their best gardeners, Martha.

After the workshop, I planned my garden and flower beds and returned to the sponsoring nursery to purchase seeds. Shopping sessions can also be viewed as consultations. After all, they occur because one person (the shopper) thinks that someone else (the provider) has information, advice, experience, or products that will be helpful in the current project.

Fortunately, Martha was available. As I completed my purchases, she asked, "Is there anything else for you today?"

Having thought of nothing more, I returned home to apply what I had learned in the workshop.

For my vegetables, I covered the existing garden with mushroom compost, lightly sprinkled seeds on top, and gently covered them with additional compost. I watered this bed carefully every day, keeping the seed bed moist until new plants appeared, just as Martha had instructed in the workshop.

Next, I turned my focus to the flower beds. I purchased ten flats of blooming pansies, planted them, and gently watered them daily.

Over the next couple of weeks, the vegetable garden was showing tiny green shoots. The seeds had germinated! The potted pansies developed more flowers and looked beautiful.

The gentle watering continued daily until one day I was shocked to see about one-third of the pansies with yellow leaves. Thinking the plants were deficient in nitrogen, I fertilized them. The yellow-leafed plants were no better in four days. I phoned Martha. She was puzzled and suggested a different fertilizer. Still there was no change in the next four days, which meant it clearly was time to present more data! I took five yellow leaves to her. She took one look and said, "Too much water."

I objected, "How can that be? I have been gently watering everything daily, just like you said in the workshop."

"No, I didn't say that. You should gently water only the *seedbeds* daily until germination occurs. You should have watered the *pansy plants* thoroughly only when you planted them. Then water them only when the soil is dry."

Let's look at this case from my perspective as the client, using the POWER process.

Prepare

The pansy case involved five interactions:

- the workshop
- the purchase of the seeds
- the purchase of the pansies
- the phone call about yellow leaves
- the visit to the nursery, carrying my yellow leaves

We will focus on the purchase of the seeds because my assumptions in that interaction led to the yellow pansy leaves and the last two interactions. Yellow leaves were certainly not the intended outcome!

1. Review the POWER process.

    Following the workshop, I developed my plan to purchase seed packets for various vegetables and ten flats of potted pansies. I did not have a wanted conversation with myself about how to grow the seeds and plants. From what I had learned in the workshop, everything looked so straightforward that I never even considered implementing the POWER process. I was in a hurry to get going.

2. Be ready for the content.

> I did not think through the entire planting and growing processes to uncover essential information for success before the seed purchases.

3. Focus.

> I did arrive at the nursery in good shape, with plenty of time to make the purchases. Focusing ended there.

In both steps 1 and 2 of *prepare*, I missed opportunities to prepare myself for an expanded wanted conversation about what to do with *all* the purchases planned. I had done many similar projects and *assumed* I could handle this one. Similar is *not* the same as identical. I was on my way toward learning once more that "you can't be aware of what you are unaware."

Open

1. Agree on the amount of time available for this interaction.

> Neither Martha nor I discussed anything about the time available for this interaction. We assumed correctly that the time required would be minimal. Assumptions are always risky. A longer conversation about my planting process may have surfaced my intention to include the pansy plants. Pausing to look at the time conversation might have triggered my memory that I was also planning to buy ten flats of pansies and wasn't sure if they were handled the same way as the seeds. Addressing this question could have averted the near calamity.

2. Have complete wanted and expanded wanted conversations.

> I told Martha that I wanted to purchase seeds for my vegetable garden. They were all available, so there was no conversation about "by when." We did not have an expanded wanted

conversation, so I neglected to tell Martha about my intention to plant the potted pansies along with the seeds. This resulted in another missed opportunity to surface the future watering problems.

> **Stepping Stone**
>
> The POWER process isn't written in stone. Rather, it is a step-by-step process that thrives on flexibility in thought and action, rather than rushing through its five steps.

3. Have a complete willing conversation.

    This conversation was not necessary, as I was given the wanted products almost immediately, indicating Martha's willingness to meet my request.

    Not every step in the POWER process is necessary in every interaction. Sometimes "willingness" is indicated by the consultant immediately responding to a request.

4. Have a complete able conversation.

    This conversation was also unnecessary, for the same reasons.

5. Treat your consultant with respect, by your consultant's standards, not yours.

    Respect was demonstrated, in large part because there was no rush to find the seeds I wanted.

Work

1. Verify that the content delivered by each party is understood by the other.

    My content was understood by Martha, as evidenced by the fact that I received the correct seeds. I understood her comments about how to plant the seeds to produce a beautiful flower bed.

2. Your answers to your consultant's questions are complete.

    I told her the entire list of seeds I wanted when asked, "What brings you in today?" However, I did not mention the pansies I planned to buy elsewhere when she asked, "Is there anything else?"

3. Use the time well. Verify with the consultant that what is being done is useful.

    The time was used well. She immediately provided the seeds I wanted.

4. Be sure that the content you give and are given will stand up to external scrutiny.

    Given Martha's experience, I was confident in the accuracy of her prediction of how well the seed mix would work. I did not ask her for input on the pansies, because I was convinced, incorrectly, that the process for the seeds would work for the flower plants as well.

5. Treat your consultant with respect, by your consultant's standards, not yours.

    Just before I paid, Martha asked, "Anything else for you today?" I gave a knee-jerk response: "No." *Part of respect is to consider questions, not just give an automatic answer.* I could have thought to myself, *What questions have I not asked that might be helpful? What information does Martha require in order to assist me?* Perhaps if I had said, "These seeds are part of a larger project that includes flowering plants," I could have grown beautiful flowers instead of yellow leaves! Another missed opportunity.

End

1. Allow enough time at the end of the session for you and your consultant to do the following:

    a. Review and agree on who will do what, by when, and to what standards.

    The interaction appeared to be so straightforward (attend workshop, buy seeds, buy plants) that I assumed the interaction was completed to the satisfaction of each when the purchases were complete. My mistake was being shortsighted; I did not look to the future and consider how to successfully grow all my purchases.

    b. Review and agree on any decisions made during the interaction.

    We verified that I had all the seeds I wanted.

    c. Agree on the time, place, and purpose of the next meeting.

    Because of the assumptions I made in this meeting with Martha, neither of us considered the possibility that there might be another meeting on this project.

2. Allow enough time at the end of the session for you and your consultant to have ample opportunity to raise any concerns about the plan developed.

    Neither Martha nor I had any concerns about the plans for the seeds. Had we at least reviewed the process for growing the seeds, we *might* have surfaced my plan to buy additional plants for the flower garden. This was another missed opportunity.

3. Identify and address any barriers to implementation.

    I did not think there were any barriers.

4. Assess whether your wants for the interaction were met. If they were not, develop a plan for how and when to address those wants.

    As I paid for the seeds, I was certain that my wants had been met. I did not look ahead at exactly how I planned to use these items.

5. As soon as possible, communicate with your consultant to verify that both of you agree on the way forward.

    Neither of us did this because of how straightforward the interaction *seemed* to be.

6. Treat your consultant with respect, by your consultant's standards, not yours.

    Overall, I thought I did, as evidenced by the fact that we have had subsequent cordial, effective interactions.

Reflect

1. What worked?

    Two days after the interaction, I judged it to be effective: it produced a plan of action that was implemented, it stood up to scrutiny, and I was planning to work with Martha again.

2. What did not work?

    After two weeks, I judged the interaction to be ineffective, as the plan no longer stood up to scrutiny: many plants were not healthy. *When* you assess the effectiveness of an interaction is an important detail.

3. How did that happen?

I did not ask about watering the plants when I made my seed purchases because I thought I knew all there was to know about watering seeds and plants.

I had numerous opportunities to ask questions that would have revealed my lack of knowledge about how to water pansy plants correctly. Yet my first reaction to the yellow leaves was to think, *Why didn't Martha tell me that this could happen? It's her fault!* I blamed her for something she could not have known unless she was a mind reader! Further, I assumed incorrectly that plants and seeds were handled in the same way. I assumed that this was a distinction that did not make a difference. Remember, assumptions are dangerous!

Whose job was it to bring up the subject of the pansy plants? Clearly, I thought it was Martha's. If this conversation in my head had been verbalized, the situation would have deteriorated. Fault-and-blame conversations are almost always adversarial and damaging to the relationship of the parties involved.

Over time, I realized that Martha did not even know about the pansies *because* I never mentioned them, let alone that I might apply her workshop information inappropriately to potted plants rather than the seeds discussed in the workshop.

Whenever a situation results in the thought "Who is to blame?" my goal now is to ask instead, "What had to be present for this breakdown to occur? And what part did I play?" Adopting this point of view requires

> **Stepping Stone**
>
> Exploring breakdowns without the intent to assess fault or blame will help your relationship become synergistic. This approach will yield information that's rarely accessed in fault-and-blame conversations.

becoming engaged in the interaction and being committed to its success, rather than thinking Martha, *the expert*, should know every potential question of concern. Being curious in a situation like this requires letting go of the thought that blaming someone else for a failure solves anything. Holding back any questions for any reason jeopardizes the chances of success for both the customer and the consultant.

4. How can this situation be better addressed in the future?

I continue to notice and analyze breakdowns, large and small, in my daily life. I now regard each one as a gift from which I can learn and grow in effectiveness.

This situation showed me that I have a penchant for making incorrect assumptions about what I know and what I don't yet know. My goal now is to identify and address my mind-set (which typically sounds like "I should already know how to do this!") before I start shopping.

I bring a list of all my questions about an anticipated purchase *or* a related product I am considering either for now or later. Before leaving, I double-check that all my questions have been addressed. My current strategy is to err on the side of getting too much information by asking the salesperson to walk me through how to correctly use each product. I then ask if there are any frequently asked questions about the use of the product that we have not yet discussed. Do I always do this? No, and when I do, my buying interactions are more successful.

Successful Medical Appointments

Working with aging relatives and friends over the past ten years has revealed that one of their greatest frustrations is appointments with their physicians. These meetings can also be viewed as consultations. After all, they occur because one person (the patient) thinks that someone else (the physician) has information, advice, experience, or expertise that will help identify and cure an ailment.

The POWER process can be applied to medical appointments to yield more effective results for all parties involved.

The *prepare* step is critical. Here is a series of activities that have served others well:

- Identify questions specifically intended for your next appointment.
- Record any changes in your medical information, as well as the results of appointments with other physicians and the results of any medical procedures, since your last appointment.
- Include information on any changes in your well-being. Be as specific as possible (i.e., if pain is the issue, identify location, intensity, type of pain—sharp, dull ache, and so on—frequency, and any other anomalies you notice).
- In addition, summarize any data collected since your last appointment on any chronic conditions you may experience.
- Summarize this information on a Physician Information Form (see table 9 for set of questions to answer on however many pages are required) and bring a copy for yourself and your physician.

Table 9. Physician Information Form

Physician Information Form
Patient's Name: Physician's Name: Date:
Nurse's Name:
Physician's contact number in evenings and on weekends:
Questions for this visit:

Why am I here? (your most important question)

Symptoms?

> Information collected relating to these symptoms (see data sheets):

Medications and other treatments used for these symptoms:

Other questions? (in triaged order)

List the questions you want to address today (with spaces after each for you to write in answers and follow-up questions):

Chronic conditions, current status, and how I am treating them:

Prescription medications regularly taken for each condition, dosage and frequency:

Vitamins, minerals, and supplements regularly taken, dosage and frequency:

Other prescription and over-the-counter medications, vitamins, minerals, and supplements occasionally taken, dosage, frequency, and for what purpose:

A list of all medical professionals who provide services for my well-being:

Under what circumstances shall I make a follow-up call to today's doctor relative to:

- procedures done in today's visit or
- today's questions or
- future treatment plans?

New information received in this meeting:

Decisions made in this meeting:

Action steps: who will do what, by when?

If new medications are prescribed today, how are they to be taken relative to meals, other medications, and supplements? What side effects may occur?

Using the ideas in this chapter can help you

- *prepare* more thoroughly for each medical appointment,
- *open* the interaction more effectively,
- *work* more efficiently with your physicians by having relevant data since your last appointment with them, and
- *end* the session more successfully by confirming and recording medication changes or any other actions that you have agreed to in the appointment.

Open the appointment by asking how much time your physician has available for this meeting. This question about time is awkward due to a long-standing tradition of hierarchical relationships between physicians and patients. Another challenge here is the increasingly stringent time limits to which many physicians are held, stemming either from the policies of their practice or the policies of the insurance companies serving their clients. Given all this, it may well be useful to preface your question with a description of your strategy. For example:

> I'm experimenting with how I can work more effectively with my doctors. I have prepared information that I hope will be of use to you and potentially save us some precious appointment time. How much time do you have available for our appointment today? Knowing this will help me to better manage my time in our appointment.

Initially, health professionals look at the Physician Information Form and the time question with puzzlement. I explain the goal of these questions, namely to create a collaborative relationship and use our time efficiently. Recently in my fourth meeting with one of my physicians, he said, "I wish all my patients used forms like this. We could do so much more." Success!

The time question produces a variety of responses. For most physicians, this is the first time anyone has ever asked. Some smile and say, "About twenty minutes, maybe more if something comes up." Others ignore the question or respond with "As long as it takes and no longer." Having an estimate of how much time is available will help you review your list of questions and concerns that, if not already in priority order, must now be triaged. This activity will be easier when you can relax knowing that your physician won't abruptly leave because their time has expired.

Learn the name of your physician's nurse. Then when you call your doctor's office and want to talk to someone, you will have a name of a person you know you can request to talk to, rather than tossing yourself into the pool of staff personnel assigned to do callbacks.

The ultimate goal is that medical appointments become a source of satisfaction for both parties rather than frustration.

When a senior is unable to manage the Physician Information Form, a family member or caregiver can assist them by completing the information for the doctor before an appointment so that the experience is less exasperating for everyone. In addition, it is important for a trusted caregiver to accompany a senior to each appointment. Seniors have enough challenges without adding solo management of medical appointments to the list. You may wonder if this process could be useful before those senior years show up. In fact, I have been using a similar form with my doctors for over twenty-five years to develop the Physician Information Form, and it has always been valuable.

Examples of such forms are now readily available because many physicians, clinics, and hospitals have developed extensive versions of this form on their websites. Another resource included on some medical websites is an extensive list of what to expect at an appointment, questions your physician may ask, and useful questions for you to ask. For starters, see the Mayo Clinic website.

Chapter 8 Activity

Role-Play

Recall a recent interaction when you were seeking advice from another. Who was the consultant/professional and why did you initiate this interaction? Do a role-play with your partner a five-minute videoed role-play playing the client/customer.

Following your role-play exercise, refer to the chapter 8 debriefing questions at the end of this chapter. Please investigate these questions with your partner *after* having completed this activity, as you will learn more from the role-play experience this way.

Recap

The POWER process can be used by either the consultant or the client; all that matters is that someone addresses the POWER steps and that each party treats the other with respect.

Frequently Asked Questions

1. So, with the pansy example, you might lose one hundred pansies that cost in total one hundred dollars. What's the big deal?

   First, though gardening is a hobby for me, I am not interested in wasting money, time, and energy on any activity. Second, this case offers an opportunity to become aware of attitudes and beliefs that may lead to essential questions not being addressed. As a young colleague says, "Every day is a school day!" Third, these issues arise in far more situations than planting pansies. For example, failing to review a doctor's instructions can lead to serious consequences, including death. Often the review is incomplete because the patient is fearful of asking the physician "too many" or "dumb" questions. Other interpersonal and intrapersonal issues can also muddy the waters here. Some examples: "I will sound like a fool if I ask this question." "It isn't appropriate to ask my physician too many questions." "My doctor should know how to make me better without hearing my complaints. After all, she spent all those years in medical school." (My grandmother's favorite!)

2. How did you become aware that you had assumed you knew more than you actually did, as was the case with the pansies?

Discovering this is tough. The short answer is that I did not stay alert to changes in the plants. I unconsciously watered them daily, not paying any attention to the changing color of the leaves. My assumption was that everything was okay. Another example of the danger of assuming!

One day while watering my pansies *more slowly than usual*, I finally *noticed that many pansies had yellow leaves*. This was a powerful enough observation to get me off autopilot! I stopped observing through the lens of my assumption that everything was okay and looked at the pansy leaves as they actually were—*yellow!* In my experience, additional information that jolts me into awareness is how I learn something of which I was previously unaware.

> **Stepping Stone**
>
> Taking care to make observations rather than assumptions is critical to avoid misjudgments.

Lesson learned: stay in the present; don't go to sleep, especially when you think you're right about your assumptions.

Once my assumptions were revealed, I became aware of my embarrassment because I thought I knew basic gardening skills. Embarrassment was acting as a barrier to becoming aware and calling the nursery sooner.

Embarrassment also serves as a barrier to medical treatment when people notice strange symptoms, especially when they are accompanied by thoughts like: *This is nothing; I should know whether this symptom matters; I don't want to waste my doctor's time with something trivial; I don't want to be a high-maintenance patient.* These attitudes often result in patients seeking medical aid later than would have been useful, thus leading to more extensive and expensive treatment, at best.

3. Do you have another example of successfully breaking through barriers like this?

Yes. Recently I had continuing pain in a tooth that was to receive a new crown within a week. I did not want to deal with the pain for the long weekend ahead, so I called the office and spoke to the dental assistant. She said that it sounded like the bite on the temporary crown was too high. She warned me that this pain would not go away. She worked me in the next day and solved the problem in five minutes. I was grateful all weekend that I overcame my reluctance to call a medical professional on what I thought might be a trivial matter.

The key step toward creating successes like this is to identify and address your barriers to asking questions quickly.

4. My physicians are never available after our appointment is over. What can I do about this?

Before the appointment is over, find out how to get follow-up help with questions that come up following this meeting and how to contact your physician at night or over the weekend. The conversation between you and your physician might sound like this:

You: How can I contact you at night or over the weekend in an emergency?

Physician: Call the office number. If it is after office hours, my answering service will take your call and refer it to the on-call physician, who will address your question.

You: And who will be on call?

Physician: Either one of my colleagues or me.

You: About how long do you think it will take for me to get a call back?

Physician: Typically, thirty minutes or less.

You: If I don't get a call in forty-five minutes, shall I call again? I don't want to be a pain. My intention is to set up a plan that will handle my concerns if I have a relapse after hours.

Physician: That's fine. We do intend to return calls within thirty minutes. Sometimes for one reason or another, we don't. So, your calling back would be a good idea.

Whenever a physical procedure is applied to you during an appointment, ask questions like: "What will I experience later (e.g., when the anesthetic wears off)? What level of discomfort is to be expected and for how long? What level of pain indicates that there may be a problem and I should call your office to check it out?"

5. Does it matter when you assess the effectiveness of an interaction?

> Yes. A classic example is the evaluation of a workshop by a sheet of questions immediately after it concludes. These sheets are often called "smile sheets" for good reason. Right after the course, many participants experience a warm glow from having learned something and having had pleasant experiences with their instructor and classmates. However, their evaluation often is different six weeks later if they have not successfully implemented any ideas from the course. Similarly, the pansies looked okay two days after planting but not two weeks later.

Chapter 8 Debriefing Questions

Which aspects of the POWER process did you employ effectively? What led you to be effective in these aspects of POWER?

Which aspects did you not employ effectively? What barriers kept you from being effective with these aspects of POWER?

PART II

Exploring the RAPID Process

Even while faithfully utilizing the POWER process, unexpected events (breakdowns) will inevitably occur. Part 2 examines a plan to recover from any interruption or anomaly that occurs so that you and your client can rapidly return to productive work.

There are five steps in the RAPID process:

> **R**ecognize your emotional cloud.
>
> **A**ddress your emotional cloud.
>
> **P**inpoint the breakdown.
>
> **I**dentify how to get back on track.
>
> **D**o it

Life is filled with opportunities to practice this process!

Chapter 9 Dissecting Mistakes and Breakdown

Chapter 10 Recognize Your Emotional Cloud

CHAPTER 9

Dissecting Mistakes and Breakdowns

When you are driving and notice that your speed has crept up to 15 mph over the speed limit, you immediately reduce your speed and continue on your journey without risking a traffic ticket. This is the gold standard for a rapid recovery from a mistake that could have had adverse consequences if not corrected. You saw the mistake and immediately took action to restore risk-free travel.

Just as some interactions are effective and others are not, some mistakes are easily addressed and quickly corrected, while others are not.

Complications often arise after a mistake is made so that the recovery process is hindered at best and aborted at worst. For example, if anger is the response to an error, damage control measures may be launched. Often we look for someone to blame. This choice may escalate until the current conversation is abandoned, leaving each participant holding a grudge against the other, thus destroying this interaction and jeopardizing all future ones.

We make many mistakes while alone, such as eating late at night or driving too fast. Other mistakes involve another person, such as when a teenager forgets to mention that his father's gas tank is nearly empty. Surprises involving machines also occur: You've been concerned about the left rear tire on your car. Suddenly it is flat on Tuesday morning when you have left yourself just enough time to drive to work for an important meeting.

These unexpected events and many more like them share the property that they are the result of "a failure [of a process] to work or function properly" (*Webster's New World Dictionary* 1980). This is the dictionary definition of "breakdown,"

> **Process**
>
> A process is a sequence of activities intended to produce a result. We engage in hundreds of them every day: getting dressed in the morning, driving to work, meeting with colleagues, eating lunch, going home in the evening, responding to text messages, to mention a few.

a word I will use to refer to this entire group of events, some of which are calamities, some minor bumps in the road. Their size depends on the severity of the consequences to everyone involved in the event. For instance, a broken fingernail may look trivial to a passerby and be far from trivial to the bride whose fingernail has broken the moment before she walks down the aisle. Upon hearing the word "breakdown,"

> **Asthma-1 Reactions to Breakdowns**
>
> Having chronic asthma has taught me much about breakdowns. The most common asthma breakdown is that something happens to trigger difficulty in breathing.
>
> Even as breathing becomes more labored, thoughts occur and have evolved during my life from, *I am not sick*; to, *I'm not sick enough to stay home; to, I am not sick enough to go see a doctor.*
>
> Asthma still threatens my ability to function periodically. However, over time I have learned to respond differently to that particular breakdown.

many think only of large breakdowns, such as totaling a car or mental breakdowns requiring years of hospitalization and treatment. The majority of breakdowns are smaller; they still require attention. If you don't attend to those small bumps, they will grow and become problems that can no longer be ignored, their consequences having escalated over time.

Breakdowns, small or large, are an inevitable part of life. You *will* make mistakes. Owning them, rather than trying to cover them up or avoid responsibility, is an essential part of developing and maintaining your professional integrity. Taking responsibility for your part in any mistake will allow you to learn how to work with mistakes effectively. An essential part of improving the quality of your services is rapidly recovering from breakdowns.

Breakdowns often have a mysterious aura surrounding them. Understanding that they are also part of a process and have a life cycle gives us entries into recognizing them and recovering from them.

The Life Cycle of a Breakdown

Figure 1. The life cycle of a breakdown

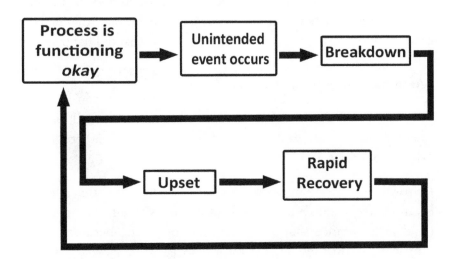

The life cycle of a breakdown begins with a process functioning as intended. Then an unintended event occurs.

Any event can be unintended in the eyes of the client or the consultant. An unintended event can occur in at least four ways:

1. A *natural disaster:* a hurricane or flood.
2. *Unmet expectations:* the client expected their consultant to be on time for their meeting today. The consultant wasn't.
3. *Blocked goals:* the client's goal was to complete their entire project in today's interaction, and due to new information, they didn't.
4. *Broken promises and lies:* we expect people to keep their word and tell the truth. When they don't, there is a serious disruption in communication.

Though each of these events is capable of producing small to large breakdowns, broken promises and lies produce the most damage to relationships. When a person makes a promise and then fails to keep it, the usual interpretation is a lack of integrity and honor. Can we work with such people? Yes, *and* a first step is to restrain from leaping to conclusions lest we create yet another breakdown. In fact, events out of a person's control may have made the promise impossible to keep. This is another situation where it is critical to manage our instantaneous reactions and stay in the conversation to clarify what did happen.

Asthma-2 Emotional Clouds

My emotional clouds always begin in response to a small, barely perceptible increase in difficulty of breathing that I either ignore or do not notice.

Growing up, my mom noticed my labored breathing often when I wanted to go outside and play. I responded with vigorous denials and an assurance that I was okay. If breathing became more difficult, I still thought, *I'm not sick enough to see a doctor.* As my situation deteriorated, eventually I was taken to a doctor.

With age and experience, I learned to take myself to a doctor before my health had deteriorated seriously and required a trip to the ER.

In any case, if one of the above four events has occurred, the process isn't functioning as intended, and a breakdown has occurred.

The moment you become aware that a breakdown has occurred, you will experience *upset*. You are now in an "emotional cloud." The larger the breakdown, the darker the emotional cloud. This cloud is a jumble of emotions that obscure your ability to see anything clearly, and it grows with every passing moment.

Upset

An intense series of physical sensations, thoughts, and emotions that suddenly sweep over you.

The RAPID process, table 10, can be used to restore a consultation to its intended mode of functioning by reducing and eventually eliminating the emotional cloud. The first step is to *recognize* that you are in an emotional cloud. This makes it possible for you to *address* your cloud and take steps toward the exit. When you are past the emotions, you are thinking clearly and are now able to *pinpoint* exactly what breakdown did occur. By specifically examining the breakdown, you are ready to *identify* the actions necessary to clean up the resulting mess. Finally, enact your plan for recovery and *"do it!"*

The life cycle of a breakdown is often more complicated than pictured in figure 1. More than one unintended event may occur, or the upset can be so intense that your partner leaves the interaction and the RAPID process is aborted.

Table 10. The RAPID process

Step	Essential Activities
Recognize	*Recognize your emotional cloud.* Identify your reactions to breakdowns. Learn to do this while you are *in* an emotional cloud.
Address	*Address your emotional cloud.* Do what is necessary to get out of it. Take a walk. Get a drink of water. Breathe! Call a trusted friend or colleague for help.
Pinpoint	*Pinpoint what the breakdown is.* Verify that your client and you agree on exactly what did not go as intended. Stay in this conversation until both of you agree on what the breakdown(s) is (are).
Identify	*Identify what it will take to get back on track.* Be sure that the cleanup addresses all concerns of both your client and you.
Do it!	*Do it.* Take action. Put the cleanup plan into operation. Don't just talk about it. Realize that this will take time, especially if this is a repeater breakdown. When you think you have done your part to clean up the breakdown, make sure your client agrees.

RAPID Scenario 1: Broken Promises

Part of this overview of the RAPID process will entail taking a closer look at three scenarios to illustrate how the process can work for you.

> You are driving home. You press the accelerator but slow down. A glance reveals no gas. Upset occurs instantly. You are now in an emotional cloud. This isn't the time to run out of gas! Earlier today, you promised your eight-year-old son, Chuck, that you would get home on time tonight for his birthday party. Remorse may hit first as you realize that you are about to break a promise to him—again!

The immediate source of the error and accompanying emotional cloud is clear: you are again breaking a promise to Chuck. How this has happened is not clear until you realize that you have ignored your personal rule to refuel when your gas gauge shows less than a quarter full.

This broken promise to yourself has led to another broken promise to Chuck. Breaking promises to yourself and others is one guaranteed way to derail relationships and may lead to giving up on making promises. Such a strategy will only result in loss of integrity and missed opportunities for success.

Now you have an emotional cloud that looks like a thunderhead, lightning bolts and all. Escaping this cloud before you walk in the door is critical even if you are late to the party! Now is the time for you to use the RAPID process.

RAPID Scenario 2: Double-Billed

I remember a time when I submitted a bill for my services as a consultant. The next day, my client emailed, saying that everything looked fine except for the fact that the bill appeared to be twice as large as expected.

I thought, *No way!* and immediately became embarrassed. What kind of a statistical consultant would make such an egregious arithmetic error? Eventually a calm look at my Excel spreadsheet revealed the problem.

I added up my daily fees to arrive at a total. Then adding my daily fees to that total, I arrived at a grand total of double my billed time! How embarrassing!

I thanked her for pointing out my error and assured her that I was most grateful that she checked my arithmetic before sending the bill to her boss! I immediately sent her a corrected version of my invoice. She wrote back and graciously thanked me for correcting the mistake. This case epitomizes my desire for how to handle all breakdowns.

RAPID Scenario 3: Scheduling Error

I scheduled a squash match with my usual partner, Gene, for Sunday at 4:00 p.m. At the appointed hour, he was not on the court. My initial and instant reaction was a flashback to high school and thinking, *Oh, no, stood up again!*

Irritation at him reigned until I recalled the times that I had kept him waiting for me. Then thoughts shifted to, *I sure hope he hasn't had a car accident.* I left a voice mail for him asking, "Are you okay? I hope this afternoon was just a scheduling breakdown between us."

Next morning, Gene left me a voice mail that he was fine; he thought we were playing at 2:00 p.m. (He, too, may have felt stood up!) He asked when we could play next, and we scheduled our next match.

Two days later, he called me. "I was cleaning my truck and found a note showing that indeed we had agreed to play at four! I apologize." Grateful for his honesty, I accepted his apology.

He expressed his appreciation for my willingness to regard this as a learning experience for both of us and not insist that either of us suffer any additional grief.

The Five Steps of RAPID Applied to Scenario 3

Here is how the five steps played out in the squash scheduling scenario.

1. *Recognize* your emotional cloud.

   My emotional cloud appeared as soon as I thought, *I've been stood up again!* I was irritated, blaming everything on Gene, until I remembered the times I too had been late. That realization deflated my self-righteousness and helped me to recognize my emotional cloud.

2. *Address* your emotional cloud.

   After I considered my own history and my excuses for producing the same sort of mistake, my concern was that there might be something wrong. This thought got me out of my cloud and moved me to call Gene to see if he was okay.

3. *Pinpoint* what the breakdown is.

   His voice mail the next day revealed that he thought the match was scheduled for 2:00 p.m., not 4:00 p.m.

4. *Identify* what it will take to clean up the breakdown.

   The question of "How did this happen?" was still unanswered for both of us. The answer became clear to Gene when he cleaned his truck and found a note that said we had scheduled our match for 4:00 p.m.

5. *Do it!*

> He called me and apologized for misplacing the note. I accepted his apology and said that it looked like there was a learning point in this mistake: we might need to reconfirm oral appointments after we look at our calendars. Since this was a rare event, we have not made any modifications of our appointment process as of now. What did happen the next time we scheduled a match was that we both repeated the match time, out loud, resolutely, half-jokingly and half-seriously.

Stepping Stone

Remember that "clients" are everywhere, from your home to the gym to the office.

There is hope! Eventually, if you persist in compassionately looking in the mirror (moving past your defenses) and keep asking, "How did this happen?" you will promptly *recognize* and *address* the emotional clouds that accompany breakdowns. Then you can *pinpoint* exactly what error did occur from your perspective. To sort out the whole mess, explore whether your client identified the same mistake or a different one. There often are at least two mistakes to pinpoint since you and your client may be upset about different incidents or in different ways and intensities. The next step is to *identify* what has to be done to recover from the breakdowns and get back on track. The final step in the process is to *do it*. The last two steps require input from both parties.

Learning to deal effectively with breakdowns is well worth the cost involved if you are committed to improving the services you provide. Pinpointing exactly what breakdown has occurred, coupled with coaching on how it happened and what alternatives are available, can produce insights strong enough to transform your world. This is what happened to me with Brenda.

My goal in part 2 is to help you learn to rapidly recover from your breakdowns. Once you have recovered from a breakdown, it is natural to ask, "How can I improve?" We will explore this question in part 3 when we discuss the LEARN process.

Chapter 9 Activity

Role-Play

Apply the five steps in this chapter to a recent breakdown.

Consider each of the chapter 9 debriefing questions at the end of this chapter. Please look at these questions with your partner *after* having completed this activity, as you will learn more from the experience this way.

Recap

Learn your early warning signs of a breakdown so that you can *recognize* when you are entering an emotional cloud, *address* and get out of your cloud, *pinpoint* what breakdown has occurred, *identify* what has to be done to get back on track, and *do it*.

Frequently Asked Questions

1. Isn't "breakdown" an unnecessarily strong word to apply to all failures of processes to function as intended? Many of these occur every day. I can't envision using the RAPID process on each one of them. Some are so trivial, like being five minutes late for a meeting.

   You have just highlighted one of the reasons for at least examining each and every breakdown that occurs. "Five minutes late for a meeting" may not be an issue for you; however, it may be an issue for your client, spouse, or boss, especially if you are perennially late for meetings and if they interpret this as a personal insult indicating that you do not respect their time.

At least examine each breakdown through the eyes of the other person. Address those that might be a source of upset that will affect the quality of your relationship both now and in the future.

2. Isn't it sometimes the case that my client is in an emotional cloud for reasons unknown to me and I'm not in an emotional cloud?

Yes, and emotional clouds are so contagious that it is a good idea to first check that you are not in an emotional cloud. If you are, *address* it. If you are not, use the RAPID steps to assist your client to deal with their emotional cloud. This is another situation in which the flight attendant's advice is useful. "In the event of an emergency, put on your own oxygen mask first before assisting others."

3. Making a mistake in school was clearly unacceptable and sometimes felt like a disaster. What is different now that I'm on the job? I still get embarrassed and flustered when I make one.

The nature of a mistake is that it can range from a misstep to a stumble to a face-plant. Not surprisingly, the consequences of making a mistake also range widely from an "oops" to a trip to the emergency room. What is different on the job is that hopefully you have developed the ability to make a distinction among different experiences of "missing the mark" and their consequences. Another difference is that the consequences of a breakdown on the job are generally more severe than were the consequences of a breakdown in school.

Your history will follow you, so being embarrassed and flustered will continue to provide useful, early warning signs that you are experiencing a breakdown and encourage you to take steps to address it. RAPID is a process for doing that.

4. Your first reaction in the squash match example was to blame everything on Gene. My first reaction is to blame everything on me. This rapidly evolves into self-talk like "I'm not a good squash player. I'll bet that's why he didn't show up." How can I rapidly recover from a breakdown when I'm in this mind-set?

> This self-shaming mind-set puts you into a dark emotional cloud, indicating that you are reacting to a breakdown. The first phase in rapid recovery is to *recognize* that self-shaming is an early warning sign that you are in an emotional cloud. The next steps are *addressing* your emotional cloud, perhaps with the help of your partner, *pinpointing* the breakdown, *identifying* how to get back on track, and then *doing* that. Chapters 10–13 explain how to proceed through each of these five steps.

Chapter 9 Debriefing Questions

Are some emotional clouds easier for you to recognize than others? What are their characteristics?

What are your typical barriers to addressing your emotional clouds?

Do you take the time to verify that your client and you have pinpointed the same incident after a breakdown?

What steps to recovery do you resist more than others?

CHAPTER 10

Recognize Your Emotional Cloud

The Onset of Emotional Clouds

An emotional cloud is triggered by a failure of which you may or may not be aware. Often there is no perceptible amount of time between the actual event and the onset of the associated cloud where your upset has taken residence. Being in an emotional cloud can feel like being overtaken by the black ink cloud that a squid sprays when threatened, the purpose of which is to obscure visibility. For humans, the dark cloud also short-circuits brain function.

Alternatively, this cloud can range from a classic San Francisco pea soup fog to a light morning mist. The thickness of the fog depends on a variety of factors, including how significant the event is in your eyes or your client's eyes, what type of relationship each of you has with the other, and the mental, physical, and emotional condition of each person when the breakdown occurs.

If you are unaware of an emotional cloud or the preceding failure, you are in a precarious position. An unrecognized breakdown can become an invisible force with the potential to destroy a relationship.

An event may be a serious mistake for you and not for your client, and vice versa. People have different expectations, standards, and sensitivities. You may regard a meeting as successful; whereas, your client may view that same meeting as littered with breakdowns. For instance, what you perceive as "good counsel" they may interpret as manipulation.

Emotional clouds gather the same way thunderstorms do. Early in the storm, only an experienced eye can identify clouds that signal the onset of a full-blown thunderstorm. If you are not paying attention to the sky, a few minutes later, a bolt of lightning, loud thunder, and drenching rainfall may be your first clues that a thunderstorm is at hand.

You may experience an emotional cloud as sensations, emotions, or thoughts that fog your brain as you become aware that an interaction is falling apart. The denser the fog becomes, the tougher to see your way ahead and move forward without hurting yourself or your client and your relationship.

The sources of fog vary from person to person. Any amount of fog is an early warning sign that you are either approaching or entering an emotional cloud. Awareness of your early warning signs allows you to take corrective measures before the interaction disintegrates. The earlier you do this, the better.

Figure 2. An emotional cloud

Early Warning Signs

Physical Sensations and Actions

Early warning signs include physical sensations you experience as you realize that an interaction isn't going well: a racing heart, sweaty palms, a tightening of your shoulders. Physical behaviors may also occur at this moment: speaking loudly, squirming in your chair, shuffling papers, doodling. Alternatively, a person may shut down: unable to move, going blank, gazing out the window.

Which of these are early warning signs for you? For your clients? Are there other physical signs that are more apparent?

> ### Asthma-3
>
> My asthma-related emotional clouds always included physical symptoms and attitudes that eventually became early warning signs for me that mold, pollen, or other substances had triggered my asthma. An attitude that signaled trouble ahead was, "I'm just fine. I can go out and play in the leaves with the other kids!"
>
> Recognizing the early warning signs and acting on them eventually eliminated asthma-induced hospitalizations from my life.

Emotions

Early warning signs also include emotions such as anger, anxiety, defensiveness, and sadness. Which of these are early warning signs for you? For your clients? Are there others that are more frequent?

Early warning signs also include mental states like confusion, a general sense of agitation, or a strong desire to flee the situation. Here, fleeing may be an emotional or mental separation from the situation or an actual physical fleeing. For some people in extreme situations, the mental confusion is so intense that the choice of whether to write with a black pen or a blue pen is overwhelming.

Thoughts

Thoughts such as judgments and evaluations can also be early warning signs. *His action was stupid. She is so inconsiderate. What was he thinking? I thought she had more sense than to say that.* Thoughts about fault and blame can also be signs. *Who made this mistake? Whose fault is it anyway? Who is to blame? Probably me—I'm always blamed when something goes wrong.*

When running late and relying on automatic pilot, you may not be aware of early warning signs, and the result can have distressing results. For example, as you head for the door, your client may suddenly announce that this meeting has not yet addressed their most immediate concern. They now demand that you extend this appointment to address at least their highest-priority item. If you brush them off with a quick reply such as, "We'll cover that next time," while you are thinking, *They should have brought this up earlier!* you have missed an early warning sign and likely added one more breakdown to this meeting.

In addition, you are now carrying an emotional cloud into the meeting with your next client. Early warning signs with this client can now be easily missed. One of the costs of not addressing mistakes as they occur is that the associated upsets persist and accumulate. They can pave the road for additional breakdowns with the next person you encounter, whether that is another client, your boss, or a colleague. An inevitable result is an unstable, ever-growing stack of emotions that crumbles much like an avalanche, a phenomenon referred to as *cascading breakdowns.*

Instead of dealing with one emotional cloud, you now find yourself digging out from under the avalanche. To avoid cascading breakdowns, become rigorous about reserving sufficient time between meetings to be able to effectively transition from one to the next, especially in case of a last-minute breakdown. Of course, you don't know what will happen in a meeting when you schedule it. However, leaving no transition time for yourself between meetings is a setup for the challenge of cascading breakdowns.

Learning to Recognize Your Emotional Clouds

When you realize that something has gone wrong, what is your immediate reaction? Do you know what your early warning signs are?

I have trouble acknowledging that I have made a mistake. Even the thought that I contributed to a mistake can trigger an emotional cloud. My first reaction under such conditions is to become defensive. I quickly check if anyone has noticed. If not, my knee-jerk reaction is to deny, cover up, or blame. Here's my historical model: if my mother discovered that half her newly baked cookies were eaten, I'd plead innocent and point to one of my two younger sisters!

> **Stepping Stone**
>
> Recognizing and addressing early warning signs quickly will allow you to avoid or mitigate impending disasters.

These defensive strategies of hiding, denying, or blaming mistakes on someone else are part of how most of us immediately and unconsciously react to breakdowns. They almost always are a part of my emotional clouds. They are excellent early warning signs. Using the RAPID process gives you and your client the opportunity to change errors from a source of shame, blame, or cover-up (all forms of defensive reactions) to a source of information for the systematic improvement of your interactions. You *can* transform breakdowns from stumbling blocks to stepping stones. The choice is yours. The choice is simple and not easy.

Your first job is to *recognize* early warning signs as indicators that you are on your way toward, or already in, an emotional cloud. How do you deal with these indicators?

- Do you get angry at them? Do you wrestle with them? Do you immediately go on a witch hunt, searching for who is at fault (not you!) or who can be blamed for the breakdown that has

> **Stumbling Block**
>
> Reacting with anger at breakdowns is another setback.

you in an emotional cloud? Or are you so devastated as to be immobilized?

Or

- Are you grateful for the information they are providing you? Do you dance with them? Are you curious about how they happened, what had to be present for them to occur, and what can be learned from them?

> **Stepping Stone**
>
> Breakdowns can uncover critical information.

When the Brenda case occurred, I judged my mistakes solely as indicators of my incompetence, revealing my negative attitude about emotional clouds. Until I shifted my attitude to being curious about how emotional clouds occur, I did not realize that I was stuck in one and could not move past my defensiveness.

For about two years, I floundered. Finally, I had an ah-ha moment and, as if for the first time, understood that the question was "How did this happen?" This realization allowed me to shift my attitude from clouds of shame (they are to be hidden, denied, or blamed on someone else) to curiosity (What can be learned? With whom can I explore this cloud?). Suddenly, I realized that hiding, denying, and blaming were early warning signs rather than effective strategies for dealing with upset. This shift in point of view had an enormous impact on all my future interactions. You and your client will make more rapid progress if you share the attitude that emotional clouds are learning opportunities to be explored.

Breakdowns provide signals that the relationship or interaction needs attention, care, or understanding. A session in which all goes well is a worthy goal; however, when mistakes do occur, they are best seen as opportunities to solve problems. A complaint may become an actual blessing. This reminds me of the time when my friend was tested for a minor illness, and a serious condition was discovered. Because the lab technician approached the minor complaint as a possible signal, a rapidly growing illness was discovered and treated. With an attitude of curiosity rather than blame, a focus on problems can generate a wealth of important information.

When you first begin to study your emotional clouds, you may not become aware of having been in one until well after it has dissipated. A learning strategy is to recall as best you can the events that occurred immediately before the cloud began to form. As you continue to do this with each episode, you will notice some events that occur regularly before your clouds form, like having your advice questioned. These events are ones that you regard as breakdowns.

Also notice the physical sensations, thoughts, or emotions that you experience immediately after you become aware that a mistake has occurred. These might include anger at someone (a subordinate who has questioned your opinion) or fear of being wrong (the subordinate might be right). This anger or fear is the beginning of your emotional cloud. If you continue this inquiry, you will become aware of other early warning signs closer and closer to the onset of a breakdown. You can learn to diffuse your emotional cloud before it becomes a thunderstorm.

Three Cases—Recognize

Mustang

There was a time when I was broke, yet I managed to save enough money to repair the dents and dings in my prized 1969 Mustang and have it painted.

At dinner the first night the car was back from the body shop, one of my sons, then nine, said, "Dad, some of the Mustang letters on the trunk are loose." I immediately reacted with exasperation, "No, they're not! I just paid a lot of money to have the car fixed and painted. It's fine!" The rest of the meal passed in silence.

Instantly an emotional cloud surrounded me, as evidenced by the wave of intense emotions that swept over me. I had invested time, energy, and all my discretionary cash in this project. To have my young son imply that my choice of body shops was mediocre was humbling at best. While in the cloud, I dismissed his input. The result was a bigger breakdown a week later.

This situation helped me to learn how important it is to recognize and manage anger in challenging circumstances. Anger is an early warning sign and part of many emotional clouds. My anger camouflaged my emotional cloud for some weeks until I was discussing this incident with colleagues during a classroom exercise in which we were examining situations in which we had been given good advice and did not take it.

Sus-Phrine

I was hospitalized on a Saturday night, recovering from the effects of an onset of the flu combined with a severe asthma attack. My physician had left a standing order that I could have an injection of 0.1 ml of Sus-Phrine once every four hours if I requested it. I began to have trouble breathing and put in such a request. Shortly the nurse arrived, carrying a syringe, and began preparing my arm for the injection. I looked at the syringe, recognized it as a 1.0 ml syringe, and noticed that it was full! It contained 1.0, not 0.1 ml, of the drug!

I reacted quickly. "Stop! This is *not* the dosage I'm to receive."

The nurse was calm and firm. "Yes, it is. That's exactly what your doctor wrote on your orders."

At this point, my anger at the nurse for selecting the wrong dose was only intensified by her abrupt dismissal of my input. I was also alarmed because the safety of the hospital had been compromised. What led to recognizing this deteriorating situation was that I had stopped to take a deep breath before continuing. I realized that this conversation could result in dire consequences for us. My choice was to calm down and not raise my voice, which would have assuredly escalated the conflict.

Sudafed

During a regular checkup, my physician and I were reviewing my current medications, which included 30 mg of Sudafed when needed. He asked, "And what color is that pill?"

"Red," I said, immediately going into a dark cloud. My thoughts were, *He knows good and well what color that pill is. He's suspicious that I'm taking the 100 mg long-acting pill, which is white. He doesn't believe me. He doesn't trust me. I can't believe that! I hate it when people think I'm not telling the truth.* And this thought process took two seconds.

I did not say a word about any of this to him.

As in the Brenda case, I stayed lost in the emotional cloud for some time.

My pride was deeply hurt, yet I was intimidated enough by the fact that he was an MD that I could not think of anything to say. I withdrew in a pout and said nothing. I stayed lost in this emotional cloud for several years. My upset was on my mind during each checkup in those years, compromising my relationship with him.

The Recognize Checklist

1. How rapidly do you recognize the onset of emotional clouds? Are some easier for you to detect than others?
2. What are your early warning signs that indicate you are on your way toward, or already in, an emotional cloud? Physical events? Emotions? Thoughts?
3. Which defensive strategies do you employ: hiding, denying, or blaming? Others?

Chapter 10 Activity

Sometimes you are fortunate and your role-play partner points out an emotional cloud to you. Timing is critical here. If you are still in the midst of your cloud, you may not be receptive to this input. Recall the year and a half that passed between when I first saw the Brenda video in front of my students and when I recognized and addressed my defensive reactions.

Pick a recent interaction with a client in which an emotional cloud enveloped you and continues to do so. Examining this event will produce information about your early warning signs.

A danger here is that your partner may be eager to start coaching while you are still entangled in your emotional cloud. One way to manage this eagerness is for your partner to begin with, "I have some observations about your incident. Are you interested?" If you are not yet ready to be coached, your responsibility is to let your partner know. Your partner's responsibility then is to honor your wishes.

Role-Play

Your job in this role-play is to repeat as best you can recall what you said and did in the interaction you have picked. The more accurately you depict the exchange you experienced, the more information you will discover from this exercise. Keep in mind that you will have to get past your pride to show your partner what you look like in your emotional cloud. If you do your job well, the effort will be worth your time and discomfort.

When you are ready to be coached, describe the context in which your recent interaction occurred to your partner in enough detail so that they can play the role of your client. Then set up the video equipment, set your timer for five minutes, and begin the role-play.

Following your role-play, explore the chapter 10 debriefing questions at the end of this chapter. Please look at these questions with your partner *after* having completed this activity, as you will learn more from the role-play experience this way.

Brenda's Case—The Recognize Checklist

1. How rapidly do you recognize the onset of emotional clouds? Are some tougher for you to detect than others?

    In the Brenda case, I did not recognize my emotional clouds for a year and a half. Since then, I have noticed that there is still a delay in recognizing my emotional clouds when I make simple mistakes, or mistakes I think I should no longer be making. That cloud is only more intense when I make a mistake while working with people who have more authority than I do.

2. What are your early warning signs that indicate you are on your way toward, or already in, an emotional cloud? Physical events? Emotions? Thoughts?

    With Brenda, one sign was my anger when she appeared to be late. Others included anxiety when she changed her research problem, the thought that she was incompetent, and my hands shaking when I had difficulty explaining basic statistical concepts.

3. Which defensive strategies do you employ: Hiding? Denying? Blaming? Others?

    All of them.

4. Are you curious about how your breakdowns occur? If not, what are the barriers standing between you and being curious?

    I am curious now, though it may take a while after recognizing a mistake before curiosity takes hold. I was not curious in the least during the Brenda case. My pride and fear of looking incompetent were major barriers there.

Recap
Be aware that your emotional clouds may come over you slowly or rapidly. Become curious about how and when your clouds appear. Continue to search for your early warning signs that a cloud is forming. Identify those defenses that hide your clouds.

Reflecting on the Brenda case and discussing it with colleagues helped me to become aware of all the above recap insights.

Frequently Asked Questions

1. I seem to have breakdowns without early warning signs. Is that possible?

   Yes. This happened to me with Brenda. I had no way of knowing that she had changed her project until she told me. At that point, several thoughts occurred that were, in hindsight, early warning signs that I was on my way to an emotional cloud: *How can she do this? She has just wasted my weekend research. She should have called me about this! I don't think she respects me.* Remember that the concept of emotional clouds was foreign to me at the time. The Brenda case prompted years of exploration that have resulted in this book.

2. I'm intimidated by some of my colleagues. Is this all bad? These are people that I have learned to be careful around.

   This isn't "all bad." It is part of your survival strategy. Unfortunately, it also compromises your relationships with those colleagues, as you may not be telling them your truth as you seek to be careful around them. In fact, you may withhold information that would be helpful to them, were you not afraid to speak up. If it is important for you to have a working relationship with one of these colleagues, examine your memory to identify what incidents were the sources of this intimidation. Examine these memories with your partner to develop a more effective strategy for dealing with them than being intimidated.

3. I get embarrassed when I can't answer a question. My attitude is that I should know the answer to all questions at all times. What can I do?

You have done the first step: *recognize* that you have the attitude that you should be an expert in all areas. The second step is harder: let go of that attitude. Many "good students" come out of school with this attitude; however, it is impossible to sustain this in the workplace. Have a conversation with the person you think expects you to be an expert in all areas. Find out what their specific standards are for you. Ask how you can work with them so that it is possible for you to meet their standards. To survive and thrive when you don't know or aren't sure, learn to say, "I don't know. I can find out. By when do you want to know?"

4. I get upset when corrected by anyone, especially a junior member of my staff. Is this an early warning sign of an emotional cloud?

For sure! A correction reveals that you are vulnerable. You may have made a mistake. Confronting vulnerability often generates upset in the form of anger. Stay in the conversation until you have let go of fault and blame and the potential error has been explored and resolved for everyone involved.

Chapter 10 Debriefing Questions

Watch the video. What did you notice?

Did you see early warning signs that you missed in the actual session? What barriers kept you from seeing them? (These are your defenses.)

What kind of early warning signs do you have? Mental? Physical? Emotional? Other?

Review your recent emotional clouds with your partner to begin to identify your early warning signs.

CHAPTER 11

Address Your Emotional Cloud

Let's suppose you have identified several of your early warning signs and occasionally *recognize* that you are in an emotional cloud during an interaction. Now what? A key question is whether you think you can *address* and exit this cloud during the interaction without causing damage. The darker the cloud, the rougher the ride as you seek to exit.

To continue the thunderstorm analogy, if you discover that you are driving in a cloudburst, a real frog-choker, you would pull off the road as soon as safely possible. If you are in a similarly dark and dangerous emotional cloud in a consultation, arrange for a break in your interaction rather than expecting yourself to perform well while in the midst of an emotional storm. A simple request for a break will suffice. Give yourself time to calm down. If necessary, extend the break to another day, preferably as soon as possible. This approach will provide time to intentionally and privately address the storm.

On the other hand, if you are cruising along as a light shower begins, you can easily continue your journey by turning on your headlights and windshield wipers. Similarly, if your emotional cloud with a client is light gray and just beginning, you can gently address the underlying breakdown without risking damage to your relationship.

Identify and Address Your Barriers

Several barriers interrupt examination of our emotional clouds. As long as they are in place, they keep us securely in the emotional cloud.

If an emotional cloud has you unnerved, you may find yourself saying words that you know you will regret the moment they leave your mouth. Being distracted by thoughts about how someone else would be handling the problem only results in missing critical information from your client. Part of dealing effectively with breakdowns is operating in a fashion that is consistent with the severity of the cloud you are experiencing. You would not increase your speed in the middle of a fog bank, would you?

> **Ask for Five … or a Day**
>
> If I am deep in the cloud, my strategy is to ask for five minutes alone to gather my thoughts. When I do *not* take a break, the result is a darker cloud, often accompanied by more breakdowns. Over the years, nearly all clients have granted my request for a break.

The goal in addressing your emotional cloud is to be confident that you can manage your emotional cloud rather than having it overpower you. When you are in charge, you know that you can have a rational conversation despite the breakdown, even though you may still be in distress. Staying in the present moment is an important part of addressing the emotional cloud if you hope to avoid cascading breakdowns.

Anger is often a reaction to a breakdown in communication and is used as a defense against the experience of vulnerability. No one is perfect, and we do not live in a perfect world. When vulnerable, I find myself using anger—toward myself and others. While anger does distract me from vulnerability, at least in the short term, it does not present a way out of an emotional cloud.

Pride interrupts the examination of our clouds. No one likes to make a mistake, though we all do. Often this threat to pride is handled by blaming the cloud on someone else: "You made me mad at lunch today." Some people develop a habit of blaming others and resist considering the possibility that they may have played a part in creating the disagreement, misunderstanding, or mistake. You may know someone like this, and most clients do too!

Anger
Anger is often a defense against the experience of vulnerability.
Additional words for anger are irritation, annoyance, and exasperation.

Fear can also drive both denial and blame. Some organizations take pride in having a "blame-free culture" where one can make mistakes without penalty, though private conversations reveal there is often a gap between the intended and actual practice of such a policy. Most of us share a history in which our mistakes and the accompanying emotional clouds have been a source of pain. Hence, our reaction has been to avoid being wrong whenever possible.

Intimidation is another barrier to asking important questions. Becoming aware of who and what intimidates you is an important step. Dangerous consequences could have occurred had I not questioned the nurse in the Sus-Phrine case. It can be difficult to be effective in conversations with persons who are intimidating. This may be a result of our early experiences with such people when we did not have the skill to deal with certain situations.

Denial sometimes shows up when we resist the fact that we are in an emotional cloud. People may say, "I am *not* upset!" "Just leave me alone!" or "Nothing's wrong!" As long as you are resisting your emotional cloud and are voicing your anger about its existence, you won't be able to help yourself. Until you address your emotional cloud, there will be no recovery from the precipitating breakdown.

Overwhelm occurs when a cloud is so intense that you are unable to address it immediately. In this situation, take a break and return when the emotional cloud has reduced in intensity. Give yourself whatever time it takes before you return to the situation.

Becoming masterful at recognizing emotional clouds during an interaction requires time, commitment, and courage. Is it worth it? Yes, indeed! Consider how long it takes to clean up one nasty comment blurted out in the midst of an emotional cloud. Sometimes our sudden exclamations, whether intended or not, are offensive, belligerent, or abusive and cannot be cleaned up. When we act irresponsibly, we run the risk of producing irreversible and painful consequences.

Notice and Act on Early Warning Signs

What to do? First, begin to notice the signs that you are in an emotional cloud and admit it, at least to yourself. We each have our own signature patterns. For example, anger and anxiety form an emotional cloud that regularly envelops me after a breakdown occurs. The progression begins with being only vaguely aware that something is wrong, long before I can pinpoint the actual breakdown. These feelings, thoughts, or hunches are my early warning signs that tell me, "There is a problem here somewhere."

> **Anxiety**
>
> "Anxiety is the anticipation of pain. It could be physical pain or emotional pain."
>
> From Christian Grillon, a neuroscientist at the National Institute of Mental Health (NIMH).

When I'm aware of these signs, I have a chance to catch myself early in the development of my emotional cloud. This is another case of the sooner the better, in that I can *address* and escape my ballooning cloud before it becomes overwhelming. Then I can shift my attention to pinpointing the initiating breakdown.

The key is to learn your own early warning signs so you can *recognize* an emotional cloud and *address* it while it is still small. Early warning signs include and are not limited to the following:

- sweaty palms or fidgeting fingers;
- increased heart rate, signaling preparation for fight-or-flight;
- derisive thoughts about your client, subordinate, or boss;
- looping thoughts such as *I should, I can't,* and *no one listens to me*; or
- interrupting anyone or prematurely changing the topic.

Take whatever steps work for you to escape the cloud so that you can rationally study the breakdown that's provoking it. Follow the spirit of the flight attendant's instruction to put on your own oxygen mask before assisting others. Get out of your cloud first. Then check to see if your client is in a cloud as well. If they are, assist them if they are willing to accept your assistance. Learning to address your emotional cloud while the interaction is taking place will take time and practice. Be patient with yourself and others throughout this process.

For some of us, leaving a good pout is a difficult step to take. Irrational perhaps, but sometimes it feels necessary to spend some time having a moan before moving on! If someone is pushing you to discuss the breakdown when you are aware that you have not yet addressed your emotional cloud, ask for a short break. A tall glass of water can be useful in such times. Be aware that your client may also find a break helpful.

Sometimes a client may not respect your boundaries in these situations. For example, they may prefer to stay in their emotional cloud and escalate the breakdown by

> **Stepping Stone**
>
> Avoid a goal of zero breakdowns. One can achieve that goal only by promising nothing and doing nothing, which is an unacceptable strategy. Instead, identify breakdowns as soon as possible and recover rapidly. The key to rapid recovery is becoming aware of one's early warning signs.

engaging in a shouting match. Address this by saying, "I understand that we currently disagree; however, shouting is unacceptable to me. Since I am interested in continuing this work, I suggest we explore ways that we can work through this disagreement. For now, I propose that we stop today and meet again when we can converse calmly. Shall I give you a call tomorrow at noon to see if we are both ready to have a conversation to recover from this breakdown?"

A clue that you have successfully addressed your emotional cloud is that you are ready to work collaboratively to resolve the error.

Goal: No Breakdowns or Rapid Recovery?

Another barrier to dealing effectively with emotional clouds is the attitude that the more breakdowns you have, the poorer the quality of your service. This point of view can lead you to take fewer risks, resulting in fewer opportunities to contribute. Certainly, if you make no promises, there is no risk of breaking a promise.

A more useful measure of the quality of your service than the number of breakdowns you have is how rapidly you recover from a breakdown. There is a memorable line in the movie *The Karate Kid* where the master is questioned about how he can perform so flawlessly. His response? "Many mistakes. Very rapid recovery." Shifting your focus from the number of breakdowns to the speed of recovery frees you to act boldly, recover quickly, and contribute generously to the people in your world. If you can't make any mistakes, you can't learn anything either.

Three Cases—Address

The following cases are examined again as an extension of the discussions from the previous chapter.

How long does it take?

As long as it takes.

Addressing an emotional cloud generally will not cause it to go away immediately. Addressing the cloud does allow one to become more aware of the factors that are impinging on a conversation about pinpointing a breakdown.

Mustang

A week after my confrontation with my son, I was pumping gas and was surprised to see that I was now the proud owner of a MU TANG. An external force (gravity) intervened; the S dropped off! Now it was impossible to ignore my son's input, no matter how much I disliked hearing it! Time and external factors often lead a person to *recognize* and *address* even the most noxious emotional cloud. I finally checked out my son's assertion. I wiggled the other six letters and discovered that three more were loose!

For me, becoming annoyed with my son was an early warning sign that I was about to unconsciously dismiss his input rather than consciously consider whether his observation had merit. From this I learned a strategy to implement when I feel myself becoming irritated: I pause to identify the source of my vulnerability and then address that feeling of dismay. For example, I could have suggested we check out which letters were loose. Implementing this strategy has helped me to stay in the conversation in many difficult situations—a large return for the cost of a single S!

Another issue that hampered my ability to deal with the cloud was my discomfort with the prospect of confronting mechanics at the body shop. I often am intimidated by experts who know more about my car than I do, so I never talked with the mechanics. This cloud was not addressed.

> **Speaking Truth to Power**
>
> This issue took hold of me during the Mustang incident. When my son spoke the truth to me about the loose letter, I did not respond well. I imagine that the irritated reaction he received served to reinforce his idea that speaking truth to power is risky business. My aversion to negative reactions was evident in my reluctance to confront the mechanics.

A conversation with the mechanic in charge of my car would have been difficult for me since I saw this incident as including a broken promise.

I was afraid that an unpleasant confrontation would ensue. For many, "speaking truth to power" is another issue in dealing with breakdowns.

Sus-Phrine

> **Stepping Stone**
>
> Emotions are data. When emotions arise, examine them. Consider both positive and negative emotions. Becoming angry, impatient, intimidated, or even elated can draw your attention away from the task at hand.

After the nurse said, "This dose is exactly what your doctor ordered," I took a deep breath. There was a long pause. "Then I refuse this dose of medicine. Call my doctor and connect him to the phone in my room." The deep breath, pause, and demand were all components of addressing this emotional cloud.

Sudafed

I did not discuss my distress and anger at my physician's Sudafed question until years later. He did not remember the incident but said that he was not surprised that he asked about the color since so many pills of so many different colors and sizes are available. It was his standard practice to ask what the color of the pill was if he had any doubt about the dosage. Ironically, this was the sort of checking that I had expected from the hospital nurse and had not received.

During the interim between when the emotional cloud occurred and when we talked about my breakdown, I held a grudge against him for not believing me. That issue was standing between us in every appointment until I finally had the courage to raise the issue with him, and together we cleaned it up.

This case taught me how a powerful emotional cloud can restrain the intent and ability to respond. Recognizing that a breakdown has occurred is a first step. Addressing any mistake is a necessary second step. Talking about the incident with someone is essential, especially when you cannot address it by yourself. Cut yourself some slack and get help!

What about you? Think back to the last breakdown you encountered. As soon as you recognized it, you had two choices: were you grateful for having the breakdown or did you become angry? How did that work for you? If you became angry, what were the barriers that kept you from being grateful—or at least accepting?

Emotional clouds come in various sizes. You always have the choice of when to deal with one, once you have recognized it.

Working with Your Partner

A partner who is committed to your growth is an invaluable asset as you learn how to *recognize* and *address* your emotional clouds. A partner who will listen can provide assistance by asking questions such as the following:

- Are you committed to getting the job done or being right?
- Are you committed to recovering or to continuing in your emotional cloud? For how long?
- What could you accomplish if you let go of your displeasure?

Your partner in the process of improvement can help you to sort out and identify the real issues relating to a breakdown, separating them from the fog and drama that thrive in emotional clouds.

The first step for your partner after observing that you are in an emotional cloud is to invite your participation with, "I have an observation. Are you interested?"

After several years of such conversations with my partner, I recognize the pattern. She will notice that I'm in an emotional cloud and offer an observation. By now, I know this is a true question, to which I may answer, "No," and she won't argue. I also know that there is something going on with me that is big enough to get her attention, even if it has not yet occurred to me. I usually say, "Yes," unless I'm already deep in my cloud. If I say, "No," she will say, "Okay, and I'm available," thus providing time and support.

If I say, "Yes," she will ask, "Are you aware you are stepping into an emotional cloud?"

> Doug: Yes.

> Partner: What happened just before you went into it?

> Doug: I don't recall.

> Partner: What were you doing?

> Doug: Answering email.

> Partner: Who were you writing?

> Doug: Greg.

> Partner: What happened?

> Doug: I got mad at him.

> Partner: How did that happen?

> Doug: Well, Greg was just being Greg. You know.

> Partner: Yes, and how did it happen that you got angry?

This dialogue is usually enough to get me started on the path of tracking down what happened before I became upset and went into my cloud. The key is that she will stay in the conversation with me until I *recognize* my breakdown and calm down enough so that I'm willing to *address* it.

The above interaction did not develop overnight. We have been working on it for years. And it does not always work smoothly! Please note once again that this coaching process requires both courage and patience to stay in the conversation until calm has been restored.

The Address Checklist

1. Do you recognize that you are in an emotional cloud? How much time passes before you are aware of this cloud?
2. Do you have a partner to help guide you as you *address* your cloud? If not, find one.
3. What are the barriers standing between you and addressing your cloud? Denial, anger, blame, pride, intimidation, guilt, and fear are frequent culprits.
4. What early warning signs between a breakdown and the beginning of your cloud are you beginning to notice?

Chapter 11 Activity

Role-Play

Reflect on the last breakdown you experienced. When that breakdown occurred, did you consider it an *opportunity* or a *failure*? Were you *curious* about the cause or were you *defensive* and looking for someone to blame? What were the results of your choices? If those results were unsatisfactory, use a different approach during your role-play.

Video a conversation with your partner about your breakdown. Your partner may wish to use questions similar to those found in the section above, "Working with Your Partner."

Following your role-play exercise, refer to the chapter 11 debriefing questions at the end of this chapter. Please consider these questions with your partner *after* having completed this activity, as you will learn more from the role-play experience this way.

Brenda's Case—The Address Checklist

1. Do you recognize that you are in an emotional cloud? How much time passes before you are aware of this cloud?

    I knew I was upset during the consultation. I thought I had nothing to do with it. It was all her fault! This thought lasted through the entire consultation.

2. Do you have a partner to help guide you as you *address* your cloud? If not, find one.

    I had a partner who asked me, "How did it happen that the session did not go well?" I wasn't willing to answer his question, as I thought he was implying that it was my fault, and I was positive it was not!

3. What are the barriers standing between you and addressing your cloud? Denial, anger, blame, pride, intimidation, guilt, and fear are frequent culprits.

    The barriers were many: anger was the underlying emotion. I was angry at Brenda for not meeting me where I expected and for changing her research question. I was angry at myself for not being able to explain a basic topic to my client's satisfaction. In addition, I developed many negative attitudes about Brenda and excused my part in the failed consultation.

4. What early warning signs between a breakdown and the beginning of your cloud are you beginning to notice?

    The main early warning sign that I missed was my anger. I did not stop to take a deep breath and recognize that anger is always a defense against the experience of vulnerability. Then I could have looked for the source of my vulnerability: by failing to plan for adjustments on her part, I had created a safety net that proved inadequate.

Another set of early warning signs that I missed was my negative judgments about Brenda and her research problem. I got swept up in my judgments and took them as truth rather than defenses against my vulnerabilities.

Recap

Identify the barriers that keep you from addressing your emotional clouds. What early warning signs are you beginning to notice that assist you in identifying your cloud sooner? Work with a partner to shorten the time between entering an emotional cloud and addressing it.

Frequently Asked Questions

1. My boss regularly gives me complex tasks to do and then expects me to leave and do the task without any further discussion. I get infuriated when this happens. How can I *address* this emotional cloud?

    First, ask your boss to meet with you to discuss your working relationship. If she agrees, request that this meeting be dedicated to how you can work together more effectively, rather than including a discussion of your current tasks. Agree on the amount of time you are both willing to reserve for this meeting.

    At the start of the meeting, explain that you are experiencing difficulty with the process used for making assignments. You would like to work with her to become more efficient when project assignments are made to assure that the outcomes meet her standards and timeframe without rework.

    Use the POWER process to structure your meeting for effectiveness and efficiency.

Chapter 11 Debriefing Questions

Watch the video. What did you notice?

What did you learn? What barriers are toughest for you to address, even with your partner's assistance?

What did your partner notice during the conversation?

What have you learned from this exercise that you are willing to implement the next time you notice yourself going into an emotional cloud as a result of a mistake? Practice what you have learned with your partner until you are confident that you will be able to implement it when dealing with an actual breakdown.

CHAPTER 12

The Heart of RAPID Recovery

In this chapter, we will explore two steps that are at the heart of RAPID recovery: *pinpoint* the breakdown and *identify* how to get back on track. As obvious as the breakdowns in this book appear, they are rarely obvious when you are a participant in the moment they occur. Only after you recognize and address your emotional cloud can you be ready to pinpoint the breakdown and identify possible strategies for recovery. Few people are comfortable with the vulnerability they experience while observing themselves on video *until* they reap the rewards of insights from using the RAPID process.

Pinpoint the Breakdown

Sometimes you recognize mistakes during an interaction, and sometimes it's a week later. As your awareness increases, you will recognize your errors as they occur, allowing you to address them more quickly. Mastering this process will save both you and your client much time, energy, and emotional distress.

Once you recognize an emotional cloud and decide to face your emotions, move on to *pinpoint* the specific breakdown.

If your client also recognizes their emotional cloud, then you can work together to identify the breakdown. Listen to see if you both are reacting to the same breakdown. Stay in this conversation until you agree on the breakdown to address.

A New Scenario to Explore

In the middle of an interaction with a client, you hear her say, "Your advice does not relate to my proposal—again!" Then you hear yourself say, "If you would just listen to what I'm saying …"

Your client is irritated that you are not addressing her proposal. In addition, both of you are now aware that this breakdown is a repeater, signaled by her exclamation of "again!"

Your breakdown is that you interpreted your client's comment as questioning your advice or even attacking your competency.

The two of you are in different clouds, reacting to different breakdowns. Unscrambling them requires patience and perseverance. First, each of you must recognize and address your emotional cloud to clear the air. A time-out may be useful. Then you can proceed as follows:

> "Whoa! Let's back up the bus. Could we review that interchange?"

> "Yes."

> "Please ask me your question again. Clearly I missed something."

Now you have a chance to recover from your knee-jerk reaction of feeling attacked while confirming that you are committed to listening. Keep in mind that her "Yes" may actually be "Maybe." If she says something like "Well, I suppose," or "It depends," explore what else may be wrong before returning to her question. She may still be in her cloud.

You might hear a response like "You have ignored my proposal three times today! I finally had to say something." Now you have an opportunity to move forward with "Okay. Thank you for that clarification. I want to take the time required to clean up my mistakes."

What happened? Both you and your client recognized and addressed your emotional clouds. Then you began to pinpoint the breakdowns. Now is the time to verify that each thinks the next task is to identify how the breakdowns occurred. If either decides the immediate task is to assign blame, the meeting will be stalled until your attitudes shift to being curious about *how* these breakdowns occurred.

Recognizing mistakes as an appealing opportunity isn't a perspective that you can dictate. You can choose to have this point of view for yourself and invite your client to also consider it. Clearly you cannot force the adoption of this attitude. Courage and patience are called for to pinpoint the mistakes that hide in what appears to be one giant disaster.

Benefits of a Time-Out

Sometimes in an intense interaction, a client can make a comment that takes me by surprise. I'm so stunned and distressed that I don't ask for a time-out. Instead, I struggle to continue the conversation and end up acquiescing to something I intensely oppose. I'm more prone to make this mistake when the interchange is especially adversarial and with someone who outranks me. My distress can be such that I can't articulate my opposition calmly and in the moment, given the intensity of my emotional cloud.

When I ask for time to collect my thoughts, nearly every client grants my request. The benefits of a time-out are shared. However, you do have to ask. To learn how and when to make such requests takes practice. Start with good friends and small upsets and gradually build your muscles in this area.

Keep in mind that your client is probably well aware that you are upset and may be confused as to how that happened. If you say nothing about your emotional cloud, you make the interaction much more challenging for both of you. Your client will be puzzled about what is going on and trying to continue in the interaction as if nothing has happened. Small wonder that some interactions crash and burn under the complexity of both parties becoming lost in several simultaneous breakdowns, recognized and unrecognized!

Clarify Causes

A key step in pinpointing a breakdown is to search for the unintended event that was the source of the breakdown. Sometimes a promise has been broken. This is certain to produce a high level of distress. Surprises and unmet expectations will also produce upset, as will blocked goals. Any one of these can derail an interaction. Sorting out which causes have occurred (broken promise, unmet expectations, or blocked goals) is the challenging work involved in pinpointing a breakdown.

Search to clarify how each of you would describe the breakdown, without resorting to fault and blame. Some useful questions for clarifying the breakdown during the interaction are: What happened? What is your perception of what happened? What is your client's perception of what happened?

After the interaction, additional questions may be useful: What is your coaching partner's perception of what happened? In which of the five parts of POWER did the breakdown occur? What results were intended? What results occurred?

Come to an agreement upon the specific mistake to address. This is difficult yet essential if you and your client are going to recover.

Managing Off-Limits Breakdowns

There may be some breakdowns that you are reluctant to examine. Some you may not even be aware have occurred. Some you may have dismissed with the thought, *It was nothing.*

A breakdown may remind you of an open wound from the past—such as an unresolved breakdown with a client three years ago. Its reoccurrence in a meeting with this same client yesterday presents you with a choice: address it and see if you can use these tools to discover a way forward *or* add one more breakdown to your stack of unresolved breakdowns with this person. My advice: *address* it. Your life is too full for you to be effective while carrying around a huge stack of unresolved breakdowns.

Examples here intrigue me. Here's one: Occasionally when I'm driving and am lost, I am finally willing to act on the suggestion that my wife made ten minutes ago, namely to ask for directions. There was a time when I was not willing to take her advice at all when I was lost, because I did not want to admit that I had made a mistake.

Often when a breakdown occurs, one party isn't willing to talk about it now with anyone—period. Pouting isn't only for children! Proficient mediators, therapists, and mentors are available to help you sort out at least your part of the problem, even if the other person involved isn't willing to talk about it. Working through your barriers to asking for help is an important step in resolving breakdowns. As a coach once asked me, "How bad does it have to get before you are willing to ask for help?"

Beware of Conflicting Commitments

Certain situations exist in which we *refuse to ask for assistance*. These situations differ for each of us yet have similar characteristics. Conflicting commitments are a stumbling block that materializes when we are more committed to appearing competent or to preserving the status quo than we are to getting the job done, which in this situation is to recover from the breakdown. Conflicting commitments can lead to unresolved disagreements.

Refusing to ask for help appears in many forms and is rationalized in many ways. "My checkbook just won't balance; there is no point in trying." Or "I can't leave the table without having a second helping." And an old favorite: "No matter how hard I try, I can't satisfy my _____ (fill in the blank—boss, spouse, relatives, parents, children)."

> **Stumbling Block**
>
> Are you more committed to looking good than you are to getting the job done?

The common element in the above situations is that your thoughts have become rules to live by. How do you change your rules? Change is always tough since rules (like beliefs) are both complex and entrenched. First, compassion is required, especially in the presence of the repeater breakdowns that created each rule in the first place. You may have to let go of a part of who you are.

Changing Your Life Rules

Here are a few examples of how your *rules* can threaten your commitment to change.

Learning from Unmet Expectations

A friend of mine was distressed by the fact that his checkbook was continually unbalanced. Out of sheer desperation stimulated by four unbalanced months in a row, he entered all the numbers from those four months into an Excel spreadsheet. Comparing the spreadsheet to his checkbook, number by number, the source of the difficulty became plain: every month he would make a few arithmetic mistakes. Seeing these multiple mistakes was a shock. He believed that as a professional mathematician, he was expected to manipulate numbers in his head. In fact, that skill had become part of his identity. To resolve this dilemma, he had to let go of his expectation and thus let go of this piece of his identity.

Working in a Marginalizing Culture

Another friend was distressed by the fact that ideas in which he saw great promise and presented to management were routinely dismissed by his superiors. This state of affairs had a negative impact on his whole work experience. His interpretation was that management had decided that only their ideas were worthy of consideration. However, he did not want to confront anyone in management to investigate this belief. Confronting a belief by checking it out may lead to a tough choice between letting go of a cherished point of view and finding new employment.

When "Being Right" Doesn't Work

Still another colleague confided that, "The newest member of our unit is questioning my judgment. I know he's wrong." With this belief in place, one may be labeled by others as "information-proof." Being right and avoiding being wrong can lead to being ignored.

An alternative strategy with more promise is to approach input with a spirit of humility. After all, you have made mistakes in the past, and your firm view *could* be wrong or at least be improved. As you open your mind to new information, you might be willing to consider revising your view! And then you may be seen as open-minded, fair, and cooperative, regardless of the final outcome.

When Mind Reading Doesn't Work

I have personally experienced this phenomenon with those who have mild to moderate hearing loss. They are often convinced that "If I ask, they'll think I'm a dummy." While some people will ask you to repeat a word they did not understand, others won't. They will just drop out of the conversation, creating a devastating impact on relationships. The desire to participate in conversation is overcome by a fear of looking dumb. This same fear may be observed in classrooms from kindergarten to corporate, with or without the presence of a hearing loss.

A Reluctance to Ask for Assistance Knows No Age Limits

Multiple interactions with seniors in their eighties and nineties demonstrate that being more committed to appearing competent than to getting the job done is a lifelong challenge. Here's a personal story that clarifies the process.

I had a wonderful friend Daniel who was in his mideighties, having survived a stroke. My wife and I were visiting him and his wife in their retirement community. They invited us to join them for dinner, which was a coat-and-tie event. All of us, except Daniel, were dressed and ready to leave for the dining room. Here's the interaction that followed between Daniel and me:

Daniel: Just go ahead. I will catch up with you.

Me: Is there anything I can do that would be of assistance?

Daniel: No, thank you. That's not necessary. I will be down in a couple of minutes.

We three waited at the table twenty minutes until Daniel appeared, looking distressed. I asked, "Are you okay?"

Daniel: Yes, it's just this darned tie. It is so hard for me to tie anymore!

After dinner, I waited until he and I were alone and asked, "How did you get it tied?"

Daniel: I tried and tried until I was really upset. An aide looked in and asked if she could help. I sheepishly asked her to tie my tie. Ach! This is the darned pride thing again, isn't it? (We had discussed pride on several earlier occasions.)

Me: I think so.

Daniel: I thought for sure that I'd be done with vanity by now.

Me: I don't know that it ever leaves, Daniel.

Daniel: It doesn't look to me like it does.

Daniel's expectation that he should be able to tie his necktie was not being met. It would continue not being met until he could accept that this task was something he could no longer do. Accepting the loss of various competencies is tough, as it indicates that he is one step closer to death. Yet, accept it he must if he hopes to move past having frustration accompany every dinner.

Three Cases—Pinpoint

Although there were distinct breakdowns in each of these cases from earlier in part 2, I had the most trouble pinpointing the second one in the Mustang case.

Mustang

The first breakdown to pinpoint was that the body shop did not attach the Mustang letters properly. The second was that I rejected input from my son, who had revealed the first one. This judgment was based solely on my assumptions about his powers of observation. Pinpointing the second mistake came to light only when I had conversations with colleagues about this event.

Sus-Phrine

My breakdown was that my nurse had made an error in filling the syringe. Clearly, she disagreed with me. From her perspective, the problem was that she had a noncompliant patient.

Sudafed

The difficulty here was that I did not ask my physician why he had asked me about the color of the Sudafed that I was taking. Pinpointing this breakdown did not occur until years after the initial interchange. I chose to revisit this issue because I did not want to continue having it in the back of my mind whenever I met with him.

As it turned out, I was the only one who remembered the interaction. On reflection, this isn't surprising since from his point of view, he was doing his job as usual. I was upset because I felt insulted. My unwillingness to address this upset was due partly to my tendency to put doctors on the authority pedestal and partly to my own embarrassment for not speaking up sooner.

The Pinpoint Checklist

1. Do you respond to comments your client makes that indicate they are upset about something?
2. Do you stay in the conversation until your client agrees that you realize what breakdown has occurred?
3. When you feel upset in an interaction, do you look for evidence of a breakdown to explain your upset?
4. Do you see a breakdown as an opportunity or a failure?
5. Do you ask for assistance when having trouble pinpointing a breakdown? If not, what barriers stop you from asking?
6. Are there some breakdowns you are unwilling to *pinpoint* because you do not want to address them? Do you count the cost of refusing to deal with these particular breakdowns?

Brenda's Case—The Pinpoint Checklist

1. Do you respond to comments your client makes that indicate they are upset about something?

    I did not speak to Brenda's refusal to take a statistics course. I was stunned that she had rejected my advice.

2. Do you stay in the conversation until your client agrees that you realize what breakdown has occurred?

    Instead of staying in the conversation with her about her upset, I went into lecture mode, explaining aspects of statistical theory that I thought were basic. My emotional cloud was thick enough that I had trouble explaining them.

3. When you feel upset in an interaction, do you look for evidence of a breakdown to explain your upset?

    I do now; I did not in the interaction with Brenda.

4. Do you see a breakdown as an opportunity or a failure?

    On good days, I now see breakdowns as opportunities. In the Brenda interaction, I definitely saw the multiple breakdowns as failures—and not mine!

5. Do you ask for assistance when having trouble pinpointing a breakdown? If not, what barriers stop you from asking?

    With Brenda, I did not ask anyone for help, though later on when I shared the video with colleagues, I received valuable coaching that changed my life. Pride is what stopped me from seeking outside assistance. Now, I often request other points of view when isolating a breakdown.

Identify—Getting Back on Track

A complete job of pinpointing the breakdown is an essential first step toward getting back on track. When you are in the early stages of developing these skills, you may find yourself pinpointing a mistake three days after the actual interaction. At that point, rejoin your client and start identifying how to put the project back on track. Completing the RAPID recovery process is essential.

Barriers to Recovery from Breakdowns

A key barrier to getting back on track is what you see as your part. Define your part and realize that you and your client may not immediately agree on who is to do what. Stay in the conversation until you both agree on the required actions.

Identify what each of you wants the other to do to clean up the breakdown. In this way, you both will discover what actions are essential for recovery. Then consider whether you are willing to do what has been asked. Agreement on a recovery plan is critical to the process of getting back on track.

The shadows of fault-blame conversations will assuredly resurface here if you did not deal with them earlier. Even if you dealt with them as completely as both of you knew how at that time, arriving at this stage may cause new, related, and unexamined issues to appear.

An underlying barrier to recovery from any breakdown is pride—thinking that the mistake was "not your fault." Further, you may expect that your client should be initiating the conversation about doing what is necessary to get back on track.

Prolonged arguments here indicate that something other than the health of the relationship is most important to one or both parties. A likely suspect is that "being right and avoiding being wrong" is driving the argument. This attitude is one of the most powerful motivators for action no matter the circumstances. Consider duels in which each party is willing to risk dying rather than admitting being wrong.

Sometimes an absolute boundary has been crossed for one party and reconciliation isn't possible. Acknowledging that this is one's attitude and owning it allows for a clear termination of the relationship and a resumption of one's life. The alternative is to live a lie and continue in the relationship while being mentally and emotionally absent. This does not work. I know. I have tried it. This produces living at odds with yourself and your values in a state that psychologists call *cognitive dissonance*.

During my worst experience with cognitive dissonance, I felt trapped and did not have the courage to express my honest feelings. Constantly angry, I had a sense of inertia that made addressing the situation even more difficult.

Finally, I felt empowered when a friend reminded me that I always have choices. It can take a long time to terminate dysfunctional relationships. In the end, it's worth it.

An Effective Apology

When you pinpoint a breakdown as a broken promise, profuse apologies such as "I'm sorry; I am so sorry; you don't know how sorry I am" won't save the day. Two steps are essential for continuing the recovery process.

> Step 1. Initiate an *effective apology* by acknowledging that you broke your promise, and then an "I'm sorry" may help. However, stopping here can lead to disaster in the long run.

> Step 2. Ask how you can address the consequences of having broken your promise. This step may feel awkward, but it is necessary for the recovery conversation to succeed.

Breaking a promise to your client always creates a disturbance. Sometimes the disruption is small; sometimes it is large. Let's look at two cases that illuminate this difference:

> *Case 1.* You are five minutes late to a meeting with a longtime friend and client.

> *Case 2.* You are five minutes late to a meeting that your client had arranged with a vice president so that your report could be heard by senior management.

In either case, identify how to get back on task by asking how you can address the consequences of your broken promise and the resulting consequences.

In case 1, your client may well say, "Oh, it's nothing, just a couple of minutes." In case 2, you may have to listen, probably after the meeting, to your client's emotional cloud, which will focus on the tension created by your late arrival. You may discover that this vice president is a stickler for starting meetings on time. The fact that you didn't know that before the meeting is no excuse. In the future, when your clients invite you to a meeting, routinely check who else will be attending and what their criteria are for a successful meeting. (Notice that this is another opportunity to employ the wanted conversation.)

Recovery is more difficult for larger breakdowns. In case 2, the best you may be able to do is promise to be early for future meetings involving your client ... and then *do it*!

Offering extensive excuses for why you were five minutes late won't clean up the mess and wastes time. A complete recovery will depend upon whether your client is willing to forgive your lateness this time and whether you keep your promise in the future. Keeping this promise is critical for rebuilding the trust that has been broken.

Recovery often takes a while and is generally not under your control. If both of you identify and agree on what it will take to get back on track, you will be headed in the right direction.

Is this hard work? Is it awkward (at best) or disconcerting? Yes and yes. To neglect the work of restoring a relationship that has suffered a fracture plants a seed of discontent in the project that can easily grow into a project-threatening cancer. Remember, "Pay me now or pay me later."

Making Considered Requests

Sometimes getting back on track is easy. For example, a problem may occur when your client immediately rejects your detailed and, from your perspective, well-thought-out proposal. Further discussion may reveal that you did not give them ample context. Your client can't understand your suggestion without sufficient background. Though

> **Stumbling Block to Stepping Stone**
>
> Whining does not produce action; requests do!

this problem may be considered small, the sooner it is recognized and addressed, the better. An attitude of "What I said was perfectly clear" (implying that the listener is somehow at fault, not you) is a setup for cascading breakdowns in the future.

If someone fails to meet your expectations, don't whine about it behind their back. A more productive action is to make a request that, if they grant it, will clear up your disappointment. You will be back on track. Whining does not produce action; requests do.

There is no future in arguing with your client about who is responsible for what percentage of the breakdown. This relates to the adage that couples who think marriage is a fifty-fifty proposition are doomed to divorce because marriage requires a total commitment from both parties. Any partnership that is working with reciprocity is most successful if *both parties* hold themselves *fully responsible* for what goes on and fully accountable for cleaning up breakdowns.

Three Cases—Identify

Here are some thoughts on identifying how to get back on track in the three cases discussed earlier in part 2.

Mustang

What had to be done to get my relationship with my son back on track was to apologize for snapping at him and discounting his input.

Had I been able to *recognize* and *address* my emotional clouds, I could have said to my son, "Really? Let's go see how bad it is." Then we would have discovered that four letters were loose. I could have returned the car to the shop the next day to get the job done right, provided I could have overcome my fears about the body shop conversation. The longer you wait to address the upset, the harder it is to deal with those fears. With each passing day, they take on a life of their own and negate any "good intentions" that may cross your mind.

In hindsight, what I learned was that embracing and exploring emotional clouds and breakdowns as soon as possible is what produces breakthroughs. Unfortunately, by the time I apologized, enough time had passed so that my son had forgotten the incident. This was a great disappointment and a lesson in humility.

Sus-Phrine

I required an injection with the correct dose of medication. It was clear to me that getting back on track required my doctor's support.

Sudafed

After the breakdown about the red versus white Sudafed pill occurred, I knew what had to be done to get back on track, namely to have a conversation with my physician about the incident. Since I wasn't willing to do that for several years and then he didn't remember the incident, I received another dose of humility. Upon reflection, one piece of advice I would pass on to others in similar situations is that procrastinating merely prolongs the agony. There is something to be said about learning to let go.

The Identify Checklist

1.   Do you make either an effective apology or a complete request when appropriate?
2.   Does each of you *identify* what you think has to be done to get back on track?

Brenda's Case—The Identify Checklist

1.   Do you make either an effective apology or a complete request when appropriate?

     I did not because I did not have any contact with Brenda after recognizing all the apologies I owed her.

2.   Does each of you *identify* what you think has to be done to get back on track?

     This did not happen since no further contact occurred.

What I have learned from these cases is to become aware of my mistakes sooner so that I can quickly and effectively apologize and hopefully get back on track.

Chapter 12 Activity

Role-Play

Identify a situation in your life comparable to the one Daniel faced with his necktie. Explain the situation to your partner, including your reasons for not accepting assistance. Create a five-minute videoed role-play with your partner in which they are playing the role of you not wanting assistance, and you are a close friend seeking to be of assistance in dealing with the issue.

Following your role-play exercise, explore the chapter 12 debriefing questions at the end of this chapter. Please consider these questions with your partner *after* having completed this activity, as you will learn more from the role-play experience this way.

Recap

When an interaction isn't going well, explore with your client what breakdowns have occurred. Stay in this conversation until you both agree on which breakdown to address first.

Make an effective apology when you have broken a promise. Acknowledge your mistake and address the inconvenience you caused your client. Work together to identify what has to be done to get back on track.

Frequently Asked Questions

1. How can I identify one breakdown when it seems to me that I'm in the midst of fifteen of them?

    When working with a client, ask for a break so that each of you can sort out the multiple breakdowns individually. After you write down each breakdown, prioritize them so that you and your client can identify the one to address first.

If your cloud is too thick for rational thought at this level, I suggest that you request a new meeting to sort out where to go from here. You might also ask yourself, "How did this happen? How did I let one or two breakdowns become fifteen?"

2. How can I *pinpoint* a breakdown when my boss operates on the basis of positional power rather than relational power? When he is operating hierarchically, I can't see a way to work with him collaboratively.

    This is a tough situation and won't be resolved quickly. To get started, request a meeting with your boss to discuss how both of you can work more collaboratively to recover from the various problems that occur in your relationship. If he agrees, this is a first step toward building a collaborative relationship with him. If he does not, keep listening for other opportunities to invite him into a more collaborative relationship with you. Keep in mind that you can still have a working relationship with him, even if he insists on it being hierarchical. What is required is that you are willing to be honest with him as you identify your aligned goals.

3. How can I *pinpoint* a breakdown that my client is upset about and that I can't even remember? It happened several months ago.

    This is what happened in the Sudafed case. Tell the truth about not remembering the incident, as my physician did. Then listen to your client's description of the situation until it becomes clear to you what is upsetting them. Do not succumb to the thought, *This cannot be a big deal. After all, it happened months ago.* Bad idea! It was a big enough deal for your client that they carried it around all these months. Try a response like, "Thanks for raising this matter. I can see that it has been bothering you.

Unfortunately, I don't remember it. Please fill me in on more details of the incident so that we will be able to clean it up."

4. How can I *identify* what is required to get back on track if my client won't speak to me?

Communicate with your client in as personal a way as possible (face-to-face, phone, email, a handwritten letter, etc.). Make sure you express your concern for the regrettable fracture in your relationship and that you are committed to working together to identify a way forward to restore communication. Then ask, "Is there anything I can do or say to get this conversation started?" If not, ask, "Do you see a way for the two of us to heal the fracture in our relationship?" If not, the relationship is dead as of now. If you wish to extend an olive branch, you may say, "If at some point in the future, you change your mind, please contact me. We can explore this matter further then."

Chapter 12 Debriefing Questions

Watch the video. What did you notice?

Review the video using the *pinpoint* and *identify* checklists. What did you learn? What did your partner learn?

CHAPTER 13

Do It!

By now, you have gone through the first four steps in the RAPID process. You have *recognized* a breakdown and the attending emotional cloud, *addressed* them both, *pinpointed* the specific difficulty, and *identified* how to get back on track. Now for the last step: *do it*.

After identifying what actions are essential for getting back on track, now is the time for action as you put the cleanup plan into operation. Don't just talk about it. Realize that this concentrated effort will take time, patience, and perseverance, especially if this is a repeater breakdown.

In the face of a breakdown, your shared goals may evaporate. The interpersonal action steps for achieving success (covered in part 1) also require the intrapersonal qualities of courage, generosity, and integrity. To generate high levels of these qualities, get back in touch with your initial commitment to the goals you share with this client, including your eagerness to progress toward them and your commitment to the relationship. When you think you have done your part to clean up the mistake, make sure your client agrees.

If you are reluctant to spend the time and effort required for this action step, consider the consequences of *not* recovering from this breakdown. Remember that problems like the present one will likely show up again. Practicing the RAPID recovery process at every opportunity will ensure less time spent recovering from future breakdowns. The choice is yours.

Barriers to Taking Action

Another aspect of taking action is staying in the conversation with your client (supervisor, subordinate, spouse, etc.) until the breakdown is resolved. This strategy is a challenge that requires you to manage your anxiety, anger, and impatience so that you can persevere until the recovery is complete.

Staying in the conversation requires looking at your vulnerability when you have been a party to a breakdown. You can ask for forgiveness for your part in creating the breakdown, *and* you cannot force your client to forgive you. This vulnerability is a consequence of creating problems (e.g., breaking promises). Keep in mind that we are all in the same boat as we seek to learn how to recover from the breakdowns that inevitably occur in our lives.

One more point: even if you have broken a promise, recognized, addressed, and pinpointed the breakdown, identified a recovery plan, and executed it, one step remains before recovery is complete: *you must forgive yourself.*

Three Cases—Do It

Mustang

It was clear to me shortly after recognizing my mistakes that to restore my relationship with my son, I had to apologize to him for both snapping at him and discounting his input. Unfortunately, I repeated my Brenda behavior and did neither one at the time. By the time an apology was offered, he had forgotten the incident. This outcome was much like the one with my doctor in the Sudafed episode. These experiences have resulted in more timely apologies and reduced the prolonged agony of fuming over an unpleasant breakdown.

Sus-Phrine

When called, my doctor arrived in twenty minutes. I received the correct dose, and he had an intense conversation with the floor nurses. The nurses worked closely with me on every medication I received during the remainder of that hospital stay. The medical system is so hierarchical that the only way I could see to resolve the problem was to seek assistance from someone who had more power in the system than the nurse.

Had this incident happened ten years earlier, I might not have said anything to the nurse since I was generally intimidated by all medical personnel. The attitudes that support intimidation complicate recognizing breakdowns. When there is a difference in status, knowledge, or authority, it is difficult for the lower-status person to say, "I think you are making a mistake." However, in this case, when my survival was at stake, pointing out her mistake was much easier than I had expected.

What I have learned is that one can be intimidated and still point out an error to the benefit of all concerned. This case was a reminder that staying present and aware of your circumstances at all times may save your life. Developing the courage to deal effectively with situations like this is an essential part of life's journey.

Sudafed

When I had the conversation with my doctor and discovered that he was asking the "red versus white pill" question to make sure that he was clear what dosage I was taking, I felt foolish about harboring a grudge and not trusting his judgment for years. Being reassured that his intentions were professional and appropriate did clear the air between us. From then on, my interactions with him became more relaxed and effective. In addition, he decided to make a change in his practice by telling his patients his strategy while treating them rather than risk such misunderstandings in the future.

Dealing with Hierarchical Relationships

We learn in childhood that relationships with medical personnel are hierarchical. Indeed, it is critical for children to obey their caregivers in *almost* all cases. Yet, as an adult, we must learn to take responsibility for our own health to interact effectively with medical professionals.

Tension arises when we have made this shift and then encounter a medical professional who has not. My interaction with the Sus-Phrine nurse was my first realization that I had grown into a different relationship with at least one medical practitioner. This experience opened up the possibility of developing cooperative relationships with authorities and thus changed how I interact with them.

There is a parallel process in education. In preschool, you carry virtually no responsibility for your education. Some parents and teachers see themselves as hierarchically responsible for their children and students throughout their school years. There can be tension between these parents or teachers and their mature students who are learning to be responsible for their own education.

In medicine, education, and even at home, many of us learn that someone who asks one too many questions, by the unstated standards of some authority, immediately is labeled a "difficult" person. In the workplace, there is a comparable tension between managers and subordinates. An attitude of superiority in each of these venues jeopardizes the quality of the results produced.

All three cases are examples of one of life's more difficult conversations: *speaking truth to power.* The Sudafed cloud was more intense than the Sus-Phrine cloud and overwhelmed me, possibly because he was an MD and she was an RN.

> **Stepping Stone**
>
> With twenty-twenty hindsight, my goal now in hierarchical relationships is to stay in the conversation and say, "I am having trouble with your question. Please help me understand what you are saying." The Sudafed case shows that withdrawal from confrontation is another early warning sign of an impending breakdown.

Examination of a New Situation—Jason's Case

I was working on a project with a colleague whom I will call Jason. We had met several times before, and each time I was late. One day, out of the blue (or so it seemed to me), he exploded when I was late yet again, launching into a scathing critique of my habitually rude behavior. Clearly, he was mightily offended.

As Jason began his scathing critique, a dark emotional cloud descended upon me, and voices were saying, "This criticism isn't fair! Why did I not receive a warning about this?" I ignored my cloud. Rather, I was silently defending myself and blaming it on him.

At that moment, our relationship was on such precarious ground that voicing my defense would indubitably have led to an escalating argument that could have produced a fatal fracture in our relationship. Somehow, and perhaps it was just shock, I was able to stand there and listen to what he had to say, which, as it turned out, was the best choice I could have made.

Early Warning Signs

Eventually I recognized my emotional cloud. The key to this was realizing that my lateness had become such a regular part of my work style that I assumed people would forgive me automatically. Assumptions rapidly become rules that defy examination thereafter. We make them up to help us get through the myriad of decisions we encounter each day. Rules can be helpful or hurtful and therefore require periodic inspection to determine their value.

Jason's intense reaction to my lateness was a sign that trouble had been brewing for some time from his perspective. Though he had not said anything to me prior to the day he blew up, my assumption that lateness was not an issue had not yet been challenged.

Being in the presence of anger is never pleasant, and to be the target of such fury was most distressing. This confrontation was enough to shock me into addressing my emotional cloud and stop blaming him. Since then, my intention is to scrutinize my interpersonal skills periodically to determine any rules that need to be questioned and addressed before another landmine explodes in my face.

Upon reflection, I realized that in the future I could support RAPID recovery from breakdowns by becoming more other-centered and address my emotional clouds as soon as I recognized them. My goal is to catch potential problems when they are small and make an effective apology.

Listen

Jason's case provided a second lesson about how to support RAPID recovery from breakdowns: when someone gathers a dump truck full of grievances about you, backs up his truck in front of you, and starts to unload, prudence demands you move. Step aside and wait until the truck is unloaded. Listen carefully. Perhaps take notes while the complaints are being deposited so that you can respond to each of them judiciously when the time comes.

As it happened, I was also working with him in a weekly meeting chaired by his boss. I was always early for those meetings. Clearly, Jason noticed the difference between my willingness to be on time for his boss. He clearly pinpointed the issue from his perspective. "You are always on time for meetings with my boss and never on time for meetings with me." He could see no reason to continue working with someone who would treat him so shabbily. I was mortified that he thought so poorly of me and intimidated by how strongly he expressed it

Again, because of being in shock, I learned another lesson about RAPID recovery from breakdowns: do not argue with your client about what they see as a breakdown, dismissing their angst as an inconsequential matter. Never try to deal with a breakdown by dismissing the event.

Fortunately, I addressed my emotional cloud by agreeing that my behavior was a problem. Remember that you and your client will likely have different interpretations of the significance of a breakdown based on your individual criteria used to assess the situation. Still, humility will move you toward reconciliation faster than defending your criteria.

Now was the time to identify how to clean up this series of breakdowns and salvage our working relationship. I could not dictate what the solution would be, but I could make a proposal that Jason could accept or reject. Happily, he accepted the proposal for me to be on time for all our meetings for the remainder of the project. Having accomplished this, we finished that project and, in the process, restored our working relationship for the future.

I'm sad to say that I continue to struggle with punctuality. My habitual lateness was too entrenched to be turned around by one interaction, even a heated one like this. However, from this interaction, I did develop an increased awareness of the potential damage that chronic tardiness can bring to a relationship. Being on time is a goal that I continue to pursue.

Working with Your Partner

Broken Promises

My recovery from the breakdown with Jason would have been smoother and less painful had I known about and used the RAPID process. The best way you can support RAPID recovery from breakdowns is to work on the recovery process with your partner. Together you can review strategies for dealing with breakdowns effectively. Key features include acknowledging that you have broken a promise and inconvenienced the other person.

Practice with your partner by addressing the inconvenience, clarifying the losses, and then exploring how you can clean these up. Work together until you are clear you can have these three conversations effectively and with integrity.

As soon as you become aware of causing or participating in a breakdown, call your client and apologize for your part, even if they may not have noticed. If you assume that your client has not noticed or has decided to say nothing, you have chosen a high-risk strategy that could blow up at any time in the future.

Often the gift of forgiveness from your client is the only way of fully recovering from a breakdown. Be willing to request forgiveness for your actions. Do not demand it. Do not expect it. Keep listening for opportunities to receive the gift. If you stop listening, you are writing off this client.

Staying Present

Early detection of emotional clouds is one of the most powerful tools for learning to rapidly recover from a breakdown. Working together with your partner, help each other discover your respective early warning signs. Another way in which you and your partner can support each other is by watching for repeater breakdowns. There can be a large return from identifying these and then learning how to rapidly recover from them in the future. Ideally, with time and practice, these repeaters can become more occasional and may disappear eventually.

Most everyone has a visceral reaction to breakdowns, such as embarrassment, anger, or defensiveness. Almost immediately, a counterreaction to the breakdown is triggered, such as laughter, put-downs, or finding fault. Being aware of this automatic process is critical so that you can choose to halt your participation immediately. Otherwise, the initial situation will suddenly become ugly, threatening to crush the relationship.

Being conscious at this level requires a high degree of awareness and commitment to staying in the present conversation. First of all, you never know the whole story (as in the Sudafed example). Second, both parties involved in a breakdown had an opportunity at some point to take a step that would avoid the problem altogether. Often being proactive isn't a part of either person's job description.

For example, Jason could have said the first time I was late, "It doesn't work for me when you are late for our meeting." I do not think it was his job to say this nor that my being late was acceptable. However, we could have avoided the substantial blowup that eventually occurred had he said something the first time or even the second or third.

In order to sustain RAPID recovery from breakdowns, speak up the first time you are aware that your client or consultant has done or said something you will get upset about if repeated.

The Do It Checklist

1. Review why recovery from this breakdown is important for you.
2. Implement the recovery plan you have created with your client.
3. Verify that this plan has addressed all the fallout from the current breakdown. If not, address the remaining upsets.

Chapter 13 Activity 1

Following your role-play exercise, explore the chapter 13 debriefing questions, set 1, at the end of this chapter. Please look at these questions with your partner *after* having completed this activity, as you will learn more from the role-play experience this way.

> **Role-Play**
>
> Identify a colleague with whom you are in a situation like the Doug-Jason one. Brief your role-play partner on the situation. Select one in which you are in the Doug role, with your partner playing the Jason role. Video a five-minute role-play that starts with "Jason" berating you for continually treating him with disrespect.

Jason's Case—The Do It Checklist

1. Review why recovery from the breakdown is important for you.

    I wanted to complete the project that Jason and I had begun. In addition, I wanted us to heal the fracture in our relationship to preserve the opportunity of working together in the future.

2. Implement the recovery plan you have created with your client.

    I was very careful to be on time to all our future meetings.

3. Verify that this plan has addressed all the fallout from the current breakdown. If not, address the remaining upsets.

    I think that it did. We completed our project. However, he did not call on me again.

> **Recap**
>
> Review why recovery from a particular breakdown is important to you.
>
> Implement the recovery plan. Verify that the results of the plan have satisfied each of you.
>
> I invite you to consider your next breakdown as an opportunity; use the RAPID process and see what gold you can mine.

Frequently Asked Questions

1. I have a client who treats me like a doormat. Every time something goes wrong, he looks to me to get things back on track because he thinks I caused the problem. How can I find the generosity to handle this repeater breakdown one more time?

    > How committed are you to working with this client? Does each project forward your career goals? If you see the value in continuing to work with this client, I suggest you arrange a one-on-one meeting for the sole purpose of sorting out mistakes by looking at how they happened rather than trying to assess who is at fault. The fault-and-blame conversation will only aggravate the situation and further compromise the quality of your relationship.

    > If your client is willing to shift his point of view on how to resolve mistakes, the conversation can focus on the cause of the breakdown. There were actions that each of you could have taken that would have avoided the problem. Recognizing these missed opportunities makes it possible to shift the conversation to "Who is willing to do what to keep this problem from recurring?"

2. How would you deal with being late to Chuck's party when you had explicitly promised to be on time (chapter 9, RAPID Scenario 1)?

    > Call home immediately and talk with Chuck. Tell him what has happened, without excuses. Ask what you can do to address this situation. Then listen. Be sure not to get upset if he is upset. Just listen. Hopefully, develop a plan together to address the situation if he is willing and able to do so now. Implement the plan.

    > If Chuck is too deep in his emotional cloud to consider resolving anything, spend some one-on-one time with him as soon as

possible after you get home each day in the next week to give him an opportunity to *recognize* and *address* his emotional cloud. Stay in the conversation until both of you have completely recovered from the breakdown.

3. I did not respond to my client's use of inappropriate language in our first three meetings. Is it too late to change this?

It's never too late, but establishing this boundary may take more patience and tenacity at this stage. The next time this occurs, acknowledge that you find this language offensive and have made a mistake by not raising your concern earlier. Request that this type of language no longer be used. If your request is denied or dismissed, you are now facing a boundary issue: do you honor your boundary or make an exception and compromise? Remember that the longer you wait to set a boundary, the more difficult setting one becomes in the future. Always consider the consequences of your choice before implementing it.

4. I get angry because a colleague is constantly teasing me about being the youngest member of the team. What can I do?

Arrange an off-line conversation whose only agenda item is to discuss this issue and how it can be resolved to the benefit of your relationship.

5. How can one deal with sexual harassment of a female consultant by one of her male clients? What is an appropriate strategy for dealing with this situation?

Sexual harassment is a difficult topic to address. Having said that, here are my thoughts.

Be aware that most organizations have specific policies for reporting sexual harassment. If you are working for such an organization, study its policies carefully. Do this now if you haven't already. Clarify any policy that is unclear to you. Be aware that most organizations have specific policies about reporting sexual harassment.

The policies of many organizations require you to immediately report the *first* comment or action that you regard as sexual harassment. You will have to decide what words or actions meet your criteria. If an incident meets your definition for harassment, be clear, be specific, and begin with a light touch. Preparation is essential to delineate your boundaries for unacceptable interactions before you are called on to declare them unacceptable. Examples:

> When you touch (or crowd or push) me, I feel uncomfortable. My request is that we keep our distance so that our working together remains professional.

> When you (*describe the offense*), I feel (*describe your reaction*). Ours is a professional relationship, and this cannot happen again.

If the person repeats another similar comment or action, terminate the meeting. Not acting upon the second incident will only make future episodes more difficult. Engaging in a debate over appropriateness will not be productive.

If you have a private practice, it might be easier to create your own policy than use something you did not create and may not understand. Then check out your policy with your attorney. If you have not done this already, do it before you see another client. Identify your own standards. Determine whether the first inappropriate joke or extended handshake meets your criteria for sexual harassment. If it does, be clear, be specific, and begin with a light touch.

Be advised that no policy can cover all the situations you will face. Prepare yourself to think on your feet about the surprises that will appear. Only you can determine your boundaries. Being thus prepared requires forethought before each interaction.

A preparation that I have found useful is to enter each interaction with a commitment to deal with whatever happens. In reality, what occurs in an interaction is often something I did not and could not have anticipated, because I cannot control what my client will do, nor am I a mind reader. If I enter a conversation with the attitude of only dealing with items that I have anticipated, I will have created a barrier to coping with the uncertainty of being out of control. Uncertainty may be the only thing we can count on. So being out of control is our natural state whether we like it or not, and learning to establish boundaries is life affirming.

Sexual overtones are not the only form of harassment that people face. Power issues are also disturbing. A frequent one is when a superior tells a subordinate to "smile." Though this is delivered as a request or faintly disguised "joke," it often is a direct order to please or appease the superior. Power harassment and sexual harassment can be delivered and received by either gender.

Sexual harassment and power issues are significant and complex. They can be managed when you are clear about your boundaries and are willing to speak your truth to anyone who crosses your line. Identify a trusted resource with whom you can discuss additional questions.

Chapter 13 Activity 2

Following your role-play exercise, refer to the chapter 13 debriefing questions, set 2, at the end of this chapter. Please look at these questions with your partner *after* having completed this activity, as you will learn more from the role-play experience this way.

Role-Play

Practice is critical for developing the ability to deal with the challenges that are present in sexual harassment situations. Create a role-play with your partner based on one of the situations below (in FAQ 6) or a situation you have encountered. Video the role-play.

6. What are examples of sexual harassment?

Hypothetical examples of sexually harassing behavior include (but are not limited to) the following:

- threatening or implying that employment may be negatively affected by rejecting a sexual advance or refusing to tolerate aggressive behavior (e.g., a supervisor suggesting to an employee that she will lose her job if she ignores his advances)
- offering or implying employment-related rewards (hiring, promotion, pay raise, etc.) in exchange for submission to sexual advances or conduct
- nonverbal sexual conduct: staring at someone's sexual body parts (buttocks, breasts, or groin), performing obscene gestures, touching oneself sexually in front of others, or making sexual sounds (such as whistling, catcalls, etc.)
- uninvited, nonconsensual sexual touching (such as patting, pinching, stroking, tickling, kissing, hugging, or brushing against someone in a sexual manner)
- continuing unwelcome sexual advances (such as flirting, requests for dates, or requests for sexual activity)
- making sexual comments about appearance, clothing, or body parts
- intrusive sexually explicit questions, teasing, or innuendos
- gender-based animosity (treating men less favorably than women or women less favorably than men)
- circulating sexual emails, texts, Instagrams, jokes, videos, letters, notes, pictures, or websites

Chapter 13 Debriefing Questions, Activity 1

Watch the video. What did you notice?

Did you *recognize* and *address* your emotional cloud and assist Jason to *recognize* and *address* his?

Did you *pinpoint* the breakdown and *identify* a way to resolve it?

Did you review why recovery from this breakdown was important for you?

What steps are required to implement the recovery plan you have created with your client?

Did you verify that the completed plan has addressed all the fallout from the breakdown that occurred? If not, address the remaining upsets.

Chapter 13 Debriefing Questions, Activity 2

Watch the video. What did you notice?

Were you clear?

Were you specific?

Did you begin with a light touch?

PART III

Exploring the LEARN Process

The POWER and RAPID processes position us to communicate with and respond to our clients more effectively. Maintaining a proactive and reasoned approach to our interactions certainly enhances our success as consultants and collaborators. There is one more step that merits careful consideration. The LEARN process is a data-based strategy for systematically improving our communications with colleagues, clients, and others.

There are five steps in the LEARN process:

Listen to your interactions.

Evaluate one of your interactions.

Act out a role-play of this interaction.

Review the video of the role-play.

Next?

Chapter 14 Setting the Stage

CHAPTER 14

Setting the Stage

L EARN develops your ability to deal with a particularly troublesome breakdown by working with it in a videoed role-play. This is a laboratory in which you can safely experiment with specific alternative methods to address gnarly interactions. Practice with your trusted partner to learn how to analyze video data to identify actions and attitude shifts that will improve your meetings.

Table 11 summarizes the LEARN process.

Table 11. The LEARN process

Step	Essential Activities
Listen	*Listen* to your interactions. Identify an interaction to improve.
Evaluate	*Evaluate* this interaction. Identify a segment of it you want to improve. Consider three alternative actions you would like to try instead of what you did. Pick one to investigate further.
Act	*Act* out a role-play of this interaction, using the alternative you have chosen.
Review	*Review* the video of the role-play. What worked? What did not? How did this happen? What did you learn? What will you do differently in the future?
Next?	Redo the role-play if you doubt that you can use what you learned. Implement what you learned in an actual consultation. Organize a different role-play relating to another issue. Look at larger questions relating to your career.

Squash Story

Playing squash has been one of my favorite activities. I played for years before hiring a coach. When I began coaching students on how to improve their consulting skills, I wanted to experience the challenge of being coached on an activity that I had done passably well for most of my life. My hope was to experience what my students were going through by using video in an area where improvement was the goal. In addition, I hoped that my experience would give me insights into the resistance that many people encounter when videoing their role-play of a professional interaction and then being coached.

My coach challenged my defective habits and the unproductive "rules" I had made up over the years. He started by going back to ground zero: "How do you hold the racket?"

Two thoughts struck me simultaneously:

Why am I paying for this? I have played for years.

Yes, and I want to play better. So listen to the coach!

Next, we worked on basic squash shots. We practiced game situations. Finally, we began to play games. He identified the weaknesses he saw in my strategy, concentration, and shot-making skills. He also used video to reveal additional aspects of my game to improve. His input helped me to improve my shots (physical) and my strategy (mental). I had not been able to achieve either of these improvements by myself.

Working with a coach is vital to systematically improving your practice. Using video in your work together is also essential. Always remember that a coach will be able to see flaws that you can't.

Building a Foundation for Improvement

The process of self-improvement is so challenging that you must begin with a solid foundation that includes your mega-vision, your mission, and your core values.

Your *mega-vision* is described by your answers to these questions:

- What are the characteristics of the world in which you want your grandchildren to grow up?
- What are the characteristics of the world in which you want to grow old?

Your *mission* is described by your answer to this question:

- What role do you intend to play in creating your ideal world?

Your *core values* are described by your answer to this question:

- What standards will guide you as you confront choices while creating your ideal world?

Not everyone has the same mega-vision. In our world today, individuals and groups have diametrically opposed mega-visions. The beauty of knowing and articulating yours is that you will then have a solid basis for identifying individuals with whom you can potentially create working and synergistic relationships.

For me, it was fifteen years before several events occurred that led me to articulate my mega-vision as *peace on earth*.

Then I began to think about my *mission*. Some time passed before it clarified: *transform relationships from stumbling blocks to stepping stones in people's lives*. This mission grew out of my passion to transform statistical education and practice. Then I began to identify partners who were aligned with these goals. Working with these colleagues (and an ever-widening circle of new ones) toward my mega-vision and mission continues to be my life work.

At this time, my core values also clarified: treat everyone with respect by their standards, be authentic, be available, and learn from every breakdown.

To learn more about mega-visions, see Kaufman and Zahn (1993).

Sources of Motivation

What is the source of your motivation to improve?

During my career at Florida State University, I often taught introductory statistics courses, many containing 250 students. These courses were required and almost universally dreaded by both teachers and students. The conventional wisdom held by both parties was that the teacher was responsible for motivating students to work hard so that every student passed. Early on, I discovered to my surprise and dismay that I was unable to motivate students; I could not compel them to be engaged in the course.

As time passed, I created assignments at the beginning of each course to help students see a link between their career goals and what was available in this course. Then they prepared for classes, participated in classes, did their homework, and even came to see me to ask additional questions. In short, they began to exhibit what is called "motivated behavior." How engaged they were depended on how far they moved themselves up the Senge-Watkins Levels of Commitment ladder (chapter 4, table 4). Internal motivation generated by the students moved them further up the ladder than any external motivation I could provide.

To access your motivation for improving your professional practice, start with identifying your mega-vision. Then describe your mission: what role do you intend to play in creating your mega-vision? Also included in mission is discerning your passion: what will be your life work? Remember that both mega-vision and mission rest on your core values that guide every step of your life journey.

With this foundation, you are ready and willing to risk videoing and evaluating your interactions—first with your partner, later with your clients. Throughout this process, you become more aware of gaps between what you do and what you *want* to do.

As you work through part 3, you will discover that working on interactions that are meaningful to you will provide the most valuable long-term results. Students who took my course as a prerequisite for their major were faced with choosing how they would respond to this requirement. Those who believed they were forced to do so often resisted the opportunity to learn, while those who thought of the course as one they had chosen in preparation for their future career learned tools to succeed in that career. It was easy to distinguish committed students from apathetic or resistant students, as one would expect from the Senge-Watkins scale.

Passion

Some people have trouble identifying their passions. If you are one of us who grew up believing that it was safer to avoid caring intensely about anything, you will have a hard time identifying any passions. I remember thinking that I did not have any passions, especially relative to my work. After many conversations with friends and professionals, I began to realize that there were some aspects of my work that did disturb me enough to risk changing them, which may well be the criterion for taking action with passion.

For example, I was disturbed by the number of students who diligently did every assignment yet failed my courses. I was unwilling to adopt the conventional wisdom that these were poor students. Likewise, I would not accept the two points of view that "Nothing can be done about them" and "You have more productive uses of your time if you hope to earn tenure." Rejecting these shared points of view raised a challenging question: what *can* I do?

The more I thought about how to work with conscientious students who nevertheless were failing, the more passionate I became about finding a way to help them succeed. This became the driving passion in my career. Additional clarifications continue to occur. Progress from apathy to commitment is a lifelong journey that has ups and downs, not unlike driving on a muddy road in a downpour.

I encourage you to search gently yet persistently for an aspect of your work you want to change, one that disturbs you, does not go well, and one you care enough about to invest time and energy in learning how to change. Invite your partner to search for a similar change to make that could make life more rewarding. Work together to apply the LEARN process to these passions.

Change

Another challenge now arises: are you willing to address the troublesome interaction you have uncovered by practicing an alternative approach and videoing your practice sessions? Though change is uncomfortable, if you don't change, you will continue to encounter the same gnarly interaction over and over. The choice is yours.

To illustrate how to go about effecting change, consider the frustration I mentioned above: the number of diligent students who failed my courses. The first step was to shift my attitudes from blaming their failures on them and labeling them "bad students." These attitudes were a barrier to any progress. Part of what made this barrier a challenge to give up was that many colleagues agreed with it.

The next step was to look at how I was teaching my courses and ask the hard question, "How are my practices contributing to their failures?" This question brought me face-to-face with my pride and my conviction that my teaching paradigm was unassailable. Yet the students continued to fail. Eventually my commitment to having my students learn the power of statistics meant I had to make fundamental changes in my teaching pedagogy.

Happily, an opportunity arose in which I could reach beyond my comfort zone and work with a professor in the College of Education. He expanded my awareness of the components of effective education practices available to me. In two years, the number of students failing my courses dropped substantially, without a lowering of standards. The practices I implemented were precursors of the POWER process.

You can use the LEARN process to analyze video data to transform breakdowns and create breakthroughs in your life. Your part is to take the risk and look in the mirror using video. My part is to provide tools to guide you through the process.

Improving Interactions

There are three principles at the core of improving interactions:

- All interactions are done in systems of interconnected processes.
- There can be a breakdown in any one of these processes.
- The keys to success are RAPID recovery and a systematic application of the LEARN process to each breakdown.

Systems and Processes

A system is defined as a group of interconnected processes. A process is a sequence of activities to achieve a result.

For example, one system involved in achieving a face-to-face interaction is transportation. You and your client may use different processes to travel to your meeting place. Perhaps you live in the suburbs, drive to the train station, park, ride the train downtown, and walk to your office, while your client lives in the heart of the city, takes a bus, and then walks to your office.

Another system is preparation. This includes doing whatever is required for each of you to be as ready as possible for all aspects of your meeting, including the physical and emotional challenges that may arise.

Having useful data on your interactions is at the heart of improving them. Often, the only data we have about an interaction are memories, as was the case in my Mustang experience. Much can be learned from memory data, especially when discussed with a partner. The sooner this conversation occurs after the event, the better.

> **Stepping Stone**
>
> The palest ink is better than the best memory.

Of course, memory has its limitations. We all remember events selectively and often differently than other parties in the interaction. Siblings reminiscing about the events of their shared childhood graphically demonstrate this phenomenon. In addition, whatever we miss during the interaction will be lost to us thereafter.

Better than memory is writing. There is a Chinese saying, "The palest ink is better than the best memory." The sooner you write down your observations about an interaction, the better.

Video is far better than the darkest ink and now is readily accessible. Video provides a way to produce high-quality data on your interaction that can expand and support your improvement efforts. Of course, this works only when you *look* at the video using the POWER process as a guide!

The utility of video was anticipated more than 230 years ago by Scottish poet Robert Burns (1786) in his poem: "To a Louse: On Seeing One on a Lady's Bonnet at Church." Here is the last stanza in modern English:

> O would some Power with vision teach us
> To see ourselves as *others* see us!
> It would from many a blunder free us,
> And foolish notions:
> What airs in dress and carriage would leave us,
> And even devotion!

What Burns did not anticipate is how strenuously we would resist freeing ourselves from blunders, even when the power of video gives us the gift to see ourselves as others see us!

Looking at yourself on a video is uncomfortable, even for professional actors. A first step toward managing this discomfort is to watch the video with your partner. This process will help you improve your interactions to make the contributions you want to make in your life. What caught my attention years ago was the comment from one of my coaches, "You know, don't you, that your client already knows what you see on the video. This is news only to you!" Do you want to know what everyone else already knows?

Though I'm still uncomfortable with the process, the lessons learned over the years from watching my videos keep me coming back to learn more. The good news is that the discomfort has decreased.

Pre-Video Questions

Here are three questions to address before you begin using video:

- **Are you willing to be videoed in an interaction?** This isn't a trivial question. I resisted video for three years even though the recommendation came from a trusted mentor. For me, pride and the fear of looking foolish on video were formidable barriers to be addressed first.
- **Do you have an appropriate venue and equipment?** A reasonably silent room that's well-lit and a smartphone can now produce high-definition video with excellent audio. Test your phone in the room before doing an actual video of an interaction to verify that you are producing excellent video *and* audio.
- **Is your partner or client willing to be videoed?** Beginning your video work in role-plays with your partner continues to be my preferred starting place. Later you may find that a videoed interaction with a willing client is more valuable. Hopefully this will be a client with whom you have at least a working relationship.

I learned a valuable lesson about client reactions to video when we introduced video-based coaching as a part of our training program. My colleagues and I feared that clients would strenuously resist being videoed and not sign our consent form. A few did. However, the large majority expressed their support with, "Wow! You're using video to help statisticians learn how to consult better? Where do I sign?"

The Learning Ladder

The learning ladder shows the challenges you will encounter as you begin to use video. We all start on the bottom step labeled "unconsciously incompetent" relative to a particular weakness in our professional practice. You are incompetent in a particular area *and* not yet aware of any need to improve current practices.

Figure 3. The learning ladder

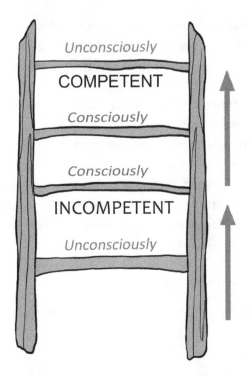

Watching the video, you become *consciously incompetent,* as you now can see your ineptitude. This is a daunting step on the learning ladder. It is embarrassing to see your inadequacies, especially if you are working with other people as you watch the video.

Courage, once again, is an essential part of moving forward. You may prefer to include only your partner when reviewing the video the first time. Stay focused on your commitment to improve your interactions to manage your embarrassment. You may soon notice that a strong commitment to improving your practice will generate the courage to use video.

As you consciously practice what is required to improve an aspect of your service, you will reach the *consciously competent* step. Working competently, you still have to focus your full attention on executing each step in the POWER process. This sense of competency is what a child discovers when first learning to balance while riding a bicycle. Balancing requires all of the child's attention.

With further practice, you can become *unconsciously competent.* Here you are focusing on creating value as you consult. No longer are you required to concentrate on each step in the POWER process as it unfolds.

Unconscious competence can be seen in easily riding a bicycle after learning to balance *and* continuing to practice. At this stage of competence, avoiding hazards and simultaneously enjoying the scenery become possible. However, even with unconscious competence in terms of balance, it is still critical to remain alert to your surroundings on the road, since surprises are always possible! The same goes for your consulting skills. You still must stay present as you attend to both the technical and relational challenges facing you.

Figure 4. The learning zones

The Learning Zones

Figure 4 illustrates another way of viewing the learning process. Typically, you live in a *comfort zone,* satisfied with your current level of competence. If you want to improve, the only way to move from the *comfort zone* to the *learning zone* is to first enter the *discomfort zone* where you become aware of those activities that you want to change. This zone will test your commitment to improvement. And, as you already know, courage will be required to move ahead. The discomfort zone and experiences associated with it are similar to those found on the learning ladder when moving from unconsciously incompetent to consciously incompetent.

Checklist for Setting the Stage

1. What are your attitudes about breakdowns, fault, blame, and the use of video?
2. When do you get defensive? Under what circumstances?
3. Have you ever worked with a coach to improve your performance? How did that go for you?
4. What are your mega-vision, mission, and core values?
5. What is a repeater breakdown that disturbs you?
6. Are you willing to be videoed? Is your partner? Is your client?
7. What is an example of an activity where you are consciously incompetent?

Brenda's Case—Checklist for Setting the Stage

1. What are your attitudes about breakdowns, fault, blame, and the use of video?

> Initially I was unaware of my attitudes about breakdowns, fault, and blame. Truly, I was unconsciously incompetent in these areas before the video was analyzed. Then I moved rapidly into both the discomfort zone and being consciously incompetent. I realized that I believed breakdowns were an indicator of failure.

The sooner I found someone else to blame, the sooner I would be off the hook.

2. When do you get defensive?

I got defensive when Brenda revealed that she had changed her request from one that I had prepared for to one that was a surprise.

3. Have you ever worked with a coach to improve your performance? How did that go for you?

I did work with a coach using the Brenda video. A long and painful process ensued as I became aware of my beliefs and attitudes that were at odds with the type of consultant I wanted to be. Eventually this process produced a transformation in my professional practice:

I shifted from seeing my attitudes as truth to seeing them as a reflection of my judgments.

4. What are your mega-vision, mission, and core values?

My mega-vision is "peace on earth." My mission is to transform relationships from stumbling blocks to stepping stones in people's lives. My core values include treating everyone as I want to be treated, being authentic, being available, and learning how to ever more rapidly recover from breakdowns. None of this was even considered, let alone verbalized, prior to the Brenda case.

5. What is a repeater breakdown that disturbs you?

I finally saw that my repeater breakdown in the Brenda case was my judgments about her that I regarded as truth. I still struggle with this breakdown while learning to recover more rapidly in the moment.

6. Are you willing to be videoed? Is your partner? Is your client?

    Yes. Yes. Some are, and some are not.

7. What is an example of an activity where you are consciously incompetent?

    Working with anyone I perceive as an authority whose attitudes are initially opposed to mine. I still have difficulty staying in the conversation with such a person and speaking my truth to power. Incidentally, staying in the conversation does not guarantee that agreement will result, only that you sought to find common ground. Not everyone has this goal. Make sure you do.

Chapter 14 Activity

Role-Play

Identify an interaction where you are consciously incompetent. Develop a role-play with your partner in which you will encounter this situation. Video a five-minute role-play of this interaction.

Following your role-play exercise, refer to the chapter 14 debriefing questions at the end of this chapter. Please explore these questions with your partner *after* having completed this activity, as you will learn more from the role-play experience this way.

Recap

Review your mega-vision, mission, and core values. Identify what motivates you enough to adjust your style of interacting so that you can overcome your barriers to change. Specify how you want to transform your practice.

Frequently Asked Questions

1. How do I get through the discomfort of climbing the learning ladder and leaving my comfort zone?

    You've heard this before, and this time won't be the last: find a partner who is willing to journey with you as you move toward improving your practice. This journey is too difficult to travel alone. In addition, reviewing your mega-vision will benefit the process by reminding you of what you are more committed to than being comfortable.

2. Why should I move into the discomfort zone?

    That move is the only way I know to get to the learning zone. For me, learning something always involves trying something new, which always involves some level of discomfort. Uncertainty, which is one of the consequences of trying something new, can be experienced as excitement rather than dread.

    Consider roller coasters. Some people are so uncomfortable with them that they refuse to ride. Others are willing to pay to experience the excitement of the ride. Since change is always a challenge, it is inherently uncomfortable. If one of your core values is to continue to learn, discomfort will be a side effect worth addressing.

3. How do I interact with my working partner as I seek to change?

    Be patient and compassionate with each other, since seeking to change increases the chances for mistakes. Mistakes, in turn, increase the incidence of upset, anxiety, and anger. Realize that emotional clouds will accompany you on this journey. When change is slow and times are tough, gently remind each other why you are seeking a particular change. Reassure each other that you are still willing to support each other.

Chapter 14 Debriefing Questions

What are your vision, mission, and core values? How are they reflected in your role-play? Which are you practicing? Which are you not practicing?

What improvements are you most passionate about making? What steps are you taking toward making some of these improvements? What are the barriers to progressing on to the others? How are these steps and barriers reflected in your role-play?

CHAPTER 15

The Listen Triad

This chapter will explore and explain the first three parts of the LEARN process, *listen*, *evaluate*, and *act*. The next chapter, Review to Learn, brings all three concepts together in a comprehensive way. The final chapter looks at the question, What's next?

Listening is a first step toward improvement. It requires intention and attention, not technology. You can do it anytime, anywhere. A key part of your listening is to become aware of the distinctions between your effective and ineffective interactions so that you can identify those that you want to keep and those you want to change using the LEARN process.

Refine Your Listening Skills

You can systematically improve your ability to stay focused on what you say, what your client says, and how your client interprets what you say. Listening from these three perspectives is essential to upgrading your interactions.

To get started, examine your calendar for the next week. Pick one interaction a day that you think might be challenging. Reserve fifteen minutes after each of these daily interactions for reflection.

In your reflection times, answer these five questions to improve your listening skills:

1. Did you clearly and completely identify what you thought your client wanted in the beginning of the consultation? Did this match what they wanted? How do you know?
2. Did you clearly articulate what you were willing and able to do in a way that was consistent with your existing commitments to your standards, boundaries, and well-being?
3. What did you do that you want to keep doing? What did you do that you want to stop doing?
4. What did you neglect that you want to attend to? What did you disregard that you want to continue to ignore?
5. Did the interaction end with a workable plan?

After a week of scrutinizing one interaction per day, review your answers and respond to the following questions:

•   What distinctions did you identify between effective and ineffective interactions?
•   Did your observations become more complete as the week went by?
•   Are there some types of interactions that are consistently ineffective for you?

During this week, have you picked an interaction to improve? If not, continue this exercise until you have selected one. Your difficult interactions are building blocks for creating role-plays that are meaningful to you.

Improve Your Observational Skills

To check the accuracy and completeness of your observations, talk with one of the individuals you met with this week, preferably on the day you met. Compare your observations to your client's memory of the interaction:

- What did you observe that your client did not?
- What did your client observe that you did not?

Often, blind spots occur when one is in an emotional cloud. This is another reason it is important to learn to recognize emotional clouds.

The gold standard for improving your observational powers is a video of an interaction. You may find it most informative to write your answers to the listening skills questions above before watching the video. Always watch the video with your partner, as well as your client when possible. Treat each other with compassion while watching the video. You will start to become aware of what you were previously unaware. This growth in awareness is uncomfortable. The discomfort, however, is good news: it indicates that you are moving toward the learning zone.

Barriers to Improvement

Barriers to Using Video

When using video to improve your listening skills, thoughts such as these may sabotage your efforts:

> Listening intentionally is too difficult.
>
> I don't want anyone else to hear what I said. In fact, I wish I had never said it.
>
> I think I'm doing well enough. Why go through all the trouble of analyzing my interactions?
>
> Things aren't so bad. What will people think if they see me using video?

Barriers to Change

Barriers of all sorts will show up as you begin to intentionally observe your interactions. There is a part of your mind that's keenly aware that these observations are dangerous to your self-image and will challenge your sense of competency. Change is risky business because it takes us out of our comfort zone and exposes us to the unknown. Also, change challenges your relationships. Those who know you and accept you as you are now may object to your making changes because they will have to adjust to a new you. Few individuals can say they like change, yet it appears to be the only way to learn and grow. Questions may form, such as the following:

- "Does changing mean that I was wrong before?" Not necessarily. It may mean that you have learned something new that is leading you to change your mind.
- "Does the no-blame policy of my workplace create a safe place to admit my mistakes?" It may. However, shifting an organization's response to an error from "blame" to "no blame" is a major paradigm shift that generally requires much time and discussion.

At some point, you must consider your response to unsettling questions such as those above. Otherwise, they remain barriers to learning and change.

Losing Concentration

Aside from concerns around the video process and the effects of change, other mental distractions block effective listening. These include letting your mind dwell on something that was said last weekend, last night, or even minutes ago, thus losing track of what is being said now. Concentration is required to listen well, focusing on the other person and staying in the present.

Once again, you face the question of whether your commitment is to appearances rather than getting the job done competently. Whenever you experience a break in concentration, acknowledge that you have lost track of what is going on (a breakdown) and find your way back into the present conversation.

Interruptions

Another form of distraction that may disturb your focus is having trouble listening when someone interrupts you. If one of your core values is that interruptions are disrespectful and therefore not acceptable, you may become angry at what the offender has to say.

Unfortunately, not everyone shares this value with you. For instance, people from large families may have the belief that the only way to be heard is to interrupt. Their habit of interruption isn't personal; they interrupt everyone.

Begin to address your boundary and consider changing your attitude about interruptions by adopting the attitude that, for whatever reason, this person has stopped you. They want to share their ideas immediately, or perhaps they have trouble managing their enthusiasm, or they may be from a large family.

In any case, quickly make a note of where you were when you were interrupted and shift to listening with intent. This shift will nourish the health of your relationship, whereas fighting for the floor will damage your relationship.

> **Stepping Stone**
>
> Focus on the person interrupting you rather than fighting for the floor. Listen!

Another way to respond to an interruption is to say, "May I complete my thought before we address your input?" If the answer is no, note where you are and then shift your attention to the present conversation. Begin to process the new information before returning to your thought. The guiding principle is to focus on your client by listening intently to that urgent message.

As you address your barriers to improvement, remember: as you become more aware of your actions either through video or your personal observations, this information will be news only to you. Your clients and colleagues already know what you do in meetings. The only question is, Do you want to be let in on the secret?

Listen Checklist

1. What did you discover in your self-reflection times this week?
2. What did you do this week to check on the accuracy and completeness of your observational skills?
3. What are the repeater barriers to your intentional listening?

Evaluate

The data you have gathered by intentionally attending to what you saw and heard in the *listen* step will give you the ability to focus on what you can change to improve your interactions.

Review with your partner your responses to the five listening skills questions at the beginning of this chapter. Evaluate which response reveals the greatest potential for improvement in your interactions.

Design a Role-Play: An Interaction to Improve

Designing a role-play begins with choosing one of your recent interactions that you particularly want to improve. One frequently chosen challenge is how to have a complete wanted conversation when your client plunges into their first identified want before you hear the rest of them. (This is sometimes called hijacking the conversation.) Before you know it, thirty minutes are gone!

Alternative Responses

Possible responses to this challenge (being hijacked) include the following:

- Take a deep breath and assure your client that you want to make the best use of your time together. Explain that to accomplish this goal, your strategy is to work with a client to identify all of today's potential topics for discussion before problem-solving begins on any one of them.

- Explain one or two consequences you have experienced in the past when a wanted conversation was not complete enough to assign priorities to all the wants before beginning work on the highest one.
- Explore whether your client's urgent project has components of varying sizes with different priorities and deadlines.

Evaluate Checklist

1. What interaction do you want to improve?
2. What are three potential actions that may improve it?

Act

Role-plays have an essential function in the LEARN process, which is designed to improve your interactions. By practicing new approaches, you will learn what works best for you in various difficult situations. The LEARN process can be used to become more proficient in the POWER and RAPID processes.

Role-Play Barriers

No one begrudges orchestras their practice time or theater companies multiple rehearsals before the final dress rehearsal and performance. Every sport, professional or amateur, is based on the discipline of practice. For some reason, role-plays of interactions are much maligned. Many people have had negative experiences doing them, which have led to negative attitudes about them. Here are a few I've heard over the years:

- I have done them before in training courses, and they never produced any value.
- I get embarrassed in role-plays. I'm not an actor.
- I'm not a people person. I can't learn how to relate to people. I wasn't born with those genes.

- It's artificial, I know it's artificial, and therefore I don't feel natural.
- If it isn't an actual consultation, then it doesn't count, and I won't take it seriously.

Attitudes like these reflect the poor reputation that role-playing has earned. Unfortunately, the practice of role-playing is a powerful tool that has been poorly used. However, using the LEARN process can change the trajectory of role-play use by creating systemic improvement in many disciplines.

Overcoming "Acting" Barriers in a Role-Play

To produce value, carefully structure each role-play to address the improvements that the creator of the role-play has identified. Use a well-defined procedure to analyze the data captured on video. These two steps of the LEARN process will convert the captured data into information that's implementable.

Role-playing a situation you find difficult is challenging. You may not be immediately pleased with the results. Sure, this is uncomfortable; that's how you know you are in the learning zone. In any case, you will have an opportunity to learn something about your personal and professional skills that you did not yet know.

Again the question arises, "To what are you more committed, hiding your incompetence or becoming competent?" Another question to consider is "Would you prefer to practice addressing this situation with nothing on the line other than your embarrassment, or would you rather wait until the situation occurs with your boss or a client and your job is on the line?"

No one has to be an actor to role-play. Just do what you would naturally do in the given situation. You can learn how to relate to people better and thus be more successful in your interactions no matter which part you play.

Of course, role-playing is artificial. So is every theater company's rehearsal, as well as every sports practice game at every level from elementary school to professional. Practice sessions produce value that's proportional to how realistically participants play their roles in the practice session.

> **Stepping Stone**
>
> The helpfulness of practice sessions is proportional to how clearly the roles are defined (without dictating a script).

Time invested in finding a situation where there is a meaningful gap between how you *actually* handled the interaction and how you *desire* to handle it in the future will pay off in your ability to produce a realistic role-play.

In addition to you (as consultant) and your partner (as client), another partner acting as a coach in the conversation about your video is most valuable. This new coaching partner must meet the qualifications that we discussed in the introduction. Someone who is well acquainted with the content of this book is essential for converting your video data into information that you can use to improve your interactions.

A wanted conversation will help clarify your desired outcomes for the role-play. For example, you may want to learn how to deal more effectively with a boss who is never willing to take no for an answer. Describe a situation that will serve as context for the role-play. Ask your two partners to interject a realistic twist based on the issue that challenges you and the skill(s) you want to improve.

Professional background in psychology, counseling, or acting isn't required. Becoming an effective player in these practice sessions involves learning to analyze interactions in a way that yields useful information for the role-play designer as well as the other two participants in the process. We will discuss this process further in the next chapter.

Effective Role-Play Construction: An Example

The next step in *act* is to video a role-play to assess whether the alternative you have picked is effective.

The Scorecard		
Role-play position	*Person*	*Actual job in the role-play*
creator	Brian	staff member
partner 1	Julie	boss
partner 2	Carla	coach

Opportunities for role-plays are abundant. The challenge is to recognize them.

For example, you may be oblivious to the fact that you are making the same mistake repeatedly with someone. This person will eventually call foul! Develop a role-play with your partners of the situation leading up to this breakdown. This role-play will give you an opportunity to develop new ways to become aware of a breakdown as it develops in the future.

Here is a practice session in which three people—Brian (creator), Julie (partner 1), and Carla (partner 2)—use video to help Brian improve:

Brian creates the scenario by identifying a recent interaction with his boss, Ralph, that did not go well. He explains the situation to Carla and Julie, using only the essential facts, rather than judging and evaluating what happened. The core issue was that Ralph would not take no for an answer. Carla asks Brian, "What did you do that you want to change? What do you want to learn in this role-play?"

"I lost my temper when Ralph insisted for the third time that I come in to do six hours of work over the weekend. I have some concerns about whether I know enough to do this work alone, not to mention I have other plans for my weekend. I want to learn how to deal effectively with Ralph when he is pressing me to do something I don't want to do."

Carla asks, "What are some alternatives?" After some thought, Brian names several:

- Take a deep breath before speaking.
- Explore whether this was a request or a command.
- Explore alternative priorities for Friday and Monday.
- Explore why it was so critical for him to do this work over the weekend rather than rearranging his priorities on Friday or Monday.

Carla says, "Pick one." Brian picks "Explore alternative priorities for Friday and Monday." All three now construct a role-play (broad guidelines for it, *not* a script) based on this information.

Build in Surprises

Then Brian leaves the room, and Carla and Julie explore how to weave a surprise into Brian's role-play. The purpose of the surprise is to make the role-play more realistic and give Brian a chance to think on his feet about this situation that matters to him. The surprise relates to what Brian has asked to get out of the role-play. The surprise is unknown to Brian, isn't over the top, and instead is something that Ralph might actually say.

When it gets to the point in the role-play where Brian is introducing the possibility of Ralph realigning Brian's priorities on Friday so that the weekend job can be done then, Carla and Julie decide that Ralph (Julie) will say, "Well, you know, Brian, annual reviews are coming up. If you step forward to handle this matter on Saturday, it would be a big plus for you on the review." Start with a role-play of five minutes. Julie won't tell Brian that she has only five minutes for this meeting unless Brian asks.

Another useful element to include is for Julie to stand and leave for her next meeting at the five-minute mark, regardless of whether Brian has had a time conversation with her.

Video the Role-Play

After the role-play is set, Brian returns to the room. Brian and Julie enact this role-play while Carla, the coach, manages the video and notes any potential learning moments as they occur. Julie seeks to recreate as accurately as possible what it is about Ralph that troubles Brian. Then the three of them watch the video of the role-play on Brian's computer. The coaching session begins.

Act Checklist

1. What are your barriers to producing a role-play of the situation you want to improve?
2. Who can help you address these barriers?

Chapter 15 Activity

Role-Play

Use all the steps in this chapter (listen, evaluate, and act) to develop a role-play with your partner and coach. Work together to be sure that the role-play addresses a skill you want to improve and contains at least one surprise.

Following your role-play exercise, refer to the chapter 15 debriefing questions at the end of this chapter. Please explore these questions with your partner *after* having completed this activity, as you will learn more from the role-play experience.

Recap

Intentionally improve your listening skills. Evaluate your practice to identify an interaction you want to improve. Create and enact a role-play that will give you an opportunity to experiment with an alternative that produces the improvement you seek.

Frequently Asked Questions

1. Sometimes my *open* conversations turn into wrestling matches in which my client and I struggle over what will be done in this session. How can I turn these adversarial conversations into collaborative ones?

    > Search for a way to restructure the interaction that would allow you and your client to get what you both want from it. Return to the wanted, willing, and able conversations until you agree on today's agenda.

2. How can I deal more effectively with a client who disagrees with me? Why did she come to see me if she isn't willing to take my advice?

    > Your client came to see you because she thought you could help her. The wanted conversation in the *open* step is used to uncover exactly what help she is looking for so that you can help her if you are willing and able. Some consultants believe that clients are required to agree with them and take their advice even when the client doesn't agree with the advice. This attitude is not productive. Your client did not take your advice because there is something that you know that she does not or vice versa. Another possibility is that your values differ. Seeking to resolve this conflict by resorting to commands will elicit reactance, which will damage your relationship. The consultant's job is to investigate the client's reasons in the expanded wanted conversation.

3. In the *evaluate* step, why do you suggest selecting three alternatives for the action you want to improve?

    > Often it takes much thought to come up with the first alternative. Once you have found the first one, a natural tendency is to apply that new strategy immediately. Instead,

I find that looking more broadly is worth the effort, as you will generate more alternatives that stimulate your creativity and very possibly develop other possibilities that prove more promising and ultimately more effective.

4. How can I be successful in my upcoming job interview?

    Construct a role-play of the job interview with your partners. Be sure to give them the context and characteristics of what you perceive as troublesome, including the questions that you are most concerned about being asked in the interview. Practice answering these questions in a videoed interview. Review the video and repeat if necessary.

5. Are fabricated role-plays as helpful as real situations?

    The quick answer is both are helpful. Sometimes when a situation is loaded with emotion or history, a fabricated situation is a good way to begin. However, the invented situation can be based on actual events that have caused you difficulty in the past. The more similar your role-plays are to the actual situation troubling you and the more variety you invent to successfully resolve the role-plays, the better chance you have to gain useful insights.

Chapter 15 Debriefing Questions

What did you discover in the process of designing and participating in your role-play?

Did any of your repeater barriers to intentional listening appear in your role-play?

Was there any aspect of your role-play that you would do differently? During the role-play, what was the barrier that stopped you from changing your approach while in the moment?

What did your coach notice on your video that you missed?

What did your partner notice on your video that you missed?

What did you see that they missed?

CHAPTER 16

Review to Learn

Prepare for the Review Step

The LEARN triad will produce a video relating to an aspect of your practice that's currently challenging you. The *review* step is the heart of the LEARN process. As you and your partners begin to analyze the video, use the *review* step to identify useful information that you can use to improve your practice. While we have discussed video throughout the book, all the main concepts related to the use of video are found in the three processes POWER, RAPID, and LEARN.

The following are guidelines for coaching sessions.

- Use the POWER process.
- Be in good shape mentally, physically, and emotionally so that issues in any one of these areas will not distract you from the coaching session.
- Tell your truth without abusing anyone in any way, overtly or covertly.
- Give complete feedback; do not withhold essential information that you are uncomfortable discussing.

Withholding information is dangerous. Be aware of topics you are uncomfortable discussing. For example, do not avoid discussing actions of the consultant that could be interpreted as sexual harassment because you are uncomfortable discussing sexual harassment. Rather, discuss sensitive topics with your partners individually, outside the coaching session, and develop a strategy for dealing with them.

- Be aware of the temptation to avoid challenging topics (such as repeatedly being late for meetings) when coaching a partner, for fear that you will be confronted with them when you are coached in the future.
- Discontinue a line of coaching if anyone says, "Stop! I do not wish to explore this any further." Disregarding this request could well cost you the relationship.

Coaching is a challenging interaction that does not always go well. If a breakdown occurs, use the RAPID process.

The following are topics and tools that consultants and coaches have found useful for understanding the activity of coaching:

- **Relationship.** Intentionally build working and, preferably, synergistic relationships with the other two members of the video team.
- **Memory.** This is often the only data we have. Write your memories as soon as possible after recognizing an interaction you want to study.
- **Video.** Plan ahead and use this whenever possible. Remember: you can always erase a video; you can't go back and video the session after it is over.
- **Systematic Strategy.** Use a systematic strategy to improve your interactions, such as the one described in chapters 14–16.
- **Psychology.** Learning the rudiments of psychology is most helpful; after all, we are interacting with people.
- **Epistemology.** This is the study of how we know what we know. Become aware of the many ways people have for deciding that they know something. Your way isn't the only way.
- **Listening.** There is always the possibility that your client may misinterpret what you intended to say. This isn't to place blame.

This is a reminder of the importance of verifying that client and consultant are on the same page. One way of testing for misunderstanding is to ask your client to rephrase what you have presented, which works better than simple repetition. You then have an opportunity to repair any misconceptions, saving you both time and frustration.

- **Reflect.** Reflect on the coaching session, preferably in writing, for future reference as you learn the role-play process.
- **Ask.** Ask the person you are coaching if the session has been helpful. If not, what would have made it more helpful? If it was helpful, what contributed to this result?

How to Review a Video to Identify a Breakdown for Analysis (Coaching for the Coach)

Brian's Case

Suppose you are the staff member (Brian) in the interaction described in chapter 15, and your partner (Julie) is the boss. Both of you have cooperatively prepared for the role-play by selecting an interaction that you want to improve. Following the video session, Carla, who joined you to construct a role-play, will facilitate your coaching conversation as you review the video.

To *open* the coaching session, Carla could ask, "What do you want to get out of this coaching session?" Here again, a wanted conversation is useful. Alternatively, she may ask, "What is the first thing you want to improve?" The answer to this question will help focus your coaching session on your highest-priority conversation.

Matters over which you have control are good candidates to explore. What isn't useful is to scrutinize matters that are beyond your control, such as a characteristic of your client you found annoying. You can only control (and change) your own actions, not those of anyone else.

When your role-play is being reviewed, pay attention to when you notice an emotional cloud gathering steam. As you become aware of the cloud, you have taken the first step toward learning from this mistake, namely to *recognize* your emotional cloud.

Your next step is to *address* your emotional cloud and find an exit! Then you can successfully *pinpoint* the breakdown and explore how it happened. Remember, the purpose of the pinpointing exercise is to improve your interactions rather than finding a scapegoat to blame.

Here are some potentially useful questions for the coach to ask as the coaching session unfolds:

- What part of the video would you like to see?
- What leads you to want to see that particular section? Were you in an emotional cloud?
- What worked?
- What did not work?
- Would you do anything differently if you were to redo the video?

Once you have pinpointed a mistake, the next step in the video analysis is to consider questions like "How did this lapse happen? What had to be present for this confusion to occur?" This process will enable you to extract useful information from the mountain of data on the video.

Consider the five parts of an interaction: *prepare*, *open*, *work*, *end*, and *reflect*. Identify in which part of the interaction the breakdown occurred. Review the checklists from part 1 to assess whether you completed the essential tasks in that part. The ones you did not complete are breakdowns, failures of the POWER process to progress as intended.

Suppose that in the *work* step of the interaction you presented two alternatives to Julie's request that you work on Saturday. Both of these were summarily dismissed. You then dug deeper and worked hard to develop a feasible plan for rearranging your schedule on Friday so that you could do the work on Friday that Julie wanted you to do on Saturday.

Julie responded with, "Well, you know, Brian, annual reviews are coming up. If you step up to handle this matter on Saturday, it would be a big plus for you." You were incensed by this blatant manipulation. In your fury, all you trusted yourself to do was to quietly agree to come in on Saturday. So you immediately left the room, furious with yourself for not having dealt with the situation more effectively.

When you begin to offer coaching, examine these three aspects of an interaction: *interpersonal, intrapersonal,* and *technical.* At least one of them contributed to this breakdown. There is so much information in any video of an interaction that it is useful to use these three facets, one at a time. Search for events or attitudes that may have led to the breakdown.

Interpersonal Checklist

First examine interpersonal aspects of the interaction, which are the *structure* of the session, the *relationship* between the parties, and the use of *language* by each party. These are externally observable events. Consider questions such as these:

In the *open* conversation:

- Have the consultant and client agreed on a time frame for the session?
- Have the consultant and client agreed on what the client wants from the session?
- What type of relationship is evolving: Hierarchical versus collaborative? Adversarial versus cooperative? Working? Synergistic? Is this in line with what you both intend?

In the *work* section:

- Do the client and consultant agree on each other's roles?

- Are requests made by both parties authentic requests, or are they commands?
- Are the requests and promises made by both parties complete? Do they specify each task to be done, including by whom, by when, and to what criteria?

In the *end* play:

- Did the consultation produce an agreed-on action plan?
- Are the requests and promises made by both parties complete? Do they specify each task to be done, including by whom, by when, and to what criteria?

Brenda's Case: Interpersonal Checklist

Looking at the interpersonal events in the Brenda case yields the following observations:

- My request for Brenda to sit at the end of the table was actually a command contributing to a hierarchical relationship from the beginning of the session.
- I was not prepared for the session to start. As she launched into her concerns for her project, I was distracted with arranging papers and pens and reviewing her New Client Information Form. In addition, though I sensed her confusion, I did not ask for clarification on potential points of confusion.
- Our relationship became more and more hierarchical and adversarial as the session continued. The important point here is that I was not attending to her.
- In preparing for the session, I created a problem for myself by investing several hours in planning for the meeting and assuming that this preparation would yield the answer to her question. It never occurred to me that she would change her question. When faced with an unexpected change, I did not stop to clarify what she now wanted from the session and how she would use these results in the future.

Brian's Case: Interpersonal Checklist

A study of Brian's role-play with Julie yields the following interpersonal observations:

- Their relationship is hierarchical rather than cooperative. Julie is telling Brian what she wants him to do rather than requesting his cooperation and exploring other possibilities when he suggested three alternatives to working on Saturday.
- Julie and Brian don't agree on how Brian would get this work done. What he could have done is to express his concerns about working alone on the project. What she could have done is to solicit the reasons for his hesitancy to work on Saturday. There was no such discussion.
- Julie's three refusals of Brian's increasingly elaborate proposals for ways to handle this disagreement suggest that Julie is not making a request but rather is making a command.

Intrapersonal Checklist

Next, observe intrapersonal aspects of the interaction, which include the attitudes, feelings, and emotions of each party. These can't be observed by watching a video of the interaction. The best we can do is watch for actions that lead us to hypothesize that certain attitudes, feelings, or emotions were present at a particular point in the interaction. Then we may be able to verify whether our theory is correct by asking each individual about what was going on intrapersonally at that point in the interaction.

Questions like these are useful in beginning an exploration of intrapersonal events in *prepare, open, work,* and *end:*

- Identify the attitudes you, as a consultant, have about your client, your client's discipline, and your client's project that were serving as barriers to effectiveness. What attitudes would be consistent with what you said or did? What was the impact of these attitudes on the consultation?

- What emotions did you experience? Two frequently occurring reactions are anxiety (apprehensive, uncomfortable) and anger (irritated, aggravated, annoyed). What was the impact of your emotions on the consultation?

Brenda's Case: Intrapersonal Checklist

Here's what I saw when watching Brenda's video:

- I was exasperated that she had changed her study over the weekend and thereby destroyed the value of my time spent in designing an experiment.
- I did not think her problem was well thought through or important.
- I was irritated to once again be dealing with someone who was trying to do a project for which, by my standards, she was not prepared.
- These attitudes, coupled with the resulting emotions of anxiety and anger, contributed to judging her rather than being engaged in a collaborative, cooperative conversation with her.

Brian's Case: Intrapersonal Checklist

Looking at the intrapersonal events in Brian's role-play with Julie yields the following observations:

- Brian reported that he was angry that his three proposals were summarily dismissed by Julie. He began to think less creatively about how to resolve their conflict.
- As the interaction continued, Brian's opinion of Julie deteriorated: she was inconsiderate, unconcerned about his well-being, and overly concerned with getting this work done her way, on Saturday. He was judging her rather than staying in a problem-solving conversation. He could not understand the

urgency that required weekend work, and he did not ask for this clarification. These attitudes and their accompanying emotional clouds blocked any opportunity to interact respectfully with Julie as the consultation continued.

Technical Checklist

To look at the technical events in *prepare, open, work,* and *end,* consider these questions:

- Is the technical material presented by the consultant clear, complete, concise, accurate, and appropriate?
- Does the client comprehend the technical tools and language used in the consultation? Is the consultant asking questions that will determine the client's level of understanding?

Brenda's Case: Technical Checklist

Here's what I noticed in the technical aspects of my interaction with Brenda:

- Early in the session, Brenda spoke of altering her study from "an experimental approach" to "a descriptive research." I assumed we were using the terms in the same way.
- Shortly, it became clear that we weren't.
- Emotions contributed to this breakdown in communication: I'm uncomfortable asking a client what she means when she uses basic statistical terms like "descriptive" or "experimental." I'm afraid that she will think I'm patronizing her by asking about such a basic term. In short, I was more focused on myself than my client. I could have simply said, "I want to be sure I understand what you mean by 'descriptive research' for your new study. Could you expand a bit on that?"

Brian's Case: Technical Checklist

Looking at the technical issues in Brian's role-play reveals the following observation and conjectures:

- Brian grudgingly agreed to work on Saturday.

  He may not have been confident that he had the technical expertise required to do the job alone. (An intrapersonal attitude related to a technical aspect of the interaction.)

  An interpersonal factor could have complicated the above attitude: he may have been afraid to reveal his lack of confidence, especially in light of the imminent annual review that his boss strategically pointed out.

  Another reason for not working on Saturday could be a family or religious one. Admittedly these personal commitments can be a challenge to bring up in a work situation, and he may have been reluctant to do so.

Reflect on the Review Process

Using the last step in the POWER process, *reflect* on the results of your coaching session on your video. Are you ready to *address* the issue that was at the heart of your role-play in an actual interaction? If your answer is yes, do so. The next section will discuss aspects of implementing what you learned in your coaching session.

If you're not ready, do another role-play addressing this issue using a different approach.

Search for anything under your control that may have contributed to the problem. Pick one of these that you are willing to explore. For example, one of your attitudes or how you explain material or even the way you open interactions is a potential alternative to explore.

Brian's Case

Brian could redo this role-play, this time saying, "Help me understand why this work has to be done on Saturday rather than Monday." If Julie's response is compelling to Brian (and set it up so that it is), then suggest that Brian experiment with a way of dealing with the fact that he has doubts that he can do this task alone, perhaps by asking if a colleague could be present as a resource on Saturday, either in person at the office or electronically via phone or email.

Repeating this role-play will give Brian a chance to grapple with the attitudes he has regarding his vulnerabilities. Acknowledging personal limitations is challenging. He could discuss different strategies with a trusted colleague until he identifies one to practice in a role-play. That role-play will give Brian a chance to evaluate how this strategy sounds and to experience the feelings attached to it.

Pick an alternative strategy for your second role-play. Either change your approach and redo the same role-play or switch parts so that Brian and Julie interchange their roles from the first role-play. Either way, much can be learned.

Implementation

When implementing any changes, take small steps. Trying to implement five new ideas at once is a recipe for failure. You are unlikely to make all these changes simultaneously. Pick one to address first.

In addition, take the first small step *in a safe environment*. Work with your friends, people who encourage you and want you to succeed. Here are four potential actions to practice:

- Check on time available at the start of a consultation.
- Start with a complete wanted conversation.

- Check whether your client understood what you just said.
- End by checking on agreements made and who will do what, by when, to what standards.

There are five levels of implementation to consider as you address change:

1. Work by yourself to implement ideas from this book. I have consistently invited you to work with a partner, yet if you are not currently willing to risk this, start working by yourself. Start in *prepare* and *open* with the wanted conversation. During the next week, intentionally use a complete wanted conversation in one interaction per day. Notice how this goes. What have you learned from your self-observation process? What's next?

2. When you are ready to work with a partner, role-play using video to implement what you learned from your self-observations. This requires that both of you sort through your attitudes toward breakdowns and being videoed. Verify that your relationship is at least a working relationship and preferably a synergistic one. Pick a short interaction involving a straightforward situation and video your first role-play. Review it and gradually work toward the tougher situations that you want to address.

3. Work with your partner and a coach to implement a video coaching process. Adding a coach to your team gives you an observer who brings a third perspective to the analysis of the role-play. Verify that all pair-wise relationships in your team are at least working relationships and preferably synergistic.

4. Experiment with a newly practiced tool, concept, or attitude in an actual interaction. Start in a supportive environment with a client you relate to well. Then, after a success here, implement this new idea with a more challenging client. Acknowledge yourself for systematically improving your relationships and interactions.

5. There is a long-standing quality movement principle: consolidate your gains before proceeding. Treat yourself with respect. Celebrate each success, small or large. Otherwise, it is

easy to become discouraged by how much improvement there is yet to do and risk giving up on the improvement process.

Review the results of your implementation activities. Notice actual interactions that you want to work on with your team. Pick one that matters to you and in which the mistakes could have serious consequences. This process is too much work to use for trivial mistakes that matter little to you, except as training exercises at the beginning of your journey.

An important part of ongoing improvement is an assessment of the effectiveness of your interactions. This involves setting a specific date in the future when you can check your progress in addressing the issue you want to change. Take steps to remember your plan and set a reminder for a month or two in the future for this appraisal to take place. Ask your partner to remind you. When the date arrives, examine the "effective interaction" questions:

- Was the plan created in the interaction implemented?
- Did the results of the implementation stand up to scrutiny by stakeholders not involved in the interaction?
- Did this client seek you out for future assistance?

If all three answers are yes, you have now sorted out this breakdown. You have reached the top of a ridge you have been climbing toward for some time. Celebrate! Enjoy the view. Having sorted your way through this problem, you have new knowledge about yourself. Perhaps you can now see a new vista that was invisible before the climb. New possibilities appear on various paths leading toward hills, ridges, and mountains ahead. What aspect of your life do you wish to improve next?

If you now are able to deal effectively with your boss who previously never took no for an answer, you may be willing to offer your ideas to them about working together more efficiently. In any case, no matter

> **Stepping Stone**
>
> Isolation is the enemy. Stay in the conversation.

what happens, you now have skills to deal with upsets. Remember to consult your partner in difficult situations. Isolation is the enemy.

The gold standard for improving an interpersonal process is to work with synergistic partners committed to their own personal improvement using video.

Brenda's Case—Video Analysis

This is a summary of what I learned from Brenda, video coaching, and the resulting suggestions for working with clients.

Prepare: Before meeting with a client, engage in only those tasks on which your client and you have explicitly agreed. Hold lightly any additional preparations you have made for the meeting, realizing that your client may have changed their mind since you last met. Verify that both your client and you know when and where your meeting is to be held. Arrive five minutes early at the meeting site.

Open: Begin with the time conversation. Engage your client in a complete wanted conversation until all wants are identified. Pursue expanded wanted conversations until it is clear how all desired results will be used. Review what you are willing and able to do and share the results of this assessment with your client.

Work: Check frequently that your client understands what you are saying. Verify periodically that your dialogue is useful to your client. If it isn't, identify what would be useful.

End: Stop at least ten minutes before the scheduled end of a one-hour session to review decisions made in the interaction. Confirm that you both agree on who will do what, by when, and to what standards.

Reflect: After the session, reflect on whether you or your client experienced any breakdowns. Assess how to address these breakdowns.

Do I use all these steps in *every* interaction I have? No. When I do, I learn from my breakdowns and recommit to the power of systematic improvement using POWER, RAPID, and LEARN.

Chapter 16 Activity

> **Role-Play**
>
> Apply the *review* step to the role-play you created in chapter 15.

Following your role-play exercise, refer to the chapter 16 debriefing questions at the end of this chapter. Please explore these questions with your partner *after* having completed this activity, as you will learn more from the role-play experience this way.

> **Recap**
>
> Work with your partner to analyze your chapter 15 role-play. Identify a breakdown in your role-play that you want to address using the tools in part 3. Identify the interpersonal, intrapersonal, and technical aspects of the breakdown. Implement the change you want to make from this analysis. You are now ready for another cycle through chapters 15 and 16.

Frequently Asked Questions

1. Is it common to discover one problem, solve it, and then discover a new problem?

    Yes. This situation occurs in quality improvement efforts in many different disciplines. Once you solve a major problem, other problems that were once obscured are now apparent. The LEARN process can then be applied to the next problem.

2. I have never coached anyone on any topic using video. Would you list just the basics to get started?

> Arrange to video an interview with your partner. Start the video. Ask your partner to describe the most successful part of their work yesterday. Then ask for a description of the least successful part. Explore with your partner what can be learned from each of these parts of their work yesterday. Stop the video.

> Watch the video. Ask your partner what parts of the conversation went well and what parts did not go well. Assess what parts were clear to you and what parts were not clear. Share these observations with your partner.

> After this exercise is over, ask your partner what parts of your coaching and observations were useful and what parts were not useful.

> Repeat this exercise using a different topic, perhaps a different day, until you are satisfied with your level of coaching proficiency.

Chapter 16 Debriefing Questions

> What is one thing that you have learned in chapters 14–16 that you are ready to implement? Do it! Did it improve some aspect of your practice? If yes, great! If not, work with your partner to identify the breakdown that occurred. Apply the tools from chapters 14–16 to this breakdown in your next role-play.

CHAPTER 17

What's Next?

On every journey, there are branches in the road; some are intentional, and some are detours. You have already made many choices at earlier branches of your life journey. Some have been mindful of your vision and mission; some have not. My hope is that you are now more aware as you make your next choices on your journey.

A book can introduce ideas. Only people can implement them. What will you do with the ideas presented here? I hope you will find a partner and explore how to be more effective in the interactions that are important to you. There is no end to the opportunities available for you to discover and learn how to make changes gracefully. This statement isn't intended to discourage you; it is intended to be a reminder that as long as you are living, growing, and experimenting, you will encounter breakdowns. Each will be an opportunity to improve your interactions.

I believe each of us has a signature contribution to make in our time on earth. There is a custom in some African villages at the time of a birth. Everyone gathers together late in the mother's pregnancy and asks, "Why is this child being born to us at this time?" Their belief is that each of us is born with a song to sing that will blend with the songs all other people on the planet have been born to sing, combining to make a magnificent chorus. You are the only one born with your song to sing. If you don't sing it, the chorus will be incomplete.

In this spirit, is the path you are on consistent with the contribution you want to make? If not, when will you move onto your path?

Hopefully, your journey through this book has given you an opportunity to discover

- the identity of your repeater breakdowns and your signature reactions to them,
- new strategies to rapidly recover from these breakdowns, and
- how to be effective in your most difficult interactions.

Insights you gain from these activities can lead you to a new place. Hopefully, you now know more about who you are, what is important to you, and what contribution you want to make.

You may find yourself called to a vision you have never considered before. Before you move toward your new vision, assess whether it is consistent with the contribution you want to make.

I wish you much perseverance as you consider the challenging questions in this chapter. These may be some of the most difficult and rewarding questions you will ever consider. I thank you in advance for the time and energy you will spend on your journey of discovery.

REFERENCES

3 kinds of power: positional, relational and expertise. 2013. Retrieved October 7, 2016. http://www.consultantsmind.com/2013/02/21/3-kinds-of-power-positional-relational-and-expertise/.

Burns, R. 1786. "To a Louse: On Seeing One on a Lady's Bonnet, at Church." Retrieved December 3, 2016. http://www.thehypertexts.com/Robert%20Burns%20Translations%20Modern%20English.htm.

Cialdini, R. B. 1993. *Influence: The Psychology of Persuasion, Revised Edition.* New York: William Morrow and Company.

"Collaboration." *Oxford English Dictionaries.* Accessed June 13, 2017.

"Consultation." *Oxford English Dictionaries.* Accessed June 13, 2017. http://www.oxforddictionaries.com/us/definition/american_english/consultation.

Cuddy, A. 2012. "Your Body Language Shapes Who You Are." Retrieved January 7, 2015. http://www.ted.com/talks/amy_cuddy_your_body_language_shapes_who_you_are?language=en.

Frequently Asked Questions. Retrieved June 21, 2016. https://knowmore.fsu.edu/faq.

Kaufman, R., and D. Zahn. 1993. *Quality Management Plus: The Continuous Improvement of Education.* Newbury Park: Corwin Press.

Kingsolver, B. 1990. *Animal Dreams: A Novel.* New York: HarperCollins.

Petersen, A. 2017. *On Edge: A Journey Through Anxiety.* New York: Crown.

Senge, Peter M. 1990. *The Fifth Discipline: The Art and Practice of the Learning Organization.* New York: Doubleday/Currency.

Vance, E., H. Smith, and D. Zahn. 2014. "Learning and Improving Skills to Become a More Effective Statistical Collaborator." Workshop presented at 2014 Joint Statistical Meetings, Montreal, Canada.

Watkins, R. 2001. "The Relationship of Some Personality and Individual Characteristics with an Individual's Commitment to an Ideal Vision for Performance Improvement." *Performance Improvement Quarterly* 14, no. 3: 117–132.

Webster's New World Dictionary, 2nd College Ed. 1980. New York: Simon and Schuster.

INDEX

mistakes, dissecting of, 173–185
motivation, sources of, 256–259
Mustang example, 192–193, 206, 207, 229, 235

N

negative feedback, 120
next? as one of five steps of LEARN, 251, 254t, 301–302
noncompliance, 89t, 126
not willing, as distinguished from not able, 63–64
not-able conversation, 62

O

observational skills, improvement of, 271–274
open
    debriefing questions, 75, 94–95
    frequently asked questions, 65–71, 92, 94
    with intention, 39–75
    most frequent mistake in, 50
    novice kayaker example, 77–80
    as one of five steps of POWER, 5, 9–10t
open checklist, 64–68
open rubric, 71, 72–74t
    required course, 80–89
    role-plays, 40, 44, 45, 50, 60, 65, 90–91
    stepping stones, 39, 48, 50, 53, 63, 64, 82
    stumbling block examples, 44, 52, 82
    your mind, 76–95
open checklist, 64–68, 138–140
open conversation, 8, 9–10t, 53, 60, 69, 71, 76, 282, 289
open rubric, 71, 72–74t
overwhelm, 203

P

palest ink, as better than best memory, 260, 261
passion, 258
perseverance, 100, 215, 234
Physician Information Form, 161–162t
pinpoint
    breakdown, 214–222
    checklist, 223–224
    debriefing questions, 233
    frequently asked questions, 231–233
    as one of five steps of RAPID, 171, 178t
    three cases of, 222–223
pinpoint checklist, 223–224
positional power, 13, 70, 83, 92, 232
POWER (prepare, open, work, end play, reflect)
    as core process, xxix
    end play, 115–132
    five steps of, 1, 3
    foundation of process of, 10–11
    open, 39–94
prepare, 24–38
process of, 9–10t
process reviewed, 24–26
    reflect, 133–150
    work, 96–114
power, use of term, 3
power harassment, 247
practice, need for, xxxiv
prepare
    construct effective role-play, 30–31
    for content, 26–28
    debriefing questions, 38
    frequently asked questions, 33–35
    get focused, 28–29
    increase your courage, 29–30
    in novice kayaker example, 79

as one of five steps of POWER, 3–4, 9–10t
prepare checklist, 30, 33–35, 138
    role-plays, 32, 36, 37
    stepping stones, 27
    stumbling block examples, 29
prepare checklist, 30, 33–35, 138
pride, 202
proactive, 151, 242, 251
process, defined, 174
promises
    broken, 176, 179, 240–241
    components of, 18
    as one of four categories of statements, 17, 18–19

R

RAPID (recognize, address, pinpoint, identify, do it)
    address, 171, 178t, 200–213
    as core process, xxix–xxx
    debriefing questions, 185
    dissecting mistakes and breakdowns, 173–185
    do it! 171, 178t, 235–248
    five steps of, 171, 178t
    five steps of as applied to scenario 3, 181–183
    frequently asked questions, 183–185
    identify, 171, 178t, 225–233
    pinpoint, 214–224
recognize, 186–199
    scenario 1: broken promises, 179
    scenario 2: double-billed, 179–180
    scenario 3: scheduling error, 180
    stepping stone, 182
rapid recovery/RAPID recovery, 173, 185, 204, 205, 214–233, 234, 239, 240, 242
reactance, in required course example, 83–84

recognition, as one of three parts of courage, xxxvi–xxxvii
recognize
    checklist, 194
    as one of five steps of RAPID, 171, 178t
    three cases of, 192–194
recognize checklist, 196
recovery, rapid. See rapid recovery/ RAPID recovery
reflect
    debriefing questions, 150
    described, 135–136
    frequently asked questions, 148–150
    as one of five steps of POWER, 8, 9–10t
    prudent reflections, 133–150
    role-plays, 143
    stepping stones, 134, 141, 146, 147
reflect checklist, 136–137, 143–148
reflections, prudent reflections, 133–150
relationship
    casual relationships, 10
    hierarchical relationships, 163, 237–238, 290, 291
    as one of three foundations of POWER, 10–11
    synergistic relationships, 10, 12–14
    working relationships, 10, 11–12
reluctant clients, examples of, 55–57, 84
requests
    considered requests, 228–229
    as one of four categories of statements, 17–18
    possible responses to, 17
required course, 80–88
respect
    barriers to, 101–103
    nature of, 76–77
review

ABOUT THE AUTHOR

Doug Zahn's passion is to help individuals in all walks of life to improve their interactions. As we know, technical expertise does not guarantee interpersonal effectiveness. Fortunately, the skills necessary to interact successfully are the same across all walks of life.

Over the years, he has listened to people leaving their statistics courses and consultations with complaints of frustration over lack of effective and supportive interaction between student and instructor, client and consultant. The persistence of these complaints propelled him to develop a method for producing successful courses and consultations. His goal is to give people a simple process using easily accessible technology they can employ to systematically improve their interactions and, thereby, intentionally enrich their relationships.

Working with students and teachers, clients and consultants who are dealing with statistical issues has proved to be an acid test for the process he has developed to interact more effectively and efficiently. In a paraphrase of Frank Sinatra's song "New York, New York," if you can make the process work in statistical interactions, you can make it work anywhere. This book now makes the process broadly available.

CPSIA information can be obtained
at www.ICGtesting.com
Printed in the USA
LVHW031452110721
692415LV00001B/123

9 781532 060885